WHAT
BUDDHISTS
BELIEVE

WHAT
BUDDHISTS
BELIEVE

Elizabeth J. Harris

ONEWORLD

OXFORD

Oneworld Publications
(Sales and Editorial)
185 Banbury Road
Oxford OX2 7AR
England

Oneworld Publications
(US Marketing Office)
160 N. Washington St.
4th Floor, Boston
MA 02114, USA

http://www.oneworld-publications.com

ISBN 1–85168–168–X

Cover design by Peter Maguire
Printed in England by Clays Ltd, St Ives plc

CONTENTS

PREFACE

In the last thirty years the West has discovered an unprecedented interest in Buddhism. With its lack of any patriarchal 'creator' god and doctrinal dogmatism; with its possibility for individual spiritual guidance and opportunity for personal transformation as the result of personal effort, Buddhism has provided an attractive alternative to post-Christian societies where all too often the concept of God has been devalued, credal formulae seem arcane and lack of strong leadership has left flocks unfed and vulnerable to the attack of wolves.

The Western Buddhist Order has been established. Tibetan refugees, victims of Chinese policies, have brought a distinctive form of Mahāyāna Buddhism, and as a result of the 1960s and 1970s, a whole generation has discovered meditation through less orthodox means. As a result of increased interest, departments of Religious Studies have included Buddhism in general courses and existing university schools have developed their studies of Pāli and Sanskrit texts. Student organizations, inspired and augmented by students from traditionally Buddhist countries, have flourished and a whole new Western perspective on Buddhism has resulted.

No religion transfers from one place to another without cultural adaptation: the presence of a Tibetan Temple complete with monks, nuns and *Dhamma* teaching on the hillsides of Scotland proves that. Samye Ling is dedicated to the teaching and practice of distinctive Tibetan Buddhism, to the preservation of Tibetan culture and to the charitable actions which are integral to Buddhism. Rokpa, the Tibetan word for charity, is the name of their charitable trust. But Samye Ling is more than a Tibetan monastery transferred to a Scottish hillside: while the traditional 'long retreat' of three years, three months, three weeks and three days is practised by some, the Abbot permits monks and nuns to take vows for a single year to test their vocation. In addition, the centre provides support for some with drug and personal problems, and on occasion, released convicts. It also promotes an active programme of *Dhamma* teaching, meditation and practical activities, including soup kitchens as far apart as Nepal and Moscow, Glasgow and Sikkim.

When the commitment to social engagement and all that implies in ecological terms is added to the traditional elements of meditation, the appeals of Buddhism to non-Buddhist societies are obvious. Not so appealing have been some recent high-profile sexual scandals surrounding certain monks, notably in Thailand, raising the inevitable question: while Buddhism has given so much to the West and non-Buddhist societies, has the growth of a Western Buddhism inspired and challenged traditional Buddhist culture?

No one is better equipped to explore the diversity of Buddhism than Elizabeth J. Harris. It was her scholarly field-researches, combined with her wide knowledge of and sympathy with Buddhist lifestyles and practices, which enabled me to produce the BBC World Services Series *The Way of the Buddha*. For me, it was a journey of genuine enlightenment: my knowledge of Buddhism was limited to studying history and text, dogma and theory, but travelling through Sri Lanka, Thailand and Cambodia with Elizabeth, I began to see at first hand the way in which a faith influences not only individuals but whole societies; where its power can transform broken and wasted lives as well as recreate new life in devastated communities.

In this book, Elizabeth has brought together both sides of a religion – the history and dogma and its practice and meditation, together with the power Buddhism can have over individuals. Not only does it explain *what* Buddhism is, it helps the reader understand *why* it is so important to those who practise *The Way of the Buddha*.

David Craig
June 1998

INTRODUCTION

Buddhism has inspired millions for almost two and a half thousand years. It has given people hope in war, conflict and bereavement. It has motivated peacemaking and selfless action. It has caused people to renounce the comforts of home life to become celibate monastics. It has cemented communities together through common patterns of devotion, morality and mutual support. Today it is an expanding religion with adherents in almost every country of the world. Particularly in the West, it is attracting many new converts.

All this was reason enough for the BBC World Service, in 1996, to broadcast a series of radio programmes called *The Way of the Buddha*. The programmes sought to bring Buddhism alive through the words of practitioners. They were aimed at the person who knew very little about Buddhism, the non-specialist. David Craig, who was then Head of Religious Broadcasting within the World Service, produced them. I was asked to write and present them. This book is based on the series, with one exception – the programme on women. This came out later, in February 1997, as an edition of *Focus on Faith*, a weekly magazine programme, but it used the same interview material.

CREATING THE RADIO PROGRAMMES

Months of discussion preceded action on the series. Numerous questions arose: How should the content be structured? Where should the material be gained? Who should be interviewed? In my own encounter with Buddhism over many years, the philosophical side had certainly impressed me but so also had Buddhism's message concerning compassionate action, peacemaking and non-violence. The programmes, we decided, must communicate both the basics of Buddhist philosophy and how this was being translated into action, commitment and devotion in different contexts. This would mean that the words of women and men, young and old, activists and academics, lay and ordained were all-important and that each programme would contain the academic and non-academic, theory and practice, the intellectual and the non-intellectual.

Buddhism is divided into three main schools or groupings. Theravāda or Southern Buddhism represents the transmission which travelled south from India from the third century BCE onwards. The main Theravāda countries now are Burma, Cambodia, Laos, Sri Lanka and Thailand. Mahāyāna Buddhism, sometimes called Northern Buddhism, developed from the Buddhism that travelled north and east from India along trade routes to Pakistan, Nepal, Central Asia, China, Korea, Japan and Vietnam. Vajrayāna Buddhism is the name sometimes given to Tibetan Buddhism, although some see this as a form of Mahāyāna. The religious texts of Theravāda Buddhism were preserved in the Pāli language and the texts of Mahāyāna in Sanskrit, although many of the latter can now be found only in their Chinese and Tibetan translations.

The countries we eventually visited to gain material for the programmes were Cambodia, Thailand and Sri Lanka, Theravāda Buddhist countries. Budgetary constraints prevented us from going further around the globe to Japan or Korea, Mahāyāna countries. Tibet was out of the question for political reasons and the next best, the Tibetan community in Dharamsala, India, was often snow-bound and impossible to reach at the time of year when we could travel, December. Therefore, we chose countries where I had close contacts or where there was a situation that cried out for coverage. Mahāyāna and Vajrayāna voices were gathered in Britain, but we also found some in both Sri Lanka and Thailand.

All three countries were places where the context became central to the message we received. In Cambodia, religion had almost been wiped out between 1975 and 1979 and reconstruction through Buddhism was being hampered by ongoing political and ecological crisis. Sri Lanka was caught in the middle of a bitter ethno-nationalist war that had produced extreme brutality as well as self-sacrificial peacemaking. Thailand at that time had a burgeoning economy and a thirst for development, which was placing pressure on religion, forcing many Buddhists to re-evaluate their priorities.

This book follows the structure of the original radio series. Rather than emphasize the divisions which some Buddhists them-selves would like to downplay, it brings out the differences between the three major schools of Buddhism in an organic way within a thematic approach. The first three chapters deal with aspects of

Buddhism central to practice and belief: the Buddha, what the Buddha taught and meditation. The fourth delves into social action, what some Buddhists are calling 'socially engaged Buddhism'. The fifth looks at the joys and struggles of women in Buddhism. The last chapter brings together a number of important faces of Buddhism in contemporary society and asks what the impact of Buddhism could be on the world, now. It looks at Buddhism as reinforcer of culture and Buddhism as challenger of culture, both in Asia and the West.

Over fifty hours of interviews were recorded for the programmes. With only three hours on air, much material in every interview had to be discarded. Only what was concise, clearly communicated and absolutely relevant to the topic could be included. For instance, a wonderfully vivid description of the Tibetan Wheel of Life and a narrative that captured with great insight the joy and challenge of forest meditation in Sri Lanka were simply unusable because of length. One of the strengths of this book is that passages such as these have not been lost. A radio programme can have a profound impact on its listeners but its effectiveness is the result of a merciless process of selection. In compiling this book, I have also had to select but I have been able to do greater justice to the rich experience of the people who so willingly gave up their time to be interviewed. Each chapter is based on one programme but includes much more interview material than we could ever have fitted into a thirty-minute radio presentation. Sections that had to be bypassed completely, although they cried out to be heard, have found life in print.

Yet, one advantage radio has over print is the creativity that can flow from sound. Our travels to Cambodia, Thailand, Sri Lanka and Scotland were filled with sound. In Cambodia, there was the eerie calm, punctuated only by crows and the horns of vehicles at Tuol Sleng, the school in Phnom Penh where Pol Pot had incarcerated the country's intelligentsia, and the rustling leaves and birdsong at Mr Chheng Ponn's meditation centre. In Thailand, there was the clicking of insects at Wongsanit ashram, the distinctive ring of coins thrown into donation bowls in front of Buddha images and the urban sounds of Bangkok's commercialism. In Sri Lanka, it was the vibrant drumming at Kelaniya Temple, soft voices chanting Pāli verses at the Temple of the Tooth in Kandy and the wind playing through the bamboos outside the remote cave of Ven. Bhikkhu Sumedha that we caught on tape. Then, in all countries, during the actual interviews, we were inspired by the voices themselves, the differences in tone, rhythm and accent and the sound 'extras' we received, whether it was the counting of breaths from the depth of the gut to illustrate Zen meditation or the chanting of Pāli texts. In print, word pictures have to suffice.

THE AUTHORITY OF THE PRACTITIONER

Central to the methodology both of the radio programmes and of this book is respect for the perspective of the practitioner. W. Brede Kristensen, a Norwegian scholar, once wrote, 'Let us never forget that there exists no other religious reality than the faith of the believer. If we really want to understand religion, we must refer exclusively to the believer's testimony.'[1] Many scholars would contest Kristensen's use of the word 'exclusively'. The study of religion is now interdisciplinary, drawing on historical studies, anthropology and sociology. Yet that does not detract from his main point that the believer's testimony is paramount when we seek to understand a religion. The radio series took this stance to heart and so does this book. The narratives of practitioners are central. Scholars of high quality were among the Buddhists interviewed, and they were asked to draw on their scholarly knowledge. But, as practitioners, they also gave from their own experience, so it would be true to say that, within these pages, personal testimony, experience and parable take an equal, if not more important, place alongside propositions or theory.

This, however, can cause problems if absolute consistency is expected within a religion, for every religion has so much internal variety that its practitioners or believers do not speak with one voice. Even in the testimony of one person, there can be variety. Different things are said in different contexts. Even the same question can be answered in different ways at different times.[2] With questions of personal experience, this is to be expected. But it is also true when doctrinal and historical questions are answered. We found variety both in the answers given to the personal question, 'What does the person of the Buddha mean to you?' and to more factual questions: 'Is Buddhism a missionary religion?' 'Does it discriminate against women?' 'How did Mahāyāna Buddhism emerge?' When personal testimony is relied on, it is much more difficult to pinpoint core features of a religion, a fact that has led some scholars to doubt whether it is possible to speak of a religion's core or essence.

Can this be resolved? Only if it is accepted that internal diversity is an inevitable part of any religion. Like the radio programmes, this book chooses to celebrate the fact that Buddhism is expressed within different contexts and cultures and by an impressively wide spectrum of people. Only by giving voice to this, we felt, could Buddhism's richness be communicated. What we discovered was that this creates patterns of unity and divergence. There is certainly variety within the voices in these chapters. Yet, across schools, countries and language (translators were used wherever necessary), the voices share much in common. We found that it was perfectly possible to speak of a well of shared perspectives and convictions binding together those we interviewed. There was unity in the diversity. Yet, with another set of people and contexts, the patterns that emerged could have been very different.

My own role as presenter of the programmes and writer of this book has been to draw the speakers together and add information where necessary. It is the role of the midwife rather than the creator. The interviews are not quotations to back up the thesis of an author. They *are* the content. I have tried to be fair and consistent. Inevitably, though, what I have added has been conditioned by my own way of seeing and experiencing Buddhism, which has been deeply influenced by the Theravāda tradition of Sri Lanka. When I was asked to present the programmes, I was a research fellow at Westminster College, Oxford but had just returned from spending over seven years in Sri Lanka, attached to the Postgraduate Institute of Pāli and Buddhist Studies of the University of Kelaniya. It is not surprising, therefore, that concepts from Theravāda Buddhism have come more quickly to my mind than those from the other schools. More quotations from Pāli texts appear in these pages than from Chinese or Tibetan, although Mahāyāna voices are not absent. That they are not more numerous is due more to the budgetary constraints surrounding the original radio programmes than to design. To be completely representative, the programmes should have included voices from Japan, Korea, Vietnam or Taiwan. I would have been more than delighted if we could have gone to one of these countries or even if more visits to centres within Britain had been possible. But there was a limit to the resources a series of six programmes could command.

To move to some more practical points, notes to what follows have been kept to a minimum. The book is not an academic treatise but a reservoir of personal insights, scholarly and non-scholarly. Readers wanting more information about topics covered should go to the suggestions for further reading at the end.

All those who were interviewed were asked whether they were willing for their names to be included in this book. In the few instances where no reply was received, I have assumed that there is no objection. By far the majority of interviewees replied in the affirmative. In the two cases where a 'no' was received, I have allowed anonymity. Throughout the book, the speakers' words have been adhered to with only minor tidying up to make for readable English.

Readers will note that one significant Christian voice has been included – Dr Aloysius Pieris SJ. He was chosen because of his Indological expertise and his present role in Sri Lanka as director of a research centre devoted to creating understanding between Christians and Buddhists. He was the first Christian priest to obtain a doctorate in Buddhism from a Sri Lankan university and has written and lectured extensively on Buddhism with great sensitivity and insight. That his voice is present parallels other, similar BBC radio series, which have included at least one significant voice from outside the tradition.

Both Pāli (P.) and Sanskrit (Skt) terms have been used. Where the speaker is a Mahāyāna Buddhist, I have retained the Sanskrit and where the speaker is Theravāda, Pāli. The equivalent in the other language can be found, if needed, in the glossary. In the text between interview extracts, Pāli terms have been used with the Sanskrit equivalent given when appropriate at the word's first appearance, except where I am speaking specifically about Mahāyāna Buddhism, in which case the Sanskrit is used first. Both Pāli and Sanskrit words are italicized. Diacritics have been included except for some proper names which enter English pronunciation without much difficulty. These are used to reduce the difficulty in reproducing Pāli and Sanskrit words in roman lettering and guide the reader into the correct pronunciation. The most frequently used diacritics are the following:

ā, ī, ū	long vowels, like *a* in 'art', *ee* in 'eerie' and *oo* in 'boot'
ḍ	pronounced as *d* in 'debt'
ṃ, ṁ	nasal *m*, like *n* in 'sing'
ṅ	pronounced as *n* in 'think'
ñ	pronounced as *gn* in 'signora'
ṇ	pronounced as *n* in 'name'
ṣ	pronounced as *sh* in 'shut' (used in Sanskrit but not usually in Pāli)
ṭ	pronounced as *t* in 'teach' (without the dot, it is pronounced as *th* in 'thatch')

Quotations from the Pāli texts and the referencing method, unless otherwise stated within the chapter concerned, have been taken from the English translations of the Pāli Text Society, Oxford, UK. Quotes from the Lotus Sutra have been taken from the translation by Burton Watson (New York: Columbia University Press, 1993).

My thanks and appreciation go to all the people we interviewed. Making the programmes and compiling this book has been a tremendous privilege. I have been humbled, inspired, challenged and warmed by the commitment and vision of the people we spoke to. My thanks must also go to David Craig, whose wisdom and expertise also moulded the programmes. But it was not only professional expertise that he offered. His personal support and encouragement has been invaluable, right up to the point of going into print. Thanks must also go to Peggy Morgan, Senior Lecturer at Westminster College, for her help and encouragement.

My hope is both that the voices in this book will make Buddhism come alive in the hearts and minds of readers and that the radical challenge Buddhism poses to us all as we go into the next millennium will be heard.

NOTES

1. Quoted by E. Sharpe, *Comparative Religion: A History* (London: Duckworth, 1986), p. 228 and Peggy Morgan in 'The Authority of Believers in the Study of Religion', *Diskus*, 4/1, 1996, p. 2.
2. See Morgan, pp. 1–10.

1

THE BUDDHA: TEACHER OF GODS AND HUMANS

Buddhaṁ saraṇaṁ gacchāmi
Dhammaṁ saraṇaṁ gacchāmi
Sanghaṁ saraṇaṁ gacchāmi

I go to the Buddha for refuge
I go to the *Dhamma* for refuge
I go to the *Sangha* for refuge

These words are chanted by Buddhists throughout the world. The language here is Pāli, used by Theravāda Buddhists, who are found in Sri Lanka, Thailand, Burma, Cambodia and many Western countries. Anyone who can say his or her sole refuge is the Buddha, the *Dhamma* (Skt *Dharma*; what the Buddha taught), and the *Sangha* (Skt *Samgha*; the community of followers), is a Buddhist. The words lie at the heart of Buddhist commitment. They are what are called the 'Three Jewels', the three precious things. They inform and infuse all that Buddhists practise and hold dear, although different schools of Buddhism will interpret the refuges in different ways or place more emphasis on one than another.

The first of the three refuges is the Buddha. This is where any study of Buddhism must start, simply because of its centrality within the life of all Buddhists. It is also the image of the Buddha, sitting serenely in meditation, standing with hand upraised or lying on his side, which stretches outside the religion, as a symbol of its content and as pointer to its meaning and practice.

There are two central questions: who the Buddha was and what he means and has meant to Buddhists. To find answers to these, religious texts, the historical development of the tradition and the contemporary experience and devotional practices of Buddhists are all equally important. One place to start is with the texts.

THE TEXTS

In the Pāli Canon, these words appear:

> Monks, there is one person whose birth into the world is for the welfare of many, for the happiness of many; who is born out of compassion for the world, for the profit, welfare and happiness of gods and humans. Who is that person? It is a Buddha, a fully enlightened one. (*Aṅguttara Nikāya*, i, 20)

A Sanskrit text puts it this way:

> The Buddhas, the World-Honoured Ones, wish to open the door of Buddha wisdom to all living beings, to allow them to attain purity. That is why they appear in the world. They wish to show the Buddha wisdom to living beings, and therefore they appear in the world. They wish to cause living beings to awaken to the Buddha wisdom, and therefore they appear in the world. (*Saddharmapuṇḍarīka Sūtra*; the Discourse on the Lotus of the True Law or, more popularly, the Lotus Sutra)

Another important definition from the Theravāda tradition was quoted by a woman academic in Sri Lanka:

> Once the Buddha was asked for the definition of buddhahood. So, he said, 'That which has to be realized with high knowledge, I have realized; that which has to be cultivated, I have cultivated; that which has to be abandoned, discarded, eradicated, I have eradicated. Therefore, I am a Buddha.'

The words *budh* or *buddhi* in both Pāli and Sanskrit mean 'wisdom' or 'enlightenment'. According to the texts and to tradition, a Buddha is one who is enlightened, who has awoken to truth, who has realized the secret of human life. Numerous Buddhas are believed to have appeared in the world. Each saw the Truth and preached it out of compassion. All schools of Buddhism agree on this, although differences of emphasis exist between the Theravāda and Mahāyāna traditions, as Ven. Bhikkhu Bodhi of the Theravāda tradition explained:

> The older portions of the Pāli Canon, the *Nikāyas* and the *Vinaya*, make mention of six Buddhas of the past, predecessors of the historical Buddha Gotama. One *sutta* [Skt *sūtra*][1] in the *Dīgha Nikāya* also mentions a future Buddha named Metteyya [Skt Maitreya], who is supposed to arise in the distant future, after the teaching of our present Buddha has disappeared from the earth.

This idea has become important in popular Buddhist practice, as many Buddhists aspire to be reborn at the time of Metteyya and to attain enlightenment under his guidance. In some later texts of the Pāli Canon the number of past Buddhas is increased to twenty-seven, while in post-canonical literature the number is increased even more. In the Mahāyāna *sūtras* the number of Buddhas is often said to be innumerable and incalculable, 'like the sands of the river Ganges'.

Each of these Buddhas is believed to have prepared for Buddhahood over countless lives. Within the Pāli Canon, the *Jātaka*, a book within the *Khuddaka Nikāya*, contains narratives of 547 of these previous births. During these lives, moral qualities or 'perfections' (P. & Skt *pāramitā*) are practised. Theravāda Buddhism speaks of ten: generosity, morality, renunciation, wisdom, energy, patience, truthfulness, determination, loving kindness and equanimity. The Mahāyāna tradition usually names six: giving, morality, patience, effort, concentration (in meditation) and wisdom. The texts are replete with epithets to describe the one who has perfected all these qualities to become a Buddha. He is teacher of gods and men, incomparable guide, endowed with knowledge and virtue, holy, exalted, a sage and a conqueror.

An Extraordinary Man

The terms 'Creator' or 'Almighty God' are never used to describe a Buddha. Some Western observers of Buddhism have assumed that Buddha must be another name for God or a god, because the devotion shown to him seems to be similar to that shown to God in the theistic traditions. However, to project onto Buddhism the concept of God found in theistic religions is a serious mistake. The Buddha is seen neither as a creator God nor as a god. This comes through in various ways. Ven. Bhikkhu Bodhi put it like this:

> We do not regard the Buddha either as a personal God or as an *avatār*, an incarnation of a God or divine reality. For Theravāda Buddhism, the Buddha always remains a human being, yet the supreme human being, 'the extraordinary man'. The texts even state that he is the foremost of all human beings, including the gods, and thus we might say that the Buddha occupies a position similar to that of God in theistic religion, in that he is the highest object of veneration. Yet his role, for Buddhism, always remains that of an exemplar and a teacher, the Supreme Teacher; he is never conceived either as a world creator or as a personal saviour.

He 'saves' others only by showing them the path by which they can save themselves.

Yet, from the religious point of view, the Buddha is the embodiment of all those excellent qualities which in theistic religion are most often associated with God. The texts describe him as the embodiment of four 'divine abodes': boundless loving kindness, compassion, altruistic joy, and equanimity. They also ascribe to him a vast range of powers of knowledge; even the complete knowledge of reality.

Richard Gombrich made the same point in a slightly different way:

> When some Christians discovered Buddhism, they were very excited about the fact that Buddhism was an atheistic religion and one of the main things which they meant by that was that Buddhists did not believe in a creator God and that is certainly true. I've never come across any Buddhist who did believe in a creator God and this is really quite clear in the scriptures and the tradition; this, and that the world as such is considered to be ethically neutral and to have no beginning. So the connection that monotheists make between God and the world, in particular that God creates the world, but also that God controls the world, having made it, is not there in Buddhism. To that extent the Buddha is wholly unlike the Christian idea of a God.
>
> The Buddha is like a God more in being an exemplar of moral perfection. In that respect he is godlike. But he's not quite godlike in that he had to work for it. He is morally perfect but he worked for that through an endless series of lives. I don't think Buddhists would admire the Buddha nearly so much if he had just been born with this moral perfection and not had to struggle for it.

Ven. Professor Dhammavihari also stressed this:

> He was not a Buddha-born. He was born a Buddha-to-be ... He tried again and again, experiment after experiment after experiment. In his own laboratory, he found the way. Eventually he got the exit right and got to the goal.

So, a Buddha is born a human being. At this stage, he is a Buddha-to-be or a *bodhisatta* (Skt *bodhisattva*). He becomes a Buddha because he becomes enlightened. After enlightenment, each Buddha becomes a teacher of gods and humans and therefore, in one sense, moves beyond both divinity and humanity. One phrase used in Pāli is *acchariya manussa*, extraordinary man. A Buddha is human and yet far more than human in his spiritual attainment. The reverence and devotion shown to his image within all Buddhist communities reflect this.

Within this era, the person recognized as a Buddha by all Buddhists is Siddhartha Gotama (Gautama in the Sanskrit tradition). Siddhartha is the name given to him by his parents; Gotama, the clan name. There is no doubt that Siddhartha was a historical person but there has been academic controversy over exactly when he lived. Professor Richard Gombrich explained:

> Different schools of Buddhists give him different dates. In most of the textbooks that you get now, you will find a date in the 480s BCE – 486 or 483 BCE – as the date of his death. As he died at the age of eighty, that means that he lived mainly in the sixth century BCE, according to that dating. But there's a very curious thing about that date. That is a date worked out by scholars in the nineteenth century, which is not the date of any of the schools of the Buddhists themselves. And scholars in fact have never been very satisfied with it. Nowadays, there's quite a different consensus among the scholars who study the subject. They are sure that the Buddha lived not in the sixth century BCE but the fifth century BCE or possibly in the fifth and fourth. The general opinion, in other words, is that the Buddha died sometime around 400 BCE at the age of eighty or maybe a bit later. I myself have a very precise theory about the dating of the Buddha. I think we can know to within a very few years when he lived. I've published an article which argues that he died around 405 or 404 BCE, although the evidence is such that there must be a margin of error one way or another. The outer limits are that the earliest possible date for his death would be 422, the latest possible date would be 399 BCE. Therefore he lived entirely in what we call the fifth century BCE.

How he came to that conclusion is rather complicated, but it begins with one of the rock edicts of the great Indian Emperor Aśoka,[2] which can be dated precisely, and then passes to the ancient historical chronicles of Sri Lanka, which trace the lineage of teachers and pupils from the time of the Buddha.[3] The important point from all this is that the Buddha probably lived in the fifth century BCE, although many Buddhists and indeed many written accounts still refer to the sixth century BCE as the time of the Buddha. But perhaps more significant than when he lived is what can be known about his life and the kind of person he was.

BIOGRAPHIES OF THE BUDDHA

Biographies of the Buddha only started to appear several hundred years after the Buddha's death, which gave time for embellishments thought worthy of so great a religious leader to be developed. One of the earliest was the *Buddhacarita* (Acts of the Buddha), written in the first or second century CE in Sanskrit by the Indian poet Aśvaghoṣa and eventually translated into Chinese and Tibetan. In what most scholars believe is the oldest extant corpus of texts, those of the Pāli Canon of Theravāda Buddhism, biographical details are scattered in different places. A hint there and a hint here appears. A woman academic in Sri Lanka gave a personal view of why this was:

> The life of the Buddha is not given in any particular *sutta*. We have to gather it from a number of *suttas*. The Buddha was not keen on perpetuating his life history as such. He spent the whole time delivering the message that he thought was the most important and that message was the way out of *saṃsāra*. I think the *Bodhisatta*, before he became Buddha, was like a man who was lost in a great forest. The forest is *saṃsāra*. He wanted to find a way out of this forest and because he had to stay in this forest for such a long time, he had to find out about its ways – in which direction there was human settlement, what the forest's beasts were like and which fruits were edible and which poisonous. But once he found the way out of the forest, he did not think it was useful for other people to know the ways of the forest. The important thing was to get them out of it. What you find in the Pāli Canon is whatever is relevant directly or indirectly to get out of this forest. What he found about the forest itself, he hardly preached. So one day he gave a simile. He took a handful of leaves and said, 'The leaves in the forest can be compared to what I understood but the leaves in my hand can be compared to what I preached because this alone is sufficient for you to make an end to *saṃsāra*.' All the other things were irrelevant.

Saṃsāra [P. and Skt] is the cycle of birth and death to which Buddhists believe beings are bound. To understand her reasoning it is necessary to know that much of the Pāli Canon is presented as the words of the Buddha. Her point is that the Buddha avoided talking about himself because the teaching was much more important. Yet the story of Siddhartha which can be extracted from the early texts and later biographies holds a place of great preciousness in most Buddhist cultures. It is taught to children in schools and temples. Numerous books exist that contain colourful pictures of the Buddha's life. The story has been interpreted and reinterpreted in temple art and iconography. It holds within it episodes replete with both human interest and spiritual truth. Now, it is almost impossible to disentangle completely historical fact from later embellishments added by adoring followers, although as a fine Sri Lankan scholar of Buddhism wrote, 'It would in any case be an exercise of little value; the essential features of the Buddha's life and teaching are quite clear, and of the rest, if many incidents did not happen as reported, they might as well have done, such is their symbolic quality.'[4] So, in what follows, history and tradition mingle, as they do in the narratives passed down from generation to generation within Buddhist families.

THE BUDDHA AS A CHILD

The Buddha-to-be was born into a privileged ruling family of the Sākyan (Skt Śākyan) clan in north-east India. India, at that time, was divided into kingdoms, ruled by royal families, and republics, governed by elected aristocracies. Siddhartha was born into the aristocracy of a republic. As Ven. Bhikkhu Dhammavihari pointed out, 'Sākyamuni [Skt Śākyamuni, sage of the Śākyas] was the son of a provincial ruler, Suddhodhana. He was not a mighty monarch but probably a rice farmer and his brothers would have been of the same name.'

Suddhodhana's wife, Mahāmāya, gave birth at Lumbini, now just inside the territory of Nepal, whilst travelling to her parent's house. One *sutta* of the Pāli Canon speaks of radiant light and seismic trembling spreading throughout the cosmos when this happened and a birth which was stainless:

> When, Ānanda,[5] the *Bodhisatta* is issuing from his mother's womb, he issues quite stainless, undefiled by watery matter, undefiled by mucus, undefiled by blood, undefiled by any impurity, pure and unstained. Ānanda, it is as when a jewel is laid on Benares muslin, neither does the jewel stain the Benares muslin nor does the Benares muslin stain the jewel. (*Majjhima Nikāya*, iii, 122–3)

A sage called Asita visited the young child shortly after his birth and wept. The reason he gave for his unusual behaviour was that the child was destined to become a Buddha and he, Asita, would not live long enough to benefit from the child's teaching. This prediction was confirmed by another seer, Kondañña, who claimed that the child would eventually renounce the world to seek enlightenment. This reading of the future horrified Suddhodhana so much that he vowed to protect his son from every intimation of suffering and pain so that the wish to renounce could not possibly arise. The luxurious mode of living this gave rise to is described by the Buddha in one Pāli text as:

By night and day a white canopy was held over me, lest cold or
heat, dust or chaff or dew, should touch me. Moreover, monks, I
had three palaces; one for winter, one for summer, and one for the
rainy season. In the four months of the rains, I was waited on by
minstrels, women all of them. I came not down from my palace in
those months. Again, whereas in other men's homes broken rice
together with sour gruel is given as food to slave-servants, in my
father's home, they were given rice, meat and milk-rice for their
food. (*Aṅguttara Nikāya*, i, 145)

As a child, he was compassionate and gifted. One story shows him
going off alone at a ploughing festival and reaching a deep stage of
meditation. Another depicts him outstripping his cousin, Devadatta,
in compassion. Devadatta shoots down a swan from the skies.
Siddhartha rushes forward to save it, reaches it first and eventually
wins the right to nurse it back to health. He is also said to have sur-
passed others in learning and sport. Eventually, he chose to marry
Yasodhara, his cousin and, when he was twenty-nine years old, a son
was born to them. Yet, by that time, so the story goes, the web of
unreality surrounding Siddhartha was being broken. An awareness of
suffering was entering. The turning-point came when he decided to
leave the palace independently. Helen Jandamit took up the story:

He was quite a revolutionary actually. He was always surrounded
by his entourage but one day he went out only with his charioteer
into the park and he saw an old man, a sick man, a corpse and also
a meditating monk. The first three made him really aware of the
suffering and the transitoriness of our existence and the monk suggested to him a way that he could practise so that he could find a
way beyond suffering.

The whole experience plunged Siddhartha into mental turmoil.
Never before had he been confronted with human mortality. The
entertainments provided by his father lost their ability to divert and
please. Even the news of his son's birth appeared a restrictive bond
rather than a joy. Determination to find an answer to the world's
pain grew. To leave home and family and become a 'wanderer', a
searcher after religious truth, seemed the only way forward, as a Sri
Lankan academic explained:

The books say that he was much loved and cuddled, that he went
from lap to lap, he was so much brought up in luxury. Later on, as
an adult, he started noticing things. Yet I don't think he really had
the opportunity to understand the limitations imposed by life until

his baby arrived. He would have seen how much his wife suffered in pregnancy. This may have worried him a great deal. Then, when the baby was born, he would have loved it but would have realized how much suffering was involved. 'Why is there so much suffering?' he started asking himself, and he saw other examples. He had a mature mind, a sensitive mind. He would have thought that maybe out of home, in the open air, he would be able to contemplate better and the religious environment of his day may have given him an example of going out, of renouncing.

RENUNCIATION

He left the palace at dead of night to begin his search. According to the tradition, gods silenced the horses' hooves. At a river, he removed his aristocratic clothes, cut his hair and left his charioteer and horse to venture alone. Helen Jandamit shared the thoughts about this which came to her one morning when looking at one of the Buddha images within her shrine:

> The Prince left everything he had ever known, everything that had surrounded him before, leaping out into the dark. He had lived in such a luxurious way, with three different palaces in different parts of the country so that when the weather got too hot he would move to another. He was surrounded by beautiful young people. He had never been exposed to illness, old age or death so when he did eventually see these things it struck him so forcefully that he had to find a way through this. He was a person who was really open and aware, going into a world he didn't know, totally alone, leaving behind everything, a young man, twenty-nine years old at that time. His body would have been so vital and alive and he was there on his own, really striving to find a way past suffering, not only for himself but for others too. This thought of a person, a young person, so aware and so open, going out there into the unknown, really brought the humanness of the Buddha to me. It was no longer a gilded image. It was a human being who'd really gone through the deepest discovery that man can make.

All Buddhist traditions are united in the conviction that it was compassion that drove Siddhartha out of his home and made him put the search for truth above his love for his wife and child. What may seem an act of irresponsibility to the outsider becomes, within the tradition, an act of supreme renunciation for the good of all human beings. It is also part of the tradition that both his wife and son eventually renounced home to become his disciples. Ringu Tulku:

What inspired him to search was not only for himself but for all
sentient beings. He actually said that without compassion one cannot even be on this path. Before he became a Buddha, he was a
bodhisattva and a *bodhisattva*, the Buddha explained, is somebody who makes a commitment to become enlightened, that
means to have the fully awakened state of mind, for the sake of all
other beings. The Buddha said that unless you have that kind of
mentality, unless you have that motivation and inspiration, you
are not a *bodhisattva* and unless you are a *bodhisattva* you cannot
become a Buddha.

There were many 'wanderers' in Siddhartha's India, men and
women who had renounced home and family to become travelling
mendicants and searchers for religious truth. Some became known
for their teaching skills, others for their austerities. As a first step,
Siddhartha tried two of the most renowned wanderers, Alāra
Kālāma and Uddaka Rāmaputta, both of whom were masters of
advanced meditation techniques. Helen Jandamit:

And he practised with two of the greatest meditation teachers of
that time in India, one after another. In each case, he reached the
highest possible level with that teacher, so much so that the
teacher asked him to take over. In each case the Lord Buddha,
who was still a seeker, knew that what he had reached was not yet
enlightenment. So he followed the highest teaching that was available at that time in India and yet he knew it was not what he was
seeking. So he went away on his own. At one point he had five followers and they practised the ascetic way – self-mortification, fast-
ing, not sleeping and so on. He followed this for almost six years,
mostly in the forest areas of the north of India. He practised austerities to the point where his body became almost like a skeleton.
He ate, they say, not more than three or four grains of rice a day,
didn't sleep and sat on rocks rather than in any comfortable
position.

Then, one day, the story goes, he heard what some people say
was Indra, one of the Hindu gods, playing a three-stringed instrument. Other people say it was a boatman. It depends on the tradition. Anyway, a three-stringed instrument was being played. The
first string was tuned too tightly so when it was plucked it let out a
very unpleasant noise. When the second string was plucked, it was
too loose so it let out a twanging sound. But when the third string
was plucked it was perfectly tuned and let out a beautiful, harmonious sound. And the Prince-monk, when he heard this, realized

what is now called the Middle Way. It's a synonym for Buddhism. He realized that practising self-mortification would be too taut and, in fact, that if he continued practising as he had, he would die before he could reach enlightenment. On the other hand if he followed a completely sensual way of life, just indulging in whatever he felt like without any restraints at all, then obviously he was not going to make progress. Therefore, he realized that the third way, trying hard enough but not too hard, was what was necessary.

ENLIGHTENMENT

The Middle Path between asceticism and indulgence led to victory. Enlightenment came on the night of a full moon when he was sitting in deep meditation under a tree at what is now Bodh Gaya, near Gaya in Bihar. The woman academic interviewed in Sri Lanka gave two vivid descriptions of what she is convinced it was like:

> His enlightenment was not according to the books. It was not the experience of a sudden flash but it was like the unfolding of a flower. It is said in one discourse that, during the first watch of the night, the night he became enlightened, he realized what is called retrocognition. He realized that he had had existences before this, that he had been born as a human being or a deity in innumerable previous existences. During the second watch of the night, he realized that this long process of births had taken place according to a pattern and that the pattern was governed by *kamma*, action – in other words that his previous births had been shaped by the moral activities he had been engaged in. And during the third watch of the night, he realized that this rebirth and *kamma* had taken place in the absence of a soul, according to the law of cause and effect. It is the law of causality that he realized during the third watch of the night. And with these three knowledges he was able to penetrate into the nature of reality regarding the human being and that gave him enlightenment.
>
> The enlightenment experience could also be like climbing a mountain, looking at the various things around. As you go higher and higher, your panorama, your vision of the environment, expands, expands, expands. The same problem is seen from different points of view and with different levels of understanding.

Ringu Tulku put it this way, 'He saw the truth. Enlightenment for us Buddhists means not only intellectually but experientially seeing things as they are, including who we are.'

From the night of his enlightenment, Siddhartha was a Buddha. Until his death at the age of eighty, he taught in north-east India, attracting many followers. His first sermon, called, in the Pāli tradition, the *Dhammacakkappavattana Sutta*, or the Turning of the Wheel of Truth Sermon, was preached near Varanasi at what is now Sarnath, to the five companions with whom he had shared a rigid asceticism earlier in his search. All became his followers.

Gradually, quite a large group of followers formed around the Buddha. In the Pāli texts there is repetition of a phrase which could have been the Buddha's first invitation, 'Come, monk, live the holy life so that you can put an end to suffering.' It was an invitation to find out through personal experience whether the Buddha's teaching made sense. But there was a cost, for it meant renouncing home and family. Those who did wore dyed robes made up of scraps of material that had been discarded. Celibacy was obligatory. Many, the story goes, became enlightened.

When sixty followers had reached enlightenment, the Buddha sent them out to teach others with these words, 'Go out, monks, and teach the truth, which is glorious in the beginning, glorious in the middle and glorious in the end, for the good of all beings.' From the very beginning, there was therefore a missionary thrust. At first, the followers disciplined themselves. A word from the Buddha was enough to guide their religious practice. Leaving home and ordination were simultaneous. Yet, as the numbers grew, restrictive regulations to prevent misunderstanding and misdemeanour became necessary. A distinction between novice ordination and higher ordination evolved. In time, a formal rule of discipline of over two hundred rules emerged, within which the following offences resulted in expulsion from the order: breaking the rule of celibacy through having sexual intercourse; taking what is not given; depriving anyone of life or encouraging another to do so; making false claim to a spiritual attainment.

In this way, a formal community of ordained monastics emerged, an Order of *Bhikkhus* (Skt *bhikṣus*). At first it included only men. Yet, eventually, the Buddha allowed women to renounce and a *Bhikkhunī* Order (Skt *bhikṣunī*) arose. The traditional story is that he was reluctant to do this and had to be persuaded by his closest aide and companion, Ānanda, that because women were able to reach enlightenment, it would be an injustice to debar them from renunciation.

At the heart of the new movement was community. Although the texts make it clear that the practice of solitary meditation was part of the training, sometimes alone in the forest, those who followed

the Buddha found themselves part of a community, with all the
challenges and difficulties that involved. Aloysius Pieris:

> At the heart of Buddhism is a community. *Sangha* really means in
> Sanskrit 'cemented together', people who are sticking together.
> The Buddha's doctrine was entrusted to a community and at the
> very inception of Buddhism, the message was preached and a com-
> munity was formed together – the monastic community. So com-
> munity is of the very essence of Buddhism. But, together with the
> monastic community, the Buddha said there were four kinds of
> disciples: monks, nuns, laymen and laywomen. From the begin-
> ning there was a tendency to define the community in terms of
> these four.

The idea of the Fourfold Society developed because many of those
who sympathized with the Buddha's teaching remained in their
families as devout laymen and laywomen. The Buddha's teaching
was not that all should leave home and family – far from it. The life
of one who had renounced could be tough, both physically and psy-
chologically. The Buddha recognized that it was not suitable for all.
Although at one point it seems he was accused of breaking up families, the *suttas* show that he did much to encourage responsible,
prosperous family life. In fact, an interdependence between the laity
and the ordained developed. Monks and nuns provided teaching
and a model of the holy life and laypeople provided food and whatever else the monastic community needed to avoid destitution.

A POPULAR TEACHER

The development of the orders of monks and nuns into institutionalized communities and evidence of a strong lay following leaves no
doubt that the Buddha's person and message appealed to many.
Why? What was it that made him so popular? Dr Asanga Tilakaratne
of Sri Lanka gave one view:

> During the time of the Buddha people came to him because he pre-
> sented a new philosophy, a new way of looking at the problem.
> India, in the sixth century BCE, when the Buddha was born, was
> actually very philosophically mature. People were very concerned
> with the existential problem of suffering and the idea of *mokṣa* or
> liberation was much in vogue. Many religious people were experi-
> menting in this area. The appeal of the Buddha was that he pre-
> sented a different path which made more sense. For instance, the
> Brahmin religion was very concerned about ritualism. The Buddha
> didn't deny ritual completely but he made it very clear that it

would not lead to liberation. So for those people who were more concerned about soteriology, about their liberation, the Buddha presented a way.

I think what also appealed to people in India was the non-dogmatic character of the teaching. During the time of the Buddha, there were so many beliefs, so many religious systems, and each religious system stressed that their own view was true and all others were false. The difference in Buddhism was that although the Buddha presented what are called Four Noble Truths, which he thought represented truth, he did not want to force them on people as dogma, as *the* truth. Mental freedom was there.

Aloysius Pieris painted another vivid word picture of India at the time of the Buddha, reinforcing Dr Tilakaratne's words and stressing Buddhism's missionary nature:

The historical context of the time was a search. There was a massive search for meaning. It was a breakdown of one model of society for another, of the village culture based on the Vedic cosmic religiosity for an urban society that developed around the cities and there was a consequent breakdown of values – overcrowding, diseases, disillusionment, violence and wars of elimination. And the search was wild. People went to all kinds of extremes. The Buddhist texts speak of many theories. The Jain texts speak of more.

Into this came the personality of the Buddha. He was certainly an extraordinary man. That is the word used in the [Pāli] texts: *acchariya puggala* or *acchariya manussa*. It means a being who is human, but human in a different way from all others. *Acchariya* means wonderful, one who creates awe and wonder.

This impression was created because he handled that situation in an extraordinary manner with his middle path, his dialogical approach and his presence in all kinds of situations of life. He was with prostitutes and murderers. He was different from many other *rishis* or sages of the time who stuck to their forest and wanted people to come to them. He was an itinerant preacher who had reached the acme of perfection in every way but was still so human, available and accessible. Certainly his personality coupled with the way he handled a confused situation made an impression on the first disciples. What is also important, compared to all other religious leaders, was that he was missionary by nature. He had a message and the message had to be given and disciples had to be formed to give the message, not to go to the forest and seek salvation. The words are almost reminiscent of Jesus' missionary mandate, 'Go you to all people who are waiting, with this doctrine which is beautiful in the beginning, beautiful in the middle and beautiful in the end.' Therefore, these elements – the way he handled a confused situation, his personality, his availability and his missionary character, all combined to give the Buddha a hearing.

In some later biographies, the Buddha's teaching career is laced with miracles or wondrous acts such as self-reproduction and clairvoyance. Yet although Buddhists believe that the Buddha possessed psychic powers to a remarkable degree, it is probable that he spurned using them to create followers. Both texts and tradition confirm this. One Pāli text shows the Buddha refusing to perform a miracle when requested to do so. He declares instead that education is the greatest wonder (*Kevaddha Sutta, Dīgha Nikāya*, i, 211ff.). In another, a person called Bhaddiya confronts the Buddha with the accusation that he is a juggler who knows tricks to entice away the followers of other teachers. Bhaddiya himself becomes a convert but the only 'trick' the Buddha uses is reasoned argument – a question and answer technique that draws on Bhaddiya's own experience (*Aṅguttara Nikāya*, ii, 190). It is a text that points both to the popularity of the Buddha's teaching and to the Buddha's methods of communication. The woman academic in Sri Lanka:

> The Buddha used so many methods of communication. One was to ask for clarification from the questioner. You are asking me what the Buddha's methods were. I can ask you what you mean by method. I can ask for clarification by asking further questions. Another method was to analyse the question – to go into detail. But there were certain questions to which he said, 'Don't ask foolish questions. Just put them aside. They are useless questions.'

Encouraging people to reflect on their own experience, using a question-and-answer technique to push the listener's thought forward, meeting his questioners where they were – all of this can be seen in the record the texts give of the Buddha's dialogues with others. Mahāyāna Buddhists place particular emphasis on what they call 'skilful means' or the Buddha's ability to increase the understanding of his listeners through giving them only what they could take in at that moment, even if it was not the whole teaching.

The overriding impression of the historical Buddha that emerges from text and tradition is of a down-to-earth, compassionate teacher and communicator who met people where they were, with teaching which spoke to their immediate need, without avoiding awkward questions. In the Pāli texts particularly, he is shown in conversation with people from all strata of society, from the rulers

of kingdoms competing for power, to merchants, craftsmen, desti-
tutes and untouchables. He is shown criticizing abuses of religion
such as overreliance on ritual or the belief that caste or age alone
determined human worth and condemning lifestyles which gave
more importance to self-centred accumulation than to generosity,
non-violence and compassion. Yet, stories of compassionate action
also abound. He is believed to have settled a dispute between the
Sākyans and the Koliyans over water rights on the River Rohini and
to have cared for sick monks abandoned by their community
because of their physically abhorrent state. He therefore comes
across as a person who was concerned both that individuals should
find answers to their questions about life and that communities
should be healthy and harmonious.

THE BUDDHA'S DEATH

The Buddha died in his eightieth year, of food poisoning, in an
insignificant village now called Kasia or Kusinagara in north India,
fifty-five miles east of Gorakhpur in Uttar Pradesh. He died, as he
was born, in the open air, surrounded this time by grieving disciples. The oldest record of this is probably the *Mahā Parinibbāna
Sutta* found in the Pāli Canon (*Dīgha Nikāya*, ii, 73ff.). This shows
him teaching to the very end, even when he no longer had the
strength to walk. He converts a person called Subhadda. Three
times he encourages his disciples to ask questions about doctrine
before it is too late. The question of his succession comes up. 'Who
will be our teacher when you go?' the monks ask. The Buddha is
recorded as saying that the ongoing teacher would be the *Dhamma*
and the *Vinaya*, the teaching and the rules of discipline. There
would be no human successor, although many of the monks had
themselves reached enlightenment through the Buddha's teaching.
His very last phrase encourages his disciples to keep striving with
energy. Global, even cosmic, grieving accompanies his final breath.
The earth quakes and thunder resounds.

After the Buddha's Death

To honour the Buddha's last instructions, a structured system was
put into place so that the teaching and rules of discipline would be
recorded, remembered and treasured as the new 'teacher'. The first
step was to hold a council soon after the Buddha's death. The most
senior disciples of the Buddha were invited. The rules of discipline
and the teachings of the Buddha were recited and a more or less

definitive version decided upon. These rules and teachings were
then taken away in the minds of those present to many different
parts of India. They were translated into local dialects and structures were put in place to ensure that different parts of the doctrine
were kept alive by different groups. Aloysius Pieris:

> From the beginning, there was a tendency to rehearse and check
> the authentic teachings of the Buddha. The scriptures themselves
> give enough hints that from the beginning there was [sic] what is
> called *saṅgīti* [councils]. Since the tradition was oral at the time,
> the only way to keep the teachings of a master alive was to
> rehearse and memorize them. We must remember that before the
> press and computer era there was a powerful and phenomenal tra-
> dition of memorizing in India. Even our older monks here in Sri
> Lanka now know their texts by heart. And in the *pirivenas*
> [monastic schools] in Burma and Sri Lanka, you find little monks
> of five or six years old memorizing whole heaps of texts. So study
> by memory rather than referring to written texts was the original
> tradition. Rehearsing these texts must have been the beginning of
> keeping these teachings stored up.

As the teachings were taken away into different parts of India, a
process of organic growth and change began, leading to inevitable
differences in interpretation and the growth of a variety of schools.
Traditionally, eighteen are said to have arisen within about three
hundred years, but in practice there may have been more.

In the years immediately following the Buddha's death, no physical
likeness of the Buddha was made. The Buddha was represented by
symbols such as a tree, a footprint, a wheel, a throne or a flame-
encircled pillar. It was as though what the Buddha represented was
simply too great for an image to be attempted. Yet there is evidence
that from a very early date devotion to the memory of the Buddha
was popular. The *Mahā Parinibbāna Sutta* itself shows the Buddha
sanctioning the offering of garments, perfumes and devotion at the
place where the ash of a Buddha rests (*Dīgha Nikāya*, ii, 142). The
movement from symbol to image was gradual; images of the
Buddha appeared for the first time only several hundred years after
the Buddha's death.

Intense devotion is shown in the presence of a Buddha image.
The exact form this takes varies from country to country. In Sri
Lanka, devotees prostrate completely so that their foreheads touch
the floor. They offer flowers, with their stems removed, and chant
verses from the Pāli texts with an intensity of feeling that is almost

palpable. This has caused some observers from monotheistic faiths to leap to the conclusion that Sri Lankan Buddhists must be worshipping an almighty God. This is what Aloysius Pieris would say to them:

> The heart of Buddhist devotion among villagers is that the Buddha is the greatest person on earth and that the Buddha has shown the path of deliverance. He is the great teacher. And therefore the first act of Buddhists in the morning is to pay their respect to the Buddha. And this showing of respect to the Buddha is different from the way they show respect to the gods.
>
> Very often observers who are not in touch with Buddhism are not able to distinguish the way Buddhists pay respect to the Buddha. I remember very clearly in 1980, when the Third Monastic Congress was held in Kandy, some Christian monks from abroad told me, 'You say Buddhists deny God, but see how they fall down and worship the Buddha.' I told them that they should observe a little more carefully. Once, I did a little survey during the *perahera*[6] season, which is when Buddhists from all over the country come to the Kandy temple. I did a random sample of fifty families. I went to the Buddhist temple, the Temple of the Tooth, and I noted families who fell prostrate on the ground and worshipped the Buddha. I then followed them to the temple of the gods and asked them questions: 'You worship the Buddha. Did you pray to him for your needs?' They answered, 'No, we never pray to him.' 'Then, why did you worship?' I countered. 'He is the greatest teacher,' was the invariable reply.
>
> And that posture of worship is the posture adopted by any Buddhist to a teacher, to the monks, to a higher spiritual person – and to their parents. They fall down on the ground. It is a sign of respect. It is not divine worship. But when they go to the gods who are lower than the Buddha, who are like animals who can be tamed through rites and used for your personal, temporal good, they kneel in the way normal Catholics or Christians would kneel in their churches. That's a lower form of worship. So the gods get a lower form of worship, what you might call a show of respect which doesn't indicate any reverence for the gods. It is the reverence you would show to any politician because you need some help. You go there, you give a bribe. Gods are simply cosmic powers you can utilize through rites and rituals. You can bribe them and get things done ... You go to a god and say, 'I want this favour done – do this for me.' The gods cannot give you salvation, neither can the Buddha. But the Buddha has shown the path of final liberation, therefore he deserves all the respect. That's the

popular devotion and after fifty families not one of them ever swerved from this.

As Aloysius Pieris implies, many Buddhists do believe in gods but their definition of a god is completely different from that of many other people of faith. They are beings from which favours can be asked rather than spiritual guides. In the Theravāda tradition, they are called *devas*. Bhikkhu Bodhi described their significance:

> Divinity as ascribed to the *devas* would in no way, in a Buddhist context, suggest the gods of polytheistic religion who have some creative or cosmic role in sustaining the universe and in activating certain forces in nature, nor does Buddhism recognize the idea of a single, all-powerful creator God, who creates the universe, who rules it and who metes out judgement. The *devas* are living beings within the round of rebirth. Those human beings who do specially lofty deeds of virtue, of merit, will very likely be reborn in the *deva* worlds. I would say that *devas* would correspond more to the heavenly beings in Christian belief than to the creator God.

In Mahāyāna countries, outward devotion to the Buddha image is as intense as in Theravāda countries, yet there are variations in what lies behind the devotion. One of the differences between Theravāda and Mahāyāna Buddhism is the way in which the concept of buddhahood developed within the two traditions. The Theravāda tradition has always looked primarily to the historical Buddha, Siddhartha Gotama. When the word *bodhisatta* is used, it refers primarily to Siddhartha, before he gained enlightenment – the Buddha-to-be. Theravāda Buddhism recognizes the existence of other Buddhas, but these are placed within previous eras of time. When it analyses enlightenment, three types are recognized, as Ven. Bhikkhu Bodhi explained:

> In Theravāda Buddhism, three grades of enlightenment are recognized, distinguished by way of the types of persons who represent them: the *Sammā Sambuddha*, the *paccekabuddha*, and the disciple *arahant*. The enlightenment they attain is identical for all, and issues in *nibbāna*, the state of perfect, spiritual freedom. The difference obtains from the conditions under which enlightenment is attained and its accompanying attributes.
>
> A *Sammā Sambuddha*, a fully enlightened Buddha, is one who discovers the path to *nibbāna* during a historical period when the *Dhamma*, the liberating teaching, is no longer known in the world. Thus at any given time there can be only one *Sammā Sambuddha*, and as long as the teaching of one *Sammā*

Sambuddha exists another cannot arise. A *Sammā Sambuddha* dis-
covers the path to liberation without outside guidance, without
relying on the instruction of a teacher, entirely through his own
innate wisdom. For countless aeons, during millions of lives, a
future Buddha must accumulate the merits, virtues and wisdom
necessary to become a *Sammā Sammabuddha*. Having discovered
the ultimate truth on his own, his specific function is to teach the
path to *nibbāna* to the world. He establishes a *Sāsana*, a
'Dispensation', the institutional expression of the path, which
enables the *Dhamma* to be passed on through many generations.

A *paccekabuddha*, a 'privately enlightened one', is one who
awakes to enlightenment through his own effort, without any
external guidance, and thereby wins the final liberation of *nibbāna*.
However, a *paccekabuddha* does not attempt to guide others to
enlightenment; he does not proclaim the path or establish a
Dispensation. He may teach others morality and meditation, but
he does not try to convey the content of his realization. According
to tradition, *paccekabuddhas* do not arise in the world during
periods when a *Sammā Sambuddha's* teaching is known.

Finally, there is the disciple *arahant*. This is a person, male or
female, who has accepted the Buddha as teacher, practised to
perfection the path taught by the Buddha, and thereby attained the
final stage of enlightenment. The *arahant* has won the same essential
enlightenment that the Buddha has won, and will enter *nibbāna* in
the same way as the Buddha did. He or she differs from the
Buddha firstly in relying on outside guidance, namely the
Buddha's, secondly in possessing fewer accompanying attributes,
such as the special knowledges and powers of a Buddha, and
thirdly as functioning *within* the Dispensation rather than as its
founder. *Arahants* may or may not guide others along the path,
depending on their own temperament and abilities.

In Theravāda Buddhism, arahantship is the ultimate aim of practice.
Mahāyāna Buddhism, on the other hand, turned away from the
ideal of the *arahant*, which they condemned as too individualistic,
and expanded the concept of buddhahood so that it embraced both
the historical Siddhartha and a cosmic principle, in what came to be
known as the doctrine of the three bodies of the Buddha, the
Trikāya Doctrine. Ven. Bhikkhu Bodhi:

In Mahāyāna Buddhism, a shift in emphasis takes place in their
view of the Buddha. I would briefly explain this shift as a stress on
what one might call the metaphysical, mystical and mythical
aspects of the Buddha's being, in contrast to the human and histor-

ical aspects of the Buddha, which are emphasized by Theravāda Buddhism. In later Mahāyāna, the Buddha becomes seen principally as a manifestation, or even 'emanation', of the fundamental universal reality, which they call, from a philosophical angle, 'suchness' or 'the Truth Body'. The Mahāyāna does, of course, acknowledge the historical character of the Buddha, but in their tradition this aspect becomes subordinated to the supramundane dimension of the Buddha's personality.

The historical Buddha, within the three-body doctrine, represents the *nirmānakāya* – the transformation or appearance body. Many Mahāyāna Buddhists do not see this as a truly physical body. It is a form that the eternal Buddha takes out of compassion for living beings. The same is true of the *sambhogakāya*, the enjoyment or bliss body, which arises in order to teach beings in the heavenly planes. The most significant 'body' is the *dharmakāya*. In this form, the Buddha is one with eternal truth, eternal *Dharma*. The Buddha becomes a cosmic principle, an absolute, ever-present, stretched across time and space, yet beyond both.

For Mahāyāna Buddhists, as for Theravāda Buddhists, the goal of the religious path is enlightenment but this enlightenment is conceptualized as buddhahood rather than arahantship. Mahāyāna Buddhism stresses that within each person lies *bodhicitta* or buddha-nature. The aim of religious practice is to realize it within oneself and so touch buddhahood. Within this framework, a Buddha is 'simply one who has fully actualized this buddha-nature', to use the words of Ven. Bhikkhu Bodhi. In the Mahāyāna worldview, therefore, many Buddhas can exist at the same time. The concept of the *bodhisattva* (P. *bodhisatta*) also takes a much more central place. If buddhahood is the aim, it follows that anyone can vow to follow the path of the *bodhisattva*, the path of one who vows to become enlightened not for personal gain but in order to help all sentient beings reach *nirvāṇa* (P. *nibbāna*). Ringu Tulku stressed that it was just because arahantship was a product of buddhahood, rather than buddhahood itself that Mahāyāna Buddhism eventually turned away from it. He added:

> There is a quotation. It says that the *śrāvakas* [disciples of the Buddha] and *pratyekabuddhas* come from the Buddha, meaning that the great monks, the great realized beings, *arahants*, can be produced by the Buddha, through practising the Buddha's teaching. It goes on, 'but a Buddha comes out of a *bodhisattva*'. In other words, without being a *bodhisattva*, one cannot become a Buddha.

Then the text says, 'What is it that makes a *bodhisattva*? It is compassion, the understanding of selflessness, and *bodhicitta* or the aspiration to work for the good of all sentient beings. These three things make a *bodhisattva*.' So, therefore, from the Tibetan or Mahāyāna point of view, the whole purpose of becoming a Buddha, the whole idea behind practising *Dharma* is centred around the concept of *bodhisattva*.

CONTEMPORARY EXPERIENCE

A question that we frequently asked our interviewees was, 'What does the person of the Buddha mean to you?' We felt that this personal dimension was most important if our listeners were to understand the significance of the Buddha today. In the responses given, the distinction between Theravāda and Mahāyāna was not as marked as might have been expected. In fact, there was a surprising convergence, which speaks of the common roots of all forms of Buddhism and of the growing amount of communication and sharing between different schools. The Buddha as a human being, a teacher who showed the way, came many times:

> He was a great human being. He has done so much, has been so kind to show us the way to liberate ourselves. We must always ask ourselves why we are born as a human being, why we are here in this world, what we should do whilst living and where we will go when we die. He is the one who tried the way, to get rid of suffering. We accept that to live, to be born is all suffering. It is all unsatisfactory. We have to get old, to get sick, to die, to leave this world. We believe that he found a way to liberate all within *saṃsāra*. (Maeji Khunying Kanitha Wichiencharoen, Thailand)

> The Buddha himself was a teacher. He himself said, 'I am only a teacher and nothing more than a teacher, a pathfinder.' I regard the Buddha as a great human being who has found a very novel path for salvation. Many of the ideas in Buddhism did exist in India before the Buddha's time – the idea of *kamma* and of *saṃsāra* or the neverending cycle of births and deaths. All those ideas were there even in pre-Buddhist times but the Buddha showed us this unique message that you have to follow the path and achieve your salvation by yourself. And to me it gives a lot of courage. (Dr Lorna Devaraja, Sri Lanka)

> I see the Buddha as a very profound, very compassionate and very wise teacher. (Ringu Tulku,Tibet and Sikkim)

The Buddha means to me enlightenment. It means release from all bonds of unhappiness, suffering and misery. That is the essence of the Buddha's teaching. We pay homage to him, we are grateful to him for having shown us the way to that highest fruit. That is what the Buddha stands for. (Mithra Wettimuny, Sri Lanka)

Then, there were those who stressed the qualities of the Buddha or his actions as recorded in biographical material as inspiration for all their actions:

The Buddha spent most of his life, forty-five years, in different parts of India, preaching to and enlightening the people. He risked his life to help the people be aware of the suffering they experience and the suffering they inflict on other people. He did all that with the motivation of compassion and wisdom. I think what I find valuable is the combination of compassion and wisdom, wisdom not only in terms of skill and intellect but in his knowledge of the real nature of the world to the extent that he could be detached from success or failure. At the same time, his compassion was also very powerful. (Ven. Paisan Wisalo, Thailand)

For me, the Buddha is a rebel and I am a rebel. His life is an inspiration for me, although our version of the life of the Buddha is a bit idealistic. He rejected the whole caste society in India and he rejected the ordinary things which human beings believe to be success in life – status, wealth, power. He said, 'This is rubbish. The meaning of life is to be just yourself, to be ordinary people, to walk in the streets like other people and have happiness from within. Status, money, power is not the answer.' Such a rebel, wasn't he? (Pracha Hutanawatr, Thailand)

The Buddha represents the best I am capable of as a human being. The Buddha himself as a historical figure communicates human qualities developed to a very high degree – kindness, generosity, clarity, fearlessness and so on. That inspires me and also that there are human beings, not just the actual founder of the Buddhist tradition, but many other human beings who've managed to make themselves a better sort of being. (Dhammacarini Saṅghadevi, Western Buddhist Order, UK)

For Aloysius Pieris, it was a quality of the Buddha expressed in traditional iconography which he picked out as inspiration for a world in which most people cannot separate themselves from feverish and often unwholesome activity:

One of the statues which attracts people in all Asian countries is
Buddha reclining and relaxing and sort of questioning you, saying,
'You are sunk in the world, sinking and sunk, whereas I keep
detached and therefore can enjoy. I can relax and can rest when
you are addicted.' The Buddha was a non-addicted person.
Iconography in the whole of Asia presents him as a person who is
free and who offers freedom, a person who is not a killjoy but who
enjoys and is happy. And this I think is a powerful message.

For many Buddhists, the inspiration given by the person of the
Buddha included the hope of enlightenment for themselves. For
Mahāyāna Buddhists, particularly, this was combined with the con-
viction that each person has the potential to become a Buddha, to
realize their own Buddha-nature. Yet, I was surprised how many
Buddhists from Theravāda countries expressed a similar hope:

> I like to have my Buddha living within me. His enlightenment was
> personal to him but as the Mahāyānists or Zen Buddhists would
> say, there's enlightenment in every grain of sand. Why not within
> me? So I've already got a pacesetter, the Buddha, set in my heart so
> that it keeps inspiring me all the time. (Ven. Professor
> Dhammavihari, Sri Lanka)

> We believe the Buddha can be seen at two levels. One is the histor-
> ical person born in India as Prince Siddhartha. He was a real per-
> son but somewhat extraordinary, a superman, not a god but a
> man, a man superior to god. The second level is not the body, not
> the face, not the bones of Prince Siddhartha but the good qualities
> in his mind which made Siddhartha, an ordinary man, to be an
> enlightened one, an awakened one. We believe that these qualities
> can be cultivated by everyone. If we accumulate compassion, purity
> and wisdom, the main qualities of the Buddha, then we can be
> Buddhas. And to achieve this it doesn't mean you ask the Buddha
> to come down and help you or protect you. It means you try to
> become what he was and what he taught us. (Ven. Dr Somchai
> Kusalacitto, Thailand)

> My son would say, 'Oh, the Buddha is there, the image, the statue
> on the shelf.' Others would show you the amulet they have around
> their neck and say, 'This is the Buddha for me.' But when we
> become Buddhists, we take refuge in the Buddha. We take refuge
> in the *Dhamma*. We take refuge in the *Saṅgha*. That Buddha.
> What does it mean to me? The Buddha who walked in India some
> 2,500 years ago. He passed away and he's long gone. How can he

be any refuge for me? How can he help me? That is not the Buddha. But there is something about him – that man who was enlightened and who is my teacher. The importance for me is the fact that he was enlightened and I believe that as his enlightenment was true for him, that enlightenment can be true for me also. This buddhahood cannot be my refuge unless and until I practise and follow the path in order that I become Buddha myself. (Dr Chatsumarn Kabilsingh, Thailand)

Everyone has the Buddha nature. I can quote the Buddha – the Truth is there, the *Dhamma* is there whether the Buddha is born or not. And the Buddha is anyone who can transform himself, herself, from a selfish being to a selfless being. That is how a person awakes. Once he or she awakes, then knowledge becomes understanding and understanding becomes love. And I see that in any great religious tradition. (Sulak Sivaraksa, Thailand)

Two women spoke movingly of the changes in their attitude to the Buddha. This is what preceded Helen Jandamit's words about the Buddha's renunciation quoted on p. 16.

It has only been recently that I've understood the human aspect of the Buddha. The very first experience I ever had of seeing a Buddha image – or it may have been a Buddhist monk, I'm not quite sure – was when I was fourteen years old. I had had absolutely no contact with Buddhists. I had never seen a Buddha image. I had never read anything about it. I came from a working-class background. There were no books in our house really. The school library had no books about this. We were not exposed to any teaching apart from Christian teaching and that was on a very superficial level. There was nothing on television about Buddhism at this time. You have to go back forty-five years. I was just lying down on my bed in my bedroom and looking across the room. It was evening, in the summer, and it wasn't yet dark. The walls were bare. They were painted light yellow. I was feeling quite relaxed and I was looking at the wall. Suddenly this image of a man of about forty years old appeared full size, three-dimensional, absolutely clearly defined, just floating, cross-legged, in the room. I looked and wondered what on earth it was. I didn't ask anything. I didn't say anything. It seemed to be completely right. Why not? Most fourteen-year-olds would probably have run out of the room. But for me it seemed so right to have this figure just sitting there and floating in the air. But I did think it was strange that he was wearing what appeared to me to be a sheet. His skin was darker than most British people's skin. His head was shaven. He was sitting there in a meditation position. It stayed for about ten minutes and I just felt incredibly calm and peaceful and happy. Eventually it just disappeared.

I went and asked my mother what this was. I'm an artist and I drew it. She had no idea. So I took it to my teacher at school. She also had no idea and told me to go and ask the art master. The art master said, 'I think it may have something to do with Buddhism. Why don't you check in the library?' Eventually I found that it was a Buddhist monk of the Southern tradition. That was my first image, if you like, of a Buddha or a Buddhist monk and it made a very deep impression, not the image itself but the calmness, the clearness and the incredible peace, and also the fact that I had no questions. In the West we're always taught to question, to look for answers, to try to look for something deeper. In this, it was quite different. It was just being there.

It was seven years later that I had any real contact with Buddhist monks and the teachings. At this time, the Buddha image appeared to me as very formal, very ritualistic, somehow out there, distant, ideal. It represented an idealized, perfect being with wonderful qualities of wisdom, compassion and purity, beyond the human. The image seemed almost too far away from anything that I could aspire to be. Yet, I knew that the meditation practice was right for me and I followed it.

In Thailand, I became more and more involved with the ritualistic aspect and with meditation. Always the image of the Buddha seemed to be ideal, out there, beyond. It was only really this year that I came to know what the Buddha was in terms of human striving. My husband died earlier this year. In meditation practice you learn how to be aware of feelings and let them come and go without being involved with them. It's a stepping back. You become adept at dealing with emotions before they become strong. You can go through life without them really touching you too much. You feel, but it doesn't overwhelm you. But, it is very easy to avoid rather than really being aware, even for meditation teachers. Of course, when my husband died, this was not a feeling I could cancel out so easily. The loss of someone you love is too strong for that. One particular morning I went into the shrine room in my house. I was lighting the candles and then incense and this incredible wave of feeling just poured over me. There was no cancelling out. I could only be there. I looked up at a Buddha image and it suddenly struck me how the Lord Buddha, when he was a Prince-monk, had left his wife and his young son and everything he had known before to go out into the unknown.

The Buddha suddenly became human for her. The change in
Niramon Prudtatorn's attitude was different again:

> I used to feel that the Buddha was just like any other man; that
> when he wanted to do some searching, he could just leave his wife,
> child and property. He had the privilege to do it. He could do it as
> a man. But I have come to see that it was good that he was from a
> rich family. His rejection of this to search for something which
> was inside rather than connected with property is now an inspira-
> tion for me. He had a palace. He had everything. But he felt that
> that was not the real essence of life. So that is something which we
> can learn – that material goods or position are simply imperma-
> nent. They do not last long. The only thing that lasts is inside you.
> If you have growth in your heart, you can go anywhere with free-
> dom. Nothing can compare with being free from greed, hatred and
> ignorance. But it is not an easy path.

The second refuge, the *Dhamma*, concerns what the Buddha taught
about greed, hatred and ignorance. We turn to that next.

NOTES

1. The word *sutta* (Skt *sūtra*) means 'thread'. It signifies a thread of doc-
    trinal teaching and is akin to a sermon.
2. Emperor Aśoka ruled most of India in the middle of the third century
    BCE. He was the grandson of Chandragupta, who founded the
    Mauryan dynasty and empire about 324 BCE. He is believed to have
    converted to Buddhism after involvement in a brutal expansionist war.
    A series of rock and pillar edicts survive as witness to the ethics he
    encouraged as a result.
3. Richard Gombrich, 'Dating the Buddha: A Red Herring Revealed', in
    The Dating of the Historical Buddha, Part 2, ed. Heinz Bechert
    (Göttingen: Vandenhoeck & Ruprecht, 1992), pp. 237–59.
4. H. Saddhatissa, *The Life of the Buddha* (London: Unwin, 1976), p.14.
5. Ānanda, according to the Pāli tradition, was the Buddha's closest compan-
    ion and attendant. Many *suttas* in the Pāli Canon are addressed to him.
6. A *perahera* is a religious procession. The town of Kandy in the central
    highlands of Sri Lanka is famous for its August *perahera* at the time of
    the full moon.

2

WHAT THE BUDDHA TAUGHT

'Dhamma [Skt *Dharma*] is Truth. It is the way things are. It is the Law of Nature.' That is the answer most Buddhists give when asked what *Dhamma*, the second refuge, is. In other words, as the last chapter stressed, Buddhists are convinced that Gotama Buddha did not invent a philosophy at his enlightenment. He saw what had always existed – the truth about existence. He then taught it and became a living embodiment of it:

> We say that the Buddha is what he taught; the Buddha and the *Dhamma* are one. The Buddha discovered the *Dhamma* but the *Dhamma* already existed before the life of the Buddha. Whether the Buddha had lived or not the *Dhamma* would still be there. The Buddha was like a scientist who discovered the law of nature. (Ven. Dr Somchai Kusalacitto)

> In the beginning was the *Dhamma*, the Truth. In the Truth is everything. (Ven. Mahā Ghosānanda)

Over the centuries Buddhists have isolated certain sentences from the texts, thought to be the words of the Buddha, which seem to encapsulate the scent, the breath, the essence of the teaching:

> One thing only do I teach: suffering and the cessation of suffering. (Theravāda tradition)

> I preach the sweet dew of the pure Law. The Law has a single flavour – that of emancipation, *nirvāṇa*. (The Lotus Sutra, Mahāyāna tradition)

> The avoidance of all evil, the undertaking of good; the cleansing of one's mind; this is the teaching of the awakened ones. (The *Dhammapada*, shared across schools in different versions)

The way to end suffering, the doing of good, purification of the mind – all are central to the *Dhamma*.

A VIEW OF LIFE

Held within the concept of *Dhamma* is both a view of life and a way of life. The view of life is a way of seeing reality rooted in experience. The focus is not metaphysical but practical and empirical. It is traced back to what the Buddha saw at his enlightenment. A Sri Lankan woman academic quoted the Pāli texts to explain it:

> As a synopsis of his understanding of the nature of things, of reality, he said *sabbe sankhāra anicca* – all component things, everything in the world, is *anicca*, impermanent. *Sabbe sankhāra dukkha* – all component things are conducive to suffering. *Sabbe dhamma anatta* – all these things cannot be considered as soul or self. This he has given as the three most important characteristics of worldly life.

These three qualities, *anicca, dukkha, anatta* (Skt *anitya, dukkha, anātman*) – impermanence, suffering and no-soul, to give rather shorthand translations – are sometimes called the three signata, the three defining signs of existence. They form the bedrock of the Buddhist view of life.

THE THREE DEFINING MARKS OF EXISTENCE

The very last words of the Buddha as recorded in the *Mahāparinibbāna Sutta* stressed *anicca*: 'Decay is inherent in all component things. Work out your own liberation with diligence.'

Everything that arises passes away. That is the message of *anicca*. Nothing in our experience can be clung to as permanent, neither health, beauty nor youth, friendship nor romantic love, possessions nor status. The Sri Lankan woman academic added, '*Anicca* is very well understood in modern science. It means that everything is dynamic. Nothing is static. So, I am tempted to say that there are verbs in nature not nouns, in the sense that everything is in a flux, changing.'

The fact of impermanence in our lives leads to the second characteristic – *dukkha*. Mithra Wettimuny gave a traditional explanation of it:

> Sickness is suffering. Old age and decay is suffering. Death is suffering. To be associated with the unpleasant, that is suffering. To be dissociated from the pleasant, that too is suffering. To not get that which one desires, that is suffering. And then you realize that, in this life, there is a load of it, a whole lot of it. So often we are associating with the unpleasant, dissociating ourselves from

the pleasant. We inevitably will get sick, grow old and die. None of these things are pleasant and they are the norm of the world; how things become otherwise. Those things we regard as lovely, delightful, they ultimately become otherwise and part from us. You can't change the norm. You can only come to realize and accept it and not be tormented or harassed by it.

The word *dukkha* is very hard to translate into English. There is no direct parallel. It points to something that is dislocated, out of joint, unsatisfactory about the nature of human existence. Both Dr Tilakaratne in Sri Lanka and Helen Jandamit in Thailand stressed this:

> *Dukkha* is usually translated into English as 'suffering'. However, this is somewhat misleading because it gives the notion that Buddhism is talking about physical pain in a very ordinary sense. It does not exclude it. But the concept of *dukkha* in Buddhism presents a more existentially important philosophical concept. It refers basically to the fundamentally unsatisfactory nature of human existence. (Dr Asanga Tilakaratne)

> *Dukkha* is translated in many different ways but I prefer the translation 'unsatisfactoriness', in this context. But it also implies changeableness as well. *Anicca*, *dukkha*, *anatta* are very closely connected. You can't separate them except to analyse them in this way. *Dukkha* is the unsatisfactory nature of our existence. Many people misunderstand this and conclude that Buddhism is a very pessimistic religion, because *dukkha* is often translated as suffering. In fact, it's far deeper than this. It's much more than suffering. It is saying that there is an inherent unsatis-factoriness in our experience of life. This doesn't mean that there cannot be happiness; that there cannot be joy and bliss. Of course, there are these experiences. But they don't last. If you think about feelings of great bliss or exaltation that you may have felt, they don't last. They have inherent within them the aspect of change. This is where it links up with *anicca*, change-ableness. (Helen Jandamit)

The teaching of the Buddha begins with this element of human expe-rience. 'If we want to see the *Dhamma*, we have to see suffering. The Buddha taught only two things: suffering and freedom from suffer-ing', Ven. Mahā Ghosānanda said to us in Cambodia. And it is the intense suffering of war and poverty, not only unsatisfactoriness, that he sees daily in Cambodia. Chapter 4 makes this clear.

Anatta, usually translated as 'no-soul', is the third quality of existence. It can be grasped most clearly when the concept of impermanence is applied to the human person. But again, there is a problem of translation. Helen Jandamit:

> *Anatta* means that you're aware of the sense of self also as something that arises because of conditions and changes according to the changing conditions. You can be aware of this intellectually. When you're a child, you have one sort of body. As you grow up, it changes. When you grow old, you get grey hairs and become stiff. But when you become aware of it in every single instant of perception as arising and passing away, you can't be attached to it. This is *anatta*.

At a conventional level, Buddhism does not deny that there are persons or individuals. The world is full of them! What it does deny is that there is any entity within the human body over and above the process of change and impermanence present within every phenomenon. To use the terminology of the Sri Lankan woman academic, Buddhism sees human beings as verbs rather than nouns, as processes rather than static entities. Seen in this light, *anatta* describes how things function within the human person. One way of glimpsing this, according to Buddhism, is to watch the body and the mind with mindfulness and to ask, 'Can I control what happens?' 'Can I dictate when the body should begin to age?' 'Can I have absolute control over my thoughts?' To all these questions, Buddhism would expect the answer 'No', because the common experience of humankind is that neither the thought processes of the mind nor the health of the body can be controlled completely. Ven. Professor Dhammavihari:

> Nothing in the world is going to stay and last as we want it. Take your own self, you have no command over whether your hair turns grey or falls off. Either personally or interpersonally, when you have no command over anything, two things become clear – that it is all impermanent and grief-generating. There is no selfhood because you have no command over it.

Mahāyāna Buddhists speak more of emptiness, *śūnyata* (P. *suññata*), than of *anatta*. All phenomenal things are said to be empty of their own nature. This is present in Theravāda Buddhism too, but it is not emphasized in the same way. Ven. Bhikkhu Bodhi:

In Mahāyāna Buddhism, a shift in emphasis takes place in the philosophical interpretation of the original teaching. In the Pāli texts, the Buddha repeatedly states that all life is marked by three characteristics: impermanence, suffering and non-self. Here 'non-self' means the absence of a permanent self, a lasting basis of personal identity. In the Mahāyāna, the teaching of non-self evolves into the teaching of śūnyata, 'emptiness', the idea that all phenomena are devoid of their own nature, that they lack any kind of substantial identity at all. This idea of emptiness is already implicit in the Pāli texts but it does not play a very prominent role there. In the Mahāyāna literature, especially of the Prajñāparamitā or Perfection of Wisdom class, it becomes the pivot around which everything else revolves.

Professor Gunapala Dharmasiri is a Sri Lankan who has become a Mahāyāna Buddhist:

In Mahāyāna Buddhism, what we see is an attempt to transmit an experience rather than a theory, a doctrine as such. If you want me to put this in a short form, I think the most significant experience the Mahāyānists were trying to convey was the idea of voidness, śūnyata. That is the basic foundation of Buddhist thought. Of all the Mahāyāna sūtras, one particular passage is quoted frequently which says that form is not different from emptiness and emptiness is not different from form. It is like a mantra.

As later sections will show, Buddhist tradition insists that the experience of both śūnyata and anatta can be positive and intensely liberating. If rightly understood, Buddhism says, the defining characteristics of saṃsāra hold within them the seeds of liberation. Mahāyāna Buddhists would go further and say that saṃsāra and nibbāna occupy the same space and therefore are not completely different.

A WAY OUT OF SUFFERING

Nineteenth-century Christian missionaries to countries such as Sri Lanka and Thailand were horrified by what they saw as the life-denying aspect of such concepts as dukkha and anatta. Fired by evangelical zeal and the optimism of the Victorian imperial venture, they seized on them as objects of ridicule. For instance, they saw the doctrine of anatta as leading logically to annihilationism and nihilism. John Murdoch's words, written in 1887, would be fairly typical: 'As the devout Buddhist counts his beads, he mutters Anitya, Dukkha, Anatta, 'Transience, Sorrow, Unreality'. Existence is a curse, and the great aim should be annihilation or nothingness.'[1] None of the people we interviewed would have agreed with him, for he overlooks one basic component of the Buddhist view of life: there is a way out of suffering. The Buddha at his enlightenment saw beings passing through countless lives of pain. He saw them being born, ageing and dying. He saw them being filled with hope only to be thrown into the swirling waters of despair, being joined with loved ones only to be violently separated. If the Buddha had only offered his followers the three signs of existence, John Murdoch's words would have been justified. At worst, the Buddha's teaching would have been nihilistic, at best, realistic. Buddhism, however, is not content with holding a mirror up to human experience. It analyses it and seeks causes. Helen Jandamit puts it to her students like this:

> The way *anicca*, *dukkha*, *anatta* are translated is so misleading, because they have this aspect of negativity built into them. Buddhism includes negativity, of course, but it is also very positive. There is a way out of this mass of ceaselessly changing sensations which cause you discomfort and pain and sometimes happiness.

This way out is not, as some early Christian missionaries concluded, that death ends all because of the no-soul doctrine. At the time of the Buddha, there were eternalists (P. *sassatavāda*; Skt *śāśvatavāda*) and annihilationists (P. and Skt *ucchedavāda*), in other words those who believed in an eternal soul and those who insisted that the material was the sum total of existence. The teachings of the Buddha as they have come down to us through the texts show that he rejected both the view that we have an unchanging, eternal soul and the view that death ends all. What he did was to chart a middle path between the eternalist and the materialist view of life, as well as between asceticism and self-indulgence.

THE LAW OF CAUSE AND EFFECT

The middle path that the Buddha put in the place of the two extremes was the doctrine that everything within *saṃsāra*, the round of rebirth, was governed by cause and effect, that everything was conditioned. The classically simple formulation of it is this: If x exists, then y exists. When x is there, then y is there. When x arises, y arises. When x does not exist, then y does not exist. When x is not there then y is not there. When x does not arise, y does not arise.

Within Buddhism, this is called the doctrine of dependent origination or *paṭiccasamuppāda* (Skt *pratītyasamutpāda*).

At first, *paṭiccasamuppāda* might seem an obvious, common-sense concept. That everything is governed by a law of cause and effect is something few would want to argue with. Yet within Buddhism, the implications that flow from this are radical. *Anicca*, *dukkha* and *anatta* are all cast in a different light. The truth of impermanence does not mean that everything is chaotic, haphazard or random, but rather that there is an underlying continuity governed by cause and effect. To say that life is unsatisfactory does not mean that unsatisfactoriness is an inherent quality of existence, but that it has a cause which can be eradicated. That there is no unchanging self does not mean that there is no continuity of being across the years or across lives. The truth of *paṭiccasamuppāda*, in fact, insists that everything within *saṃsāra* is held together in a radical interdependence governed by cause and effect, an insight closely connected with the Mahāyāna concept of voidness or emptiness.

In the case of the human being, Buddhism asserts that it is made up of five strands or aggregates (P. *khandha*; Skt *skandha*) held together in continuity through cause and effect. Dr Asanga Tilakaratne drew on Pāli terminology to explain it:

> If you accept the concept of a transmigrating soul, it's very easy to explain rebirth. In Indian religion, rebirth is almost a universal characteristic and it is usually explained without much difficulty by the acceptance of a soul which transmigrates from one birth to the other. It is a challenge to accept rebirth on the one hand and on the other to deny the soul. What Buddhism has done is to show that the human being is a combination of five aggregates, which are *rūpa*, the physical aspect; *vedanā*, feeling; *saññā*, perception; *saṅkhāra*, mental volitions; *viññāna*, consciousness. So, according to Buddhism, human beings are made up of these five. I would imagine Buddhism explains rebirth through the process connected with *viññāna*. I said, 'I would imagine' because in the early discourses the Buddha did not go into the exact mechanism or details of this. This was a theoretical question which came later. During the time of the Buddha, continuity across births was more or less taken for granted. But it must be remembered that *viññāna* is understood as a process, not as something static. It continues unbroken but still it is a process, one thing causing another.

According to this, what continues through death, therefore, is not a static entity but an ongoing process or energy connected with these aggregates. The doctrine of *kamma* (Skt *karma*) or action, looked at later, explains this a little more.

THE FOUR NOBLE TRUTHS

The law of cause and effect lies at the heart of the Four Noble Truths, which many Buddhists see as the most important summary of the Buddha's teaching. The way out of suffering is central to them. The first Noble Truth is the truth of *dukkha*, the truth of unsatisfactoriness in our lives. It gives the analysis or the diagnosis of the human condition. The other three give the cause and cure. Again, taken together, they cast a completely different light over the three signs of existence. What might seem pessimistic appears full of opportunity. Mithra Wettimuny:

> The heart of Buddhist teaching are the Four Noble Truths. First comes the truth of *dukkha*. Now this word *dukkha* should be understood as unhappiness, unsatisfactoriness or suffering. We will use the term 'suffering' in English. So, the first is the truth of suffering. Then the next is the cause for the arising of suffering. The third is the cessation of suffering and the fourth is the path leading to the cessation of suffering. It is important to note that the first truth must be known. The second, the cause for suffering, must be set aside. Then the third, the cessation of suffering, should be realized. And the fourth, that is the path which leads to the cessation of suffering, must be developed.

Asanga Tilakaratne was more specific:

> The malady is *dukkha*. The cause of this, according to Buddhist diagnosis, is *tanhā* or craving, the thirst for satisfying desires. The third one, the cessation of suffering, is the eradication of *tanhā*. When you eradicate your *tanhā* the suffering is eradicated. The fourth is the path or the method you need to follow. This method is generally called the Eightfold Path.

The Four Noble Truths identify craving or thirst (P. *tanhā*; Skt *tṛṣṇā*) as lying at the root of the unsatisfactoriness of our existence. Sometimes three words are used to pinpoint this further: greed, hatred and delusion: *lobha, dosa, moha* (Skt *lobha, dveṣa, moha*). Using these three, the cause of our dissatisfaction in life then becomes greed and hatred springing from delusion or ignorance. Delusion or ignorance, according to Buddhism, is, very simply, not knowing what human existence really is. It is to believe that the impermanent is permanent and that the self is a distinct and separate entity which must be protected, promoted and gratified. It is to see everything through 'I', 'me' and 'mine'. It is to cling to the illusion that happiness is something that can be gained permanently by the accumulation of possessions, human and material. It is to be swayed continually between the two poles of attraction or greed for the pleasant, and hatred or aversion for all that is not pleasant.

Within Buddhist text and tradition, ignorance, together with the greed and hatred that flow from it, is a form of mental derangement or disease, and the consequences of it are horrific, far more horrific than recognizing the truth of *dukkha*. The true horror, according to Buddhism, is found where humans do not know the problem of existence or its cause, where the right questions are simply not asked. Buddhist texts use the simile of fire to describe this:

> Monks, all is burning. And what is the all that is burning? Monks, the eye is burning, visible forms are burning, visual consciousness is burning, visual impression is burning. Also, whatever sensation arises on account of the visual impression, that too is burning. Burning for what? Burning with the fire of greed, with the fire of hate, with the fire of ignorance. I say it is burning with birth, age-ing and death, with sorrows, lamentations, with pains, with griefs, with despairs. (*Ādittapariyāya Sutta*, *Saṃyutta Nikāya*)

In the Lotus Sutra (*Saddharmapuṇḍarīka Sūtra*) of Mahāyāna Buddhism, there is a vivid illustration of a father tempting his sons to escape from an old, rotting, decaying house containing goblins, evil spirits and poisonous animals. Fire suddenly breaks out and engulfs it. Ridgepoles, beams, rafters and pillars explode and roar into collapse. The animals scurry in terror and eat one another. But the sons hardly notice, so engrossed are they in amusements and pleasure. It is only when the 'father' uses 'skilful means' to move their thinking on through promising further gratification that they come out. This, Buddhism says, is the human condition.

All Buddhist schools equate a world enmeshed in ignorance and craving with a world on fire. But, if craving is eradicated, then suffer-ing cannot arise, according to the doctrine of dependent origination. This is the essence of the Third Noble Truth. Together with the Fourth Truth, it places responsibility firmly in the hands of human beings, by stating that the cause of *dukkha* can be eradicated and that the way to do this is through human action. Strictly speaking, there is no room for chance or coincidence. The truth of dependent origination as expressed in the Four Noble Truths means that the cause of suffering can be analysed, charted and eradicated.

One traditional way of illustrating the process through which existence within *saṃsāra* is relentlessly perpetuated through craving and ignorance is by pinpointing twelve factors linked through the principle of dependent origination. Indeed, the twelve are sometimes named *paṭiccasamuppāda*. Each factor is conditioned and also conditions. Ignorance is usually placed first. Because of ignorance, volitional actions arise. Through volitional actions, consciousness arises. Through consciousness, name-and-form arises (the five aggregates or *khandhas*, i.e. the human person). Through name-and-form, the five senses and mind arise. This in turn causes contact or sense impressions to arise. Through this contact, sensations or feelings are caused. Sensation then gives rise to craving (*taṇhā*). Craving then produces clinging or attachment. This attachment then causes the life process to continue, the process of becoming. Becoming gives rise to birth, or rebirth, and we are back to ignorance and the repetition of the cycle, for birth gives rise to old age and death, decay, lamentation and pain. The cycle cannot be broken until craving rooted in ignorance is eradicated. It is because of these two that humans are tied to continual rebirths, according to Buddhism. Ven. Professor Dhammavihari put it this way:

> A process is at work in the human being which gathers momentum. As a man thinks, so does he get more and more momentum to drive on to a next birth. It is a power which cannot be quantified. As the mind works, it gathers its own inclinations such as greed and hatred. This is a power which does not get wasted and at the conception of a new baby it has an impact on it. To us, each little foetus in a mother's womb has some predeterminant, giving it its own timbre or resonance and this comes from its previous life. The previous life impacts on each new birth. Triplets in a mother's womb will run three different streams of consciousness. This is what determines individuality.

The Preciousness of Human Life

The message of the Buddha, therefore, was: 'The way you see the world and act within it is wrong. Change! Root out greed, hatred and delusion from your mind and heart. If you do this, you will see that *dukkha* is not inherent within your life. You will smell the scent of liberation, the fragrance of the deathless. You will see that happiness and peace can be yours.' And Buddhists see human existence as particularly good for this. According to Buddhist cosmology, there are five realms – or six, according to which school of Buddhism you belong to – into which beings can be reborn, stretching from hells to heavens. These realms are what Buddhists call *saṃsāra*. The human realm is a kind of crossroads between the miserable states where little spiritual growth is possible and the heavens where things seem so pleasurable and permanent that there appears no reason to reduce craving. Ven. Bhikkhu Bodhi:

> Buddhism teaches the reality of rebirth – that all unenlightened beings pass through a repetitive cycle of birth, ageing and death. According to the early texts, rebirth can take place in any of five *gati* or realms of existence. These are: the hells, realms of intense suffering; the realm of the *petas* or unhappy spirits, ghostly beings who are tormented by strong desires which they can never satisfy, particularly insatiable hunger and thirst; the animal realm; the human realm and the heavenly realms, inhabited by beings called *devas*, gods, who have immensely long life spans and enjoy great happiness, beauty and glory.
>
> The first three realms are called 'the unfortunate destinations' (*duggati*) because those reborn in them must experience intense suffering and find little opportunity for spiritual progress. The human realms and the heavens are called the 'fortunate destinations' (*sugati*). The heavenly realms are very blissful and the life span there is extremely long, so beings in those realms often buy into the illusion of permanence. Carried away by their glory and beauty, they forget that this sublime estate must eventually end. They are unable to see the unsatisfactory nature of sentient existence, the intrinsic suffering of all conditioned being, and thus they remain fettered to the round of becoming. Buddhism teaches that human existence is a kind of crossroads between the two. In the human realm there is both a certain degree of stability – for example we might live for seventy or eighty years – and also evident impermanence; there is sufficient comfort and security to practise the teaching, and enough pain and suffering to motivate us to practise it. For this reason Buddhism teaches that human existence provides the best opportunity for understanding the true nature of life and for treading the path to liberation.

Over the centuries, there are many people who have been drawn to the Buddhist path because bereavement or personal tragedy has brought them face to face with the fact that life is not perpetually beneficent; that at the very point when the future seems secure, all that is hoped for and enjoyed can disintegrate into dust. It is just because human existence holds within it this possibility that Buddhism considers it precious. It is a chance both to discover what *dukkha* is within a relatively secure environment and to see the need to eradicate its cause.

THE WHEEL OF LIFE

The Wheel of Life used in Tibetan Buddhism illustrates the Buddhist view of life in a most striking way. It hangs as a massive sphere in a squarish frame in many Tibetan temples and Buddhist centres. According to Tibetan tradition, it is one of the oldest symbols of Buddhism in existence and was first created under the instruction of the Buddha for the King of Magadha, who had come to the Buddha to ask what he could give to a king in the south of India in return for a priceless gift given to him. The Wheel of Life was the result. Ringu Tulku described it:

> The most important thing is in the centre where there are three animals, intermingled, each holding the tail of the other: a snake, a pig and a bird. These three animals represent the three basic conflicting or afflictive emotions. The pig represents ignorance, not knowing, not understanding the way things are, not knowing who you are. And from there come two things, aversion and attachment. The snake represents aversion, anger, short-temperedness. Then, the bird or cock represents attachment or desire. Because of our ignorance, we react to things either with aversion or attachment. These three things are the cause, the seed, of the whole *saṃsāric* state of mind. That is why they are in the centre.
>
> Then, around that, are pictures in a circle. Half of the circle is white and half is black. In the white part, you can see some people going up, led by a *lama*. Then, on the other side, there is a black strip, where people are going down, head first. This indicates cause and effect related to action, *karma*. If you do positive deeds then you go up, in the light. If you do negative things, you go down, towards darkness. Then, around that, there's a bigger circle divided into six sections, in which the six realms are depicted. At the top is the gods' realm. Next to it is the demi-gods' realm. To the left of it is the human realm. Then below, at the bottom, is the hell realm. To the right is the realm of the hungry ghosts. And to the left is the animal realm. Now, these six realms represent the result of our six

kinds of emotions. The gods' realm represents the emotion of pride; the demi-gods', jealousy; the human realm, desire; the animal realm, dullness; the hungry ghost realm, stinginess, miserliness and the hell realm, hatred and anger. The six realms are the whole of the *saṃsāric* state of mind. They depict the whole of *saṃsāra*. Wherever you go in these six realms there's no complete peace, no complete happiness. It's always covered, overpowered, by greed, hatred and illusion.

Then around that there's another smaller circle, with twelve pictures in twelve small sections, which represent the twelve dependent originations which illustrate how we get reborn again and again. They show the process through which we move through the *saṃsāric* world, the wheel of life, being born again and again. It starts with ignorance, which is depicted as an old person who is blind. The second picture is of someone who is making pottery. That represents concepts. Because of our ignorance, because we do not know we are conscious, we make lots of concepts. These two together then give rise to the whole thing. The chain then covers name and form – our physical body – and then the six senses. Six senses develop into contact with objects and when we have contact with objects through the six senses, sensation arises. Then, when we have feeling, we have grasping, attachment to it. Then, if it is a nice sensation and we like it, we become attached to it and if it is not so nice we feel aversion, we are afraid of it. This fear and attachment create *karma*. When this *karma* ripens through grasping it is what we call becoming. There is no other possibility but to become – to take the next stage. If it is a rebirth, then the next rebirth. If it is a momentary thing, then the next moment of the *saṃsāric* mind. Then there is the depiction of a child being born, representing birth. Then you have old age and death. Once we are born, there is no other way but to go on to old age and death. It then again starts with ignorance, for we go on and on as in a circle.

The whole thing is carried by a wrathful-looking, ferocious person, who is eating it up in his mouth. That represents time, Yama-rāja, the Lord of Death, which is impermanence. So the whole of this cycle of life is impermanent. It is eaten up by the Lord of Death all the time. Then, out in one corner, you can see a Buddha pointing towards the sky. This shows there is a way out of the *saṃsāric* state of mind. The Buddha who shattered the chain of dependent origination got rid of the *karma* and fled the *saṃsāric* chain of action and reaction. So that is freedom, *nirvāṇa*. Then there is also a small stanza in Tibetan saying the same thing in verse.

Within the Buddhist view of life, therefore, lies the possibility of liberation. This has two components: wisdom (P. *paññā*; Skt *prajñā*) and compassion (P. and Skt *karunā*). These are the two poles of the Buddhist path. Wisdom arises when greed, hatred and delusion die but, without compassion, wisdom cannot be wisdom and without wisdom, compassion cannot be compassion. Ven. Bhikkhu Bodhi:

> Wisdom and compassion are the twin pillars of Buddhism. The two have a very profound interconnection. On the one hand, considered as abstract faculties, they tend to point in opposite directions; but in *real* life, where they must meet, they support, reinforce and complete one another by reason of their intrinsic opposition. Wisdom is the faculty that understands the true nature of phenomena. When we understand things with wisdom, we understand them as they really are – as bare, impersonal phenomena, coming into being and passing away in accordance with conditions. From the standpoint of wisdom there are no real selves, no living beings, no persons. Compassion steps in to round off this picture by taking up the 'conventional' point of view. With compassion, one looks out upon the same world viewed by wisdom and sees that even though there are no ultimately real selves, no truly existent persons, from the relative perspective there are living beings, beings who, like ourselves, seek happiness and are afflicted with suffering. When the mind looks out upon the world from this point of view, when one sees living beings undergoing immeasurable suffering, then compassion spontaneously arises, as the wish to alleviate their suffering, to rescue them from the ocean of affliction. Wisdom is directed initially towards one's personal liberation, but when, through compassion, one empathizes with the suffering of others, one becomes eager to help them to tread the path of liberation. But to do so one needs wisdom. Wisdom thus comes into play again, giving one the means to help others; for it is only by helping them to understand the nature of reality that one can truly benefit others in the highest degree.

THE PATH

When the woman academic we interviewed in Sri Lanka was speaking about *anatta*, she said this:

> What is denied is the presence of an unchanging soul, but that there is a changing individuality is never denied. You could not have rebirth of an individual if there was no changing individuality. Once the Buddha took a little bit of dust on his nail and said, 'If

there is something equivalent to this bit of dust in the human being which defies change, which is permanent, then you cannot make an end of *samsāra*.' You cannot make an end of suffering, because that bit cannot be changed. By nature if something cannot be changed it cannot be changed for the better or for the worse. Because there is the possibility of change there is the possibility of change totally for the better.

The Buddhist way of life is about change. In its simplest form, it is a path that asks the right questions and promotes action on the answers. The right questions are: Why do humans suffer? How do greed, hatred and delusion arise? How can they be eradicated? In order to act on the answers, faith in the truth of the Buddha's teaching is necessary. This is the first step on the path. It is not a blind faith that demands unquestioning acceptance, it is faith in the sense of trust and confidence that what the Buddha taught is worthy of commitment. Ven. Professor Dhammavihari:

A certain amount of acceptance of the message of Buddhism has to come first – call it faith, call it *saraṇaṁ gacchāmi*, 'I take refuge in', call it whatever you will. There must be the willingness to be initiated into the new thinking. There's no denying this. You have to accept the Buddha as teacher, take his message and in your own life say it is true.

This faith is expressed in the outward sign of taking refuge in the Buddha, the *Dhamma* and the *Saṅgha*, described in chapter 1. It is shown in the devotional practices that flow through the Buddhist world and make up such an important part of Buddhist piety. It is a moving towards the 'Three Jewels' in confidence and thankfulness. Yet, after taking this step of confidence in the teacher and the message, the path is one of action, of practice. The responsibility for progress rests with the individual. The Buddhas and, in the Mahāyāna tradition, the *bodhisattvas*, are drawn on as a source of strength and inspiration, but personal effort is obligatory. As Ven. Professor Dhammavihari added, 'Perhaps the Buddhists and the Jains[2] were the first to say that individuals ran their own stream of existence.'

THE LAW OF *KARMA*

At his enlightenment, the Buddha saw, according to text and tradition, that his rebirths had been governed by *kamma* (Skt *karma*). *Kamma* literally means 'action' and an understanding of what

Buddhists mean by action is very important when looking at the Buddhist path. Action begins in the mind with volition. According to Buddhism, volition itself is an action. Each action then bears fruit according to the law of cause and effect. What is most important, however, is that wholesome action is believed to result in wholesome fruit, and unwholesome action in unwholesome fruit. Because of this, the law surrounding action is one that says unequivocally, 'you can mould your own future by whether you do good or ill in the present.' Dr Chatsumarn Kabilsingh:

> Buddhism is a religion which has a free spirit. There is no 'have to'. It depends on what you do. If you do good, you carry the result with you. If you do bad, you know it. You will carry the result of that *kamma* yourself. No one is going to interfere with you. Nobody can take away your bad *kamma* or your good *kamma* for you. You are on your own. You are master of your own life. But you must also hold responsibility for what you do.

The woman academic we interviewed in Sri Lanka said that she had come to the conviction that the very cells of our body are morally sensitive, that the consequences of good and bad action bear fruit not only in external developments which affect us but in our bodies as health or disease.

THE MIDDLE WAY

Central to Buddhism is the 'faith' that wholesome action will have wholesome results and that we need not be imprisoned by the fruit of unwholesome actions in the past if we are determined to act differently in the present. But what kind of action? One key can be found in the term used to describe Buddhism: the Middle Way. That the Middle Way is a synonym for Buddhism has already been mentioned. Philosophically, the Buddha steered a middle path between eternalism and materialism or annihilationism. In his action, he also steered a middle path between the lifestyles connected with these two poles, between the extreme asceticism of his early companions, which was in effect an attempt to free the soul from the constraints of the body, and the luxury of his upbringing, which seemed to take no account of moral responsibility. Neither, he discovered, could lead to spiritual progress. Only the path which steered clear both of over-indulgence and of self-punishment could bring wholeness, and he expected his followers to honour this. Those who renounced family life did not punish their bodies. Good health was promoted as a prerequisite for good practice. Joy was taken in beauty and friendship, yet over-indulgence to gratify selfish urges was discouraged. The ideal lives on throughout the Buddhist world. It is central to the path.

THE EIGHTFOLD PATH

The traditional formulation of the Buddhist way, its *magga* (Skt *mārga*), is the Eightfold Path which forms the Fourth Noble Truth. Dr Asanga Tilakaratne itemized it, using the Pāli terms of Theravāda Buddhism:

> The Eightfold Path starts with *sammā diṭṭhi*, right view, and progresses to *sammā sankappa*, right thought; *sammā vācā*, right word; *sammā kammanta*, right action; *sammā ājiva*, right livelihood; *sammā vāyāma*, right effort; *sammā sati*, right mindfulness; *sammā samādhi*, right concentration. These eight aspects fall into what we call a threefold discipline, namely *sīla*, or morality, *samādhi*, or concentration and *paññā*, or wisdom.

Right view is similar to Ven. Professor Dhammavihari's formulation of faith. It is a recognition that the teaching of the Buddha is true and worthy of following. Right thought is the mental effort and good intention that precede action and practice. Right word, right action and right livelihood relate to ethical living or *sīla* (Skt *śīla*). Right effort, right mindfulness and right concentration refer to meditation practices (P. and Skt *samādhi*). Wisdom is the fruit of the eight, their logical outcome.

MORALITY

Ethical living or morality is the practical foundation of the path. No progress, according to Buddhism, can be made without it. Especially in Theravāda countries, it takes the form of the Five Precepts. In countries such as Sri Lanka and Thailand it would be almost unthinkable for a layperson to visit a temple without chanting them:

> *Pāṇātipātā veramaṇī sikkhāpadaṁ samādiyāmi*
> *Adinnādānā veramaṇī sikkhāpadaṁ samādiyāmi*
> *Kāmesu micchācārā veramaṇī sikkhāpadaṁ samādiyāmi*
> *Musāvādā veramaṇī sikkhāpadaṁ samādiyāmi*
> *Surāmeraya majjha pamādaṭṭhānā veramaṇī sikkhāpadaṁ*
>   *samādiyāmi*

I undertake the precept to abstain from killing living beings
I undertake the precept to abstain from taking what is not given
I undertake the precept to abstain from sexual misconduct
I undertake the precept to abstain from false speech
I undertake the precept to abstain from liquor that causes intoxication and heedlessness.

The Precepts are not commands. There is no almighty being to give them. They are voluntarily undertaken commitments. At their heart is non-harming – not harming self and not harming others. Ven. Dr Somchai Kusalacitto:

> To observe the Precepts needs discipline. You actually have to promise yourself to follow them. The Buddha's teaching has nothing to do with a god or the supernatural. Everything depends on you. A Precept is not a commandment from the Buddha. It is something you really see the advantage of observing. You yourself see the reason why you should be a moral person. And then you take a vow. You say, 'Hereafter I will keep this Precept – I will not break it even if I die.' Your commitment has nothing to do with the Buddha. You have to see the reason clearly for yourself.
>
> The Buddha said the Precepts are more valuable than any dress or treasure. If you observe them, you are more beautiful than any dress or decoration on your body. But you have to decide by yourself and make a personal commitment.

In the *Dhammapada*, this kind of morality is compared to the most beautiful of scents:

> The smell of flowers does not go against the wind, nor the smell of jasmine nor incense nor sandalwood, but the smell of the good does go against the wind. A good person perfumes all directions.
>
> Sandalwood or incense, lotus or jasmine, among these kinds of perfume, the perfume of virtue is supreme.

> (Pāli *Dhammapada*, verses 54 and 56)

On the surface, the Precepts speak only of refraining from doing, yet the morality that undergirds the Buddhist path is much more than this. It is more than restraining the selfish acts that harm and oppress others, although this is certainly an important part of it. It involves practising positive qualities, such as kindness and generosity. In fact, another threefold path, different from that mentioned by Dr Asanga Tilakaratne earlier can be found in the traditional teaching given to lay Buddhists in Theravāda countries such as Sri Lanka, one that begins with generosity (*dāna*).[3] Each Precept can also be seen as embodying the positive, by implication: dedicating oneself not to harm any living being implies caring for them; not taking what is not offered implies respecting the rights and feelings of others. What might seem to be couched in negative language holds the positive within it, as socially engaged Buddhists are quick to stress. Mahā Ghosānanda, when asked about how the situation in Cambodia could be improved, replied:

> The cause and condition of violence is greediness, anger and ignorance. The cause and condition of peace is non-greediness, non-anger and non-ignorance. To overcome hatred we have to be compassionate. To overcome miserliness we have to be charitable, we have to put charity into practice. To overcome ignorance, we have to practise wisdom.

LOVING KINDNESS AND COMPASSION

In addition to the Five Precepts, each Buddhist tradition possesses powerful pictures of what generosity, charity and non-greed are. All relate to the qualities epitomized by the Buddha. Theravāda Buddhism has four *brahmavihāras*, or divine abidings: loving kindness (*mettā*); compassion (*karunā*); appreciative joy (*muditā*); equanimity (*upekkhā*). Ven. Professor Dhammavihari:

> You begin to look at others with the same love as you bear yourself. That's compassion to me. If you love yourself, for the same reason, cause no harm or pain to the other. It's a high ideal. Some may say that it is not possible to practise it. But I tell you that if you don't practise it you pay a price for it at some stage or another.
>   There are three important words here. Loving kindness, *mettā*, friendliness, is the keynote of Buddhism. That I believe is the reason why the future Buddha is named *maitri*. With any coming of a new Buddha, a messianic person, it is love that will come – universal loving kindness which expects no rewards in return. But that is not enough. The world is in distress, in pain. To stretch your hand out to help people when they are in pain is what we call *karunā*, compassion, to tremble as it were with the painful tremblings of others. Then, when you go past that, you have to come to a stage which the sophisticated find difficult to practise. *Muditā* is not sympathetic joy. It's appreciative joy. When you neighbour's son has come out with first-class honours whilst your own son has failed the BA, can you rejoice over that? *Muditā* is that. It is the

ability to appreciate and rejoice over the greatness of others. These are three strains of love which Buddhism practises, direct from person to person, not via a mediator.

Upekkhā means equanimity or the ability to engage with the world without being swayed by attraction or aversion, which cloud objective perception and hinder wholesome decision-making. It has nothing to do with indifference or apathy and everything to do with effective action rooted in wisdom.

As chapter 1 stressed, Mahāyāna Buddhists believe that *bodhicitta*, the Buddha nature, lies within each person. The *citta*, the human mind and heart, is normally clouded by defilements but, according to Mahāyāna Buddhism, it is naturally pure. The path thus becomes a movement towards discovering within oneself all the qualities inherent in *bodhicitta*. These include the six *pāramitās*, perfections, and also compassion. Ringu Tulku:

> *Bodhi* means 'enlightenment'. *Citta* is the mind or heart. So, 'the enlightened heart' it could be called. It has two aspects. One aspect is compassion. The other is wisdom – seeing things as they really are. Compassion is usually described as relative *bodhicitta* and wisdom as the ultimate *bodhicitta*. It is understood that when you see things as they are in a direct way, then compassion naturally and spontaneously arises, because when you see all the pain that you had before you understood the true nature of things, and realize it to be unnecessary and useless, compassion arises for all the others caught in that pain. *Bodhicitta* is when wisdom and compassion come together, inseparable.

The path also involves seeing *śūnyata*, emptiness, as a positive force. For *śūnyata* is not blankness: in some forms of Mahāyāna Buddhism, to experience the truth of *śūnyata* to its greatest depth is akin to enlightenment. It is liberation. It is a seeing into the interconnectedness of all things. Ringu Tulku:

> I'm not sure whether 'emptiness' is the right word in English for *śūnyata*. Many different words are used nowadays. Emptiness is used. Voidness is used. I've seen one translation of the Heart Sutra in Zen which gives the word 'pureness' for emptiness. Whatever you may use, what we mean by *śūnyata* is the understanding of interdependence. Every phenomenon is an interdependent thing. There is no one substance in any thing or any phenomenon which is completely, totally, independent, one and unchanging. So because there is no one thing which cannot be changed, cannot be

affected by other things, which is not related to other things, which is not made in connection with other things, there is no independent existence. The nature of everything is in this order. It's not that the thing is not there. It is there as it is. You can see it. You can touch it. You can experience it, but its ultimate nature is interdependent.

It is important to understand this not just in an intellectual way but in an experiential way, because we ourselves are like this too. If we see ourselves as also like this, then our strong sense of separateness from all other things, our strong sense of egocentrism, becomes less strong. Then, we can also understand the problems of others. Then, slowly, we can see things as they really are in a clearer way.

ROOTING OUT THE UNWHOLESOME

The *brahmavihāras* and the qualities inherent in *bodhicitta* go beyond moral action, as do the words of Mahā Ghosānanda above. Exercising choice to embrace a moral way of living, which harms no one and prepares the ground for loving and compassionate action, is the foundation of the Buddhist path. Weakening the defilements of greed, hatred and delusion by practising their opposites such as *mettā* and *karunā* flow from it. Yet, changing the heart and mind is also essential. All three should be practised together. Vital to the Buddhist path is pulling out the roots of greed, hatred and delusion from what Buddhism calls *citta*, a term that embraces both the mind and heart. This involves knowing how one's mind and heart function and purifying them. According to the Eightfold Path, this cannot be done completely except through meditation. Since the focus of the next chapter is meditation, I will not deal with it in detail here, merely stressing that according to Buddhism, rooting out the causes of suffering cannot be achieved simply by virtuous living. It involves work on one's thought processes and conditioning so that there is a complete change in the way the world is viewed and engaged with, and this is exactly what meditation is about. In the process, hatred becomes non-hatred (*adosa*) and greed becomes non-greed (*alobha*), words couched in the negative but which, again, carry within them the positive qualities of loving kindness and generosity.

STAGES ON THE PATH

The different schools of Buddhism have different ways of describing the stages along the path. Helen Jandamit spoke of Theravāda

Buddhism, which thinks in terms of gradually breaking a series of fetters[4] that bind humans to rebirth:

> Within the *vipassanā* tradition, someone who has broken through ignorance and gone beyond self the first time is considered to be a stream-enterer or someone who has entered the stream of enlightenment just once. This person will understand something about real freedom within life but not yet everything. Someone who goes through a second time is considered to be a person who will not be reborn so many times and has broken through more and more of the fetters or the problems that link us to this life, the problems that cause us to cling to our understanding of life. Someone who has broken through a third time is considered to be a non-returner, someone who does not need to come back to this human existence again. That does not mean that that person may not do so, but that person does not have to be drawn into this cycle of rebirth, suffering again and again and again. And someone who has broken through a fourth time is considered to be an *arahant* or a completely enlightened being. Now that person is the one to ask about *nibbāna*.[5]

In the Mahāyāna tradition, it is the ideal of the *bodhisattva* that inspires those who follow the path. Stages along the path are therefore related to how close one is to that ideal. In the Tibetan tradition, this can be symbolized by rituals of initiation. As chapter 1 stressed, *bodhicitta* and *bodhisattva* are closely linked. A *bodhisattva* is one who practises the *pāramitās*, which inspire and motivate in a similar way to the *brahmavihāras* in the Theravāda tradition. The threefold discipline of morality, concentration and wisdom can clearly be seen in the *pāramitās*, but their focal point for Mahāyāna practitioners is developing the mind and heart of the *bodhisattva*. Professor Gunapala Dharmasiri:

> The concept of the *bodhisattva* is not specifically Mahāyāna. It is perhaps one of the most common bridges between Theravāda and Mahāyāna. The interesting thing is that in Theravāda there is only one *bodhisattva*. In Mahāyāna there are millions. What the concept holds within it is a fantastic message of altruism, total commitment to others and the ultimate expression of the doctrine of interdependence. You start seeing everything as related to you and so you dedicate yourself to the whole. Through understanding voidness and interrelatedness, you develop this incredible compassion and thereby forget yourself and sacrifice yourself for others.

Some Mahāyāna Buddhists take what is called the *Bodhisattva*
Vow, seeing it as binding not only for the present life but all future
ones. Ringu Tulku gave the exact wording of the vow as present in
the Tibetan tradition:

> As the Buddhas of the past generated the *bodhicitta* and practised
> the path of the *bodhisattva*, stage by stage, in a gradual way, so I
> would also like to take on the precepts of a *bodhisattva* and like
> them would like to work on it stage by stage, in a gradual way.

He continued:

> *Nirvāṇa* is not something you enter and can then do nothing. That
> is not the Mahāyāna way. From the Mahāyāna point of view, the
> great *nirvāṇa* is buddhahood and buddhahood gives one the high-
> est capacity or ability to help all sentient beings. So everybody who
> wishes and intends to become a Buddha wants to do that. But
> certain *bodhisattvas* also make the promise that they will not enter
> into buddhahood until all other beings have become Buddhas, as a
> kind of token, symbol or expression of their great desire to remain
> and be equal as it were to those who are not recognized as Buddhas.
> That kind of *bodhisattva* has already realized what buddhahood is.
> So, in a way they are already Buddhas.

He was then asked whether everyone should aim to be a *bodhisattva*:

> Everyone should *aim* to be a *bodhisattva*. At the very beginning, it is
> enough to start with the intention. To have the idea that only I am
> important does not lead to happiness for myself and does not lead to
> happiness for others either. So, if that is the case, we can adopt a
> slightly different attitude, with the understanding that we still have
> selfishness and weakness. It's very important not to overestimate
> ourselves, not to blind ourselves with an ideal and then think we are
> like that. We can start little by little to do better. That is the usual
> method recommended by the Buddha. At first, if nothing else, the
> aspiration is needed. Then, starting from good motivation, you start
> doing things, little by little, and then slowly it becomes easier and
> your understanding deepens. Then you become a better and better
> *bodhisattva* and then becoming a *bodhisattva* doesn't seem some-
> thing unnatural.

RENOUNCING HOME AND FAMILY

A number of the people interviewed had left family life to become
monastics. But what place does this have in the path outlined so
far? Do Buddhists believe that the monastic life is the best life for

religious practice? Both Ven. Professor Dhammavihari and Nyanasiri renounced lay life at a late stage in their lives, in order to be more orientated towards *nibbāna*. For both the decision was quick but decisive:

> It didn't take me half an hour one morning. As I stepped out of the house and went to the bank to deposit some money, I took a decision never to return home. That was my great renunciation! It's the wisest thing I've ever done. (Ven. Professor Dhammavihari)

> I just thought, 'If I do not go into robes I might just as well be dead, because life has no meaning without robes.' It was just like that. Actually, I was at Barberyn Reef. I was lying on the beach and I had an Agatha Christie novel. The palms were swaying and it was absolutely gorgeous. And I looked at it all and I said, 'This is empty, totally empty.' I was a guest at the hotel because the owners were friends. But I said to myself, 'What am I here for?' and I returned to Kandy, went to Ven. Nyanaponika and said, 'I have to be in robes.' (Nyanasiri)

Maeji Khunying Kanitha Wichiencharoen became a nun in Thailand after forty-five years of married life. Her family were opposed to the idea but she insisted:

> I even wrote a letter saying that if I died before I became a nun they should shave my head and dress me in the white robe which I had prepared for becoming a nun. So they agreed.

The experience of all three suggests the arising of an inner imperative which made renunciation the only path for them, as it has for countless others since the time of the Buddha. All three radiated happiness when interviewed. Ven. Professor Dhammavihari, speaking of his time since he had renounced at the age of sixty-nine, actually said, 'From the ages of sixty-nine to seventy-five, six years now, I don't think I've ever enjoyed such joy and happiness. The freedom! There's more beauty in everything I see.'

   Did the Buddha teach that a person has to renounce family life in order to practise the religious path? The simple answer is, 'no'. The Buddhist texts are full of spiritually gifted laypeople. Yet, in all Buddhist traditions, except within some Japanese groups and some forms of Buddhism now developing in the West, there is a distinction between laypeople who remain within family life and monks and nuns who have renounced it. This distinction is not based on the carrying out of priestly functions as in some other religions,

although, in practice, in many countries ordained Buddhist monks
and nuns are involved in rituals of blessing. It is based on the idea
that the ordained life offers a better environment for religious practice, for the discipline needed if greed, hatred and illusion are to be
rooted out of the mind. Ven. Professor Dhammavihari, by speaking
personally, gave the traditional Theravāda viewpoint:

> A good disciple at some stage pulls himself out gradually from
> society so that the determining factors from outside are less on
> him. For instance, I pulled out because I thought if I pulled out of
> society and lived the life of the cloister I could with ease say to
> society, 'No thank you, I'm not controlled by you.'

As Nyanasiri said:

> I'm free from having to go to parties, having to entertain people,
> having to go out at night. When I don't want to do something, I
> can now cheerfully say to people, 'I'm sorry' and they understand
> or, if they don't understand, they'll accept. I'm free to spend my
> time trying to establish mindfulness at all times and examining the
> qualities of the luminous consciousness. It *has* qualities – equanimity,
> expansiveness, openness – and, of course, there can be no ego
> problem, because no ego identity is possible at that stage.

In this context, lay life is seen as tying individuals to responsibilities –
family, home, employment, earning enough to live – that can hinder
religious practice. For this reason the Theravāda tradition continues
to maintain that a monk or nun can move more quickly along the
path towards *nibbāna* than the layperson. Ven. Dhammavihari:

> A good illustration is the difference between an ordinary aircraft
> such as a KLM plane and Concorde, the supersonic jet. A monk is
> capable of reaching his goal much sooner than the layman because
> the household life has its own attractions and distractions. But the
> fact that one has shaven one's head and put on a different
> coloured garment does not necessarily make one nearer the goal.
>
> Simplification of lifestyle, even externally with the shaven head
> and the plain robe, is the thing which makes it easier for the monk
> to practise his religious life of renouncing not only the externals
> but also the internals of life. That makes a difference. Detachment
> gives us freedom of action. If you have your yardstick right you
> can reject everything. Renunciation, letting go, is the hallmark of
> reaching *nibbāna*. This is certainly too much to ask the layperson.
> We cannot ask him not to think of his children. He must find a
> school somewhere by paying this much or that much to get his

child in. To make even an honourable living many fraudulent activities have to be indulged in. Society is always driving people into areas of questionable behaviour, even ministers and heads of state. This is why the Buddha said that the more you move away from it, the better it is.

It is not only in the Theravāda tradition that the lay–ordained distinction is present. Those who renounce do not become indifferent to the pain of the world, but they do free themselves from any responsibilities that involve keeping a home and family alive and prosperous. Such duties have traditionally been seen as obstacles to the pure spiritual life, or at least as hindering uninterrupted practice of morality, meditation and wisdom. Yet, no Buddhist would deny that the path is open to anyone who is truly motivated to try it. The path of morality, concentration and wisdom is open to all.

NIBBĀNA

The goal of the Buddhist path is *nibbāna* (Skt *nirvāṇa*). According to Buddhist text and tradition, it is the end of suffering. It is the end of the craving that fuels rebirth. It is where greed, hatred and ignorance have no place. It is freedom and bliss. It is the ultimate security. It is the perfection of wisdom and the perfection of compassion. But it is also beyond our linguistic categories, beyond the immediate experience of most people. Dr Asanga Tilakaratne put it this way:

> Technically, *nibbāna* means the state in which the mind is completely empty of craving or thirst, indeed of all the defilements or *kilesas*, which are basically threefold: *rāga*, attachment; *dosa*, hatred and *moha*, illusion. According to Buddhism, the entire human predicament is traced to these internal defilements. So the attainment of *nibbāna* is not being born into some kind of heaven, not attaining a transcendental state, but simply cleansing your mind. This cleansing means that you are a completely pure person. That is the end of suffering. So the whole idea of *nibbāna* is not something you attain after your death but happiness and peace in this very life.

Ringu Tulku's words, from the Tibetan tradition, were very similar:

> *Nirvāṇa* has different meanings, different stages. One form of *nirvāṇa* is when somebody gets deep enough into understanding through meditation that he or she is completely peaceful, meaning that he or she is without the negative emotions. Another word used for *nirvāṇa* is when an enlightened being passes away and

you say he has gone into *nirvāṇa* or *parinirvāṇa*. Another way of looking at it is as the opposite of *saṃsāra*. *Saṃsāra* is a state of mind where we have delusion; where, through ignorance, we react in two ways, either with attachment or aversion. Then we just run and run and run through fear and want. It is a state of mind where we can never be peaceful. That state of mind is *saṃsāra*. When you get rid of that state of mind, and you have done away with ignorance, that is *nirvāṇa*.

Ven. Professor Dhammavihari put it this way:

There is a well-known passage in the Pāli texts which the scholars call *Udāna* 8[6] which says, 'If there was not an unborn, uncreated...' and so on, 'there would be no escape from the born and the created'. Seeing here what is born and created, if it is not satisfactory, we believe it is possible to bring about its non-existence. Therefore, *nibbāna* is the non-existence of a state which with conviction we have made up our mind to reject. To reject what is visibly seen here as unpleasant, what is *dukkha*, that is the very joy of *nibbāna*. It brings about the cessation of birth. So it is the unborn, therefore the unageing, the unpainful.

Happiness in this very life was also stressed by Helen Jandamit:

What I understand *nirvāṇa* to be is freedom from the sense of self. It is an awakening to the joy and wonder of life in all its aspects. It's being really aware of the present without running away from it or running into it but just being fully there. And it represents an amazing freedom and happiness – not something out there but something that is right here, now, in this present moment.

The woman academic in Sri Lanka also made the important distinction between *nibbāna* in this life, now, and *nibbāna* after death:

What the state of *nibbāna* is after death is not stated but you can become an *arahant* at the stage of sixty and live up to a hundred. What you are during that time is said to be so blissful. But what it is after death the Buddha said was a useless question, because someone who has not attained arahantship will not be able to understand and somebody who has attained it will not need to be told.

She gave two similes to hint at the pointlessness of trying to grasp exactly what it was through words alone:

On the other hand, if I was to ask you whether you can describe the taste of a kiwi fruit to me, can you describe the taste of a kiwi

fruit to a person who has never seen it, so that he experiences it?
It's impossible! Personal experience cannot be communicated. It
has to be personally understood, personally experienced. So if
describing a mundane experience like eating a fruit is difficult, how
much more difficult is it to explain an experience like *nibbāna*.

Once the Buddha used a simile. He asked, 'If there is a fire in
front of you, will you know that there is a fire burning?' The person who is asked the question says, 'I will.' 'If the fire went out, will
you know that the fire has gone out?' He says, 'Yes, I will know the
fire has gone out.' But the question is asked, 'Did the fire go to the
east or the west or the south or the north, how will you answer?'
And he says, 'That's a foolish question.' So, it's just like that. We
are now on fire. We are on fire because there is greed, hatred and
delusion. We are burning with greed. We are burning with aggres-
sion, hatred. We are burning with ignorance. Once this fire has
gone out, there is wisdom, but to ask what that state is at the end of
life is like asking where the fire went.

To many Buddhists, *nibbāna* seems a distant goal. Yet, just a
glimpse of its texture can generate a tremendous sense of liberation
and happiness in the present and total faith concerning the nature of
the path. Nyanasiri:

> The Buddhist position is total liberation even from the concept of
> a god, even the concept of Buddhism. The Buddha said, once you
> have crossed the river, you discard the *Dhamma*. But you must
> remember that someone who has crossed the river is the *Dhamma*.
> It's the only religion which self-destructs once you have freedom.
> What we mean by freedom in Buddhism is freedom from all the
> greeds – the subtle ones, the mental ones, the emotional ones, the
> ones which we are DNA-coded to have, and all the angers, fears
> and anxieties which, again, we're DNA-coded to have or else we
> don't survive. And it's freedom from the most terrible prisoner of
> all – the self, the I. So it's freedom from these three and with it
> comes freedom from death. There is no fear of death, no fear of
> living. It's a true freedom in which you're free of everything, espe-
> cially the fictive idea of self.

Ven. Professor Dhammavihari almost echoed her words, 'One of
the greatest assets of *nibbāna* will be that not even the minutest
speck of "I" and "mine" will be there. It will be completely erased.'

Since the time of Gotama Buddha, Buddhists have struggled to
find words that might describe *nibbāna*. From the ethical point of
view, it can be seen as the highest state of goodness, since it involves

the elimination of all the fetters and defilements that hinder the wholesome, the good. Greed and hatred are no more. Self-centredness is destroyed, replaced by a compassion that seeks nothing in return and a radical awareness of the interdependence of all things. It is also the highest, the purest form of happiness. There can be no higher form of happiness than *nibbāna*, according to Buddhism. From a philosophical point of view, it is an ending, an ending of suffering, not only one's own but that which one gives to others. Nyanasiri:

> Now there's a mistaken idea that one wants or seeks enlightenment because one wants to put an end to one's suffering. That's not technically true. What you're putting an end to is the concept of suffering, not only the suffering one individually puts up with but that which one gives to others. By the very fact that we exist, we cause other people pain. And if we have put an end to future lives, look at all the suffering we have eliminated, which is not strictly our suffering because when reborn we're both the same and different. It is truly putting an end to any pain we give to others.

In addition, it is attainable. The first sixty disciples the Buddha sent out to preach the *Dhamma* were enlightened, according to the Pāli texts. But, for many Buddhists now, it is the hope of *nibbāna* and the occasional intimation of what true liberation from suffering must be like, which inspires and motivates action.

NOTES

1. John Murdoch, *Buddha and his Religion: Compiled From the Works of Gogerly, Hardy, Kellogg, Titcomb, Davids, Oldenburg, Bigandet and Others* (Madras: SPCK Press, Christian Vernacular Education Society, 1887), p. 32.
2. The Jains were a significant religious group in India in the fifth-century BCE. One of their great teachers or *jinas* (spiritual victors), Mahāvira, was a contemporary of the Buddha. Mahāvira and the Buddha were both part of what can be called the *śrāmaṇic* religious tradition of India, as opposed to the brahmanic. Jainism is still a vigorous religious tradition today.
3. The threefold classification is: *dāna, sīla, bhāvanā* (generosity, particularly almsgiving to members of the *Saṅgha*; morality; meditation).
4. In the Pāli tradition, there are ten fetters (*saṁyojana*): belief in the ego or the 'I'; sceptical doubt; clinging to rules and ritual; sensuous craving; ill-will; craving for material existence; craving for immaterial existence; conceit; restlessness; ignorance.
5. The Pāli terms are as follows:
   a. *sotāpanna*: stream-enterer or stream-winner, who has got rid of the first three fetters;

b. *sakadāgāmī*: a once-returner, who having got rid of the first three fetters and having reduced greed, hatred and delusion, will only return once more to human existence before putting an end to suffering;

c. *anāgāmī*: the non-returner or one who has got rid of the five lower fetters and so will reappear in a higher world from where *nibbāna* will be reached;

d. *arahant*: one who has destroyed all the fetters.

6.   The complete quotation from the *Udāna* (Part 8.3) is as follows:

There is, *bhikkhus*, a not-born, a not-brought-to-being, a not-made, a not-formed. If, *bhikkhus*, there were no not-born, not-brought-to-being, not-made, not-formed, no escape would be discerned from what is born, brought-to-being, made, formed. But since there is a not-born, a not-brought-to-being, a not-made, a not-formed, therefore an escape is discerned from what is born, brought-to-being, made, formed. (*The Udāna: Inspired Utterances of the Buddha*, trans. John D. Ireland [Kandy, Sri Lanka: Buddhist Publication Society, 1990], p.109)

3

MEDITATION: THE WAY TO ENLIGHTENMENT

One of the most popular images in Buddhism is that of the Lord Buddha in meditation, back erect, legs crossed, often in the lotus posture, hands resting in the lap, eyes downcast. It is an image which breathes peace and relaxation, inspiring both devotion and emulation. Its serenity has an almost timeless quality, which seems to rise above the joys, fears and pains of human life. But what kind of serenity is found in meditation? Is it the serenity of non-involvement or withdrawal from the world? Is it the serenity of one who has risen above the world? Or is it the serenity of one who has probed the depths of human suffering and yet can be peaceful? Some people assume that meditation is an individualistic practice of withdrawal from the world of human suffering and conflict. To the social activist, it can appear to be an opting out. To the person torn apart by bereavement, it may appear to offer nothing but a false escape from the real world. But would this be a fair assessment? 'No!', according to all the people interviewed.

Let us take the social activist first. Some seventy kilometres north of Bangkok lies Wongsanit Ashram, a centre of the International Network of Socially Engaged Buddhists. To reach it, one leaves the heavy, polluted air of Bangkok with its traffic congestion, building sites and road-widening schemes to enter a rural world of canals and rice fields. Wongsanit was once just a series of rice fields. Now, the land has returned to a more natural state. It is filled with the sound of insects and birdsong. The chemical fertilizers that were used when the land produced rice have been banned. Its founder is Sulak Sivaraksa, a prominent layperson, who has consistently urged Buddhists to speak out against social evils. But for him, activism is not enough by itself:

> We stress that to have the social dimension, Buddhists must also have personal transformation through deep meditation. You must

synchronize your heart with your head. You must have a sense of peace within. But this sense of peace must not be only to feel, 'I'm all right, Jack.' This peace must be the basis of a positive, activist, view of the world which would include non-hating, non-violence.

One person who has been connected with the ashram for many years is Pracha Hutanawatr. After three years as an active Marxist, committed to the political transformation of Thai society, he felt distracted, empty and disillusioned. A friend suggested he enter a Buddhist monastery as a monk for a short while to sort himself out. In Thai society, this is quite acceptable. Many young men enter a monastery for a limited period, almost as part of their education. There, in the monastery, Pracha discovered meditation. More of his story is told in chapter 4. Now it is enough to note what he said about meditation:

> Meditation helped me develop a deep sense of humour. And this is very important for life, because, as an activist, you are so serious. You want to change the world. You want to change the people. You want to change the social structure and all sorts of things. But in meditation you can see that all the oppressive forces are also within you at the same time. You know that, when you are accusing this oppressive, exploitative, authoritarian system, you also have that tendency within yourself too. You see that you and the oppressive structures are not separate. And that gives you a sense of humour. Then, you can tease your seriousness because, after all everything is so impermanent. If you have no sense of humour, you burn yourself out. So, meditation is important to give me calm, to help me understand myself.

Another member of the ashram is Niramon Prudtatorn, who contributed to chapter 1. Before joining the ashram, she was a journalist working for the Friends of Women Foundation, an organization committed to promoting human rights for women and improving the lot of those who are sexually exploited. Like Pracha, she rejected Buddhism in her youth but found her way back to it. She realized it was only institutionalized Buddhism which she had rejected, not the heart of Buddhist practice. What she gained in coming back was:

> to have the opportunity to do meditation, to look inside myself, to learn how to cope with greed, anger, hatred and ignorance. This has been very helpful in my life, for my spiritual development. If women have more spiritual sanctuary, women can gain self-esteem. As activists, we can help them to be more peaceful, not to

be just angry, protesting all the time. If we can help women activists to practise meditation, it would help them to be broader in their ideas, so that they can go further than merely rallying on the street. If we practise more, we will gain more compassion and more calm to deal with the many issues, not just prostitution, but also rape cases and many other injustices in society.

Ven. Yos Hut Khemacaro is a Cambodian Buddhist monk who was in France when the government was overthrown by the Khmer Rouge under Pol Pot in 1975. In the four years that followed, the elimination of intellectuals and religious leaders almost destroyed the Buddhist heritage of the country. The number of Buddhist monks fell from sixty thousand to about two thousand.[1] Libraries, temples and teaching centres were razed. Buddhism almost disappeared. Chapter 4 tells the story in greater detail. Ven. Yos Hut was able to return to Cambodia in 1992 and is now involved in social reconstruction. This is how he and others have coped with the situation. They have strengthened themselves in such things as compassion:

> through increasing our own education in *Dhamma* and *Vinaya* but also through insight meditation, so that we could be mindful within ourselves and create peace within our own hearts in order to help create peace for others around us and within the whole of society.

Mrs Renee Pan, President of the Cambodian Children's Education Fund, whose whole story will be also told later, simply said:

> Without having a quiet time or meditation to start my day, I cannot stand. I have to start with it and it is so much joy to do my work alongside Buddhism. I can work more. I can use my time wisely.

Social action is one response to the suffering and pain in the world and many Buddhists, lay and ordained, are socially involved, as the above words show and as the next chapter will illustrate further. Yet, most of them are also meditators. Experience has proved to them that meditation is both central and indispensable within Buddhism. This section aims to show why this is so. Helen Jandamit in Thailand gave one of the most traditional understandings of meditation, by quoting the verse from the *Dhammapada*, which many Buddhists see as a summary of the *Dhamma*:

> The teaching of the Buddha is, 'Do good, avoid evil and purify the mind.' Meditation is about purifying the mind. It is very difficult to avoid evil if your mind is not pure because you're dragged in there whether you want to be or not. And it is the same for doing

good. Sometimes we're doing good for all the wrong reasons, but if you purify your mind then you're able to see clearly what you are doing and determine how much or how little to do and what is right and what is wrong.

The Pāli and Sanskrit word translated as 'meditation' is *bhāvanā*, which means 'becoming'. It is a word that implies growth, development. One way of looking at meditation is to see it as development of the heart and mind. The last chapter emphasized that greed, hatred and delusion lie at the heart of human dis-ease and that the roots of these are embedded in the mind. It also suggested that they could not be rooted out completely without knowing and transforming the mind. According to Buddhist teaching, meditation is the only way to do this. Without it, most Buddhists would say, greed, hatred and delusion cannot be eradicated and wisdom cannot be gained.

Several striking images of meditation emerged from the interviews. Ven. Professor Dhammavihari stressed removing poison or contamination from the mind:

> *Bhāvanā* should not be the mere ability to fix your mind on the bulb that is burning on the ceiling or the glow of a light on the wall, but it is to know that you have gradually peeled off the stains of contamination in your mind – conflict, ill-will, jealousy, rivalry. It is a question of how clean your inside is.

Geshe Lhudup Sopa stressed the traditional image of the lotus:

> The lotus is born from the mud. It is mud-born. But when it comes out it is very beautiful, clear and pure. Like that, we are born in impure water, in *saṃsāra*, the realm of rebirth, a muddy situation. But if we practise, study, meditate, we can get free of mud, free of the impure water.

Dr Aloysius Pieris drew a picture of greedlessness:

> The ultimate goal of meditation is greedlessness, *taṇhā nirodha* [the cessation of craving], which is really a definition of *nibbāna*. The purpose of meditation is that. It's not just an ego trip to another world. It is simply a hard, committed, continuous, uninterrupted effort at eradicating the egocentric building of a world around yourself. It is to break those barriers and to be free enough not only to enjoy the freedom yourself but to share it with others.

Meditation, therefore, has little to do with trance-inducement or an escape from reality, two popular stereotypes. It is not primarily concerned with achieving an out-of-body experience or a transcendent 'high'. It is hard work, committed to eradicating what is negative in the mind and heart. It is a form of mental culture.

Within Buddhist tradition, there are two main forms of meditation: *samatha* or tranquillity meditation and *vipassanā* (Skt *vipaśyanā*) or insight meditation. All traditions of Buddhism agree on this, although methods vary. Ringu Tulku, a Tibetan teacher, explained, for instance:

> Meditation as a whole is two things in Buddhism, nothing else. One is *samatha* meditation, which is to make the mind calm and clear. The other is what we call *vipaśyanā* meditation, that is to see the truth, inside. All meditations are included in these two.

Mithra Wettimuny, a Sri Lankan teacher of meditation in the Theravāda tradition, paralleled these words almost exactly:

> There are two major areas of meditation. There is the path which leads to concentration and serenity. Then there is the path which leads to insight, knowledge, wisdom, which is our ultimate goal. Finally, these will have to be yoked together. But initially, a meditator or a beginner can always sit down to practise and acquire some level of concentration and serenity, tranquillity, calmness of mind.

TRANQUILLITY MEDITATION

Tranquillity meditation uses an object to concentrate the mind and bring one-pointedness. In many traditions, the most popular practice is to concentrate on the breath. Mithra Wettimuny went on to explain, as he would to a beginner, how to start:

> This particular meditation requires a certain posture, which means your back, your spinal column, must be upright. So you should sit down in such a manner that your back is straight. Even if you sit on a chair it is OK provided that you keep your back straight. Then, close your eyes gently and first and foremost visualize the posture of your body. Now as you keep visualizing the posture of your body, gradually settle your mind onto your nosetip where the breathing strikes. There is a point of contact at your nostril where you will perceive the breathing when it passes that point, both in and out. That point of contact is very vital. It's the sign of this

practice. Now you must keep your attention on that point of contact. Always ensure that your breathing is natural. Never try to breathe artificially in deep or in short rapid breaths. Allow the natural process to take place.

Another important point is that your mind should not follow your breath to the stomach. It should stay at the point of contact at the nosetip. Now, keep watching the breath passing that point, both in and out. Don't try too hard. Relax the mind as far as possible. Now there's also another important aspect. You must try to control your thinking and pondering process. Most of the time people are thinking, but this thinking is not usually very productive. Now, when an external stimulus arises, if you think about it, it will stay in the mind. If you don't think about it, it will just pass through. It will not harass or occupy the mind. Therefore, we must restrict our thinking process. Our thinking should be restricted to the function of breathing. So when you breathe in, if you want to think, you may think, 'in'. When you breath out, think 'out'. Now this practice can be done both with thinking and without thinking. Without thinking is better. However, you may not be able to come to that point straight away. Therefore, start with the thinking process but restrict it to the breathing function.

Now, you must also know how to control the diffusion which takes place in the mind, because inevitably your mind will begin to run from one object to another. Do not get perturbed or worried when it happens to you, because it happens to all. You must be patient. Now, there's a technique which you must develop in order to prevent that diffusion. When the mind strays to another object, what you must do is to bring forth mindfulness again. Be mindful that it has strayed. Don't try to force it back to the breath, because when you force you get tired and fatigue is not good for this practice. Patiently wait, being mindful and aware that your mind has strayed. When you are mindful and aware, it will naturally come back to your main object, which is the breathing. Even here, it is right mindfulness that is used.

However, there may be the odd occasion when your mind is straying very rapidly. If you do experience that, then on that occasion take three deep breaths, slowly and mindfully. That is the only occasion when you actually and intentionally determine the extent of your breath. But the normal technique is to be mindful and aware that it has strayed. Now if you keep developing this then you will gradually find that your level of concentration will grow.

As you practise, you may begin to see various lights, like twin-kling little stars, very attractive, very pleasant. Do not get absorbed in them. Do not delight in them. They are merely symptoms of some progress in this path of concentration. If you delight in them, you will not only lose those things, you will also lose your concentration. Therefore, try to be calm towards them. Pay no attention to them. Pay attention to the breath all the time.

One more point, do not expect results very quickly because this is not an easy task. The fruits are very high. Therefore, the practice is also quite demanding.

This is how one Sri Lankan woman described her own experience of this practice:

Our senses are all the time passing messages into our minds, see-ing, hearing, touching, tasting. And our minds are all distracted. But in meditation we try to keep the mind on one object, that is bodily contact at the nose, where the breath comes in and out. We concentrate on that, so that the other distractions are kept at bay. As I concentrate, I find there is a certain amount of satisfaction. The mind is calmer and thoughts such as anger or jealousy keep out because when the mind is concentrated, the mind becomes pure. But first of all, before I start on this concentration, I take refuge in the Buddha, in the *Dhamma*, that is his teaching, and the *Saṅgha*, so that my concentration is rooted in Buddhism, because I have firm confidence in the Buddha and his doctrine. Of course, it's very, very difficult, because distracting thoughts keep coming to the mind – ideas, the sounds I hear and so on. But with my eyes closed, I don't see anything. And concentration comes gradually. The mind becomes calmer and a feeling of joy and happiness comes in.

Both serenity and insight meditation are rooted in what Buddhists call 'right mindfulness' (P. *sati*; Skt *smṛti*). Mithra Wettimuny defined it in this way:

The heart of all meditation practice is right mindfulness. That is its base. Therefore, it is the development of right mindfulness which will ultimately lead you to concentration. It means to be mindful and aware of the present, keeping your mind in the present. Let me give you a simple example. When you eat, it means to be mindful and aware that you're eating. If you're talking and eating, that is wrong mindfulness. When you brush your teeth, it means to be mindful and aware that you're brushing your teeth. If your thoughts are far away in what you're going to do during the day, what you did yesterday, at that time there is wrong mindfulness. So right mindfulness means to be mindful of the action you're performing at the time you're performing it. Living in the present – that is right mindfulness.

In serenity or *samatha* meditation, right mindfulness is directed towards the breath or another object. In some traditions, the eyes are closed; in others they remain partly open, focused about five feet ahead. Watching the breath at the nosetip is the usual method in Sri Lanka. One Burmese tradition, however, encourages meditators to watch the rising and falling of the abdomen, as air is inhaled. A word such as *Buddho* can also be repeated in a rhythmic way as the breath passes in and out. Whatever the object, one's whole attention goes to it, in the present. When thoughts of the past and the future come, they are not repressed but they are not allowed to develop either. Awareness of the object is returned to.

INSIGHT MEDITATION

Insight meditation is rooted in the same concept of mindfulness but mindfulness is used in a slightly different way. Godwin Samararatne, meditation director at Sri Lanka's Nilambe Meditation Centre for laypeople, which will be mentioned in more detail later, encourages new meditators to use a technique that combines elements from both serenity and insight meditation:

> When someone comes for meditation, the first aspect that I try to emphasize is the practice of awareness, mindfulness or bare attention. And, while emphasizing that, I encourage the technique of developing awareness in relation to one's breathing. When sitting in meditation, I tell them that it is natural that they will have thoughts. It is natural that they will hear sounds and experience physical pain and discomfort. So, as the whole emphasis is on awareness and mindfulness, I encourage meditators just to know these things and not to see them as disturbances and distractions but simply to come back to the breath. And sometimes I call breathing the primary object and whatever else is happening the secondary objects. This is so as not to create a tension when the attention is on the primary object or the secondary objects.

Godwin's words suggest that it is all right to focus attention on a secondary object if it is difficult to return to the breath. This means a mosquito buzzing near the ear can become an object of meditation, as can pain in the knees, the howling of a dog, the fall of rain or the persistent entry into the mind of any thought. The key to such practice is awareness of the present moment and what is happening to body and mind, whilst still keeping the breath as the dominant object. In his emphasis on the breath, Godwin's advice to newcomers is close to traditional *samatha* meditation. In his encouragement of a wider awareness, he touches *vipassanā*. Helen Jandamit:

> *Vi* means 'clearly' and *passanā* means 'knowing' or 'seeing' in the sense of 'I see, I understand'. *Vipassanā*, then, means, 'seeing clearly'. Seeing what clearly? Seeing the body and the mind clearly. This involves being open to the present moment. And being open means just that. It means tuning in to the body and the mind in the present moment. One could just say, 'I'm going to be open' but it doesn't work. So lots of exercises have been developed over the last 2,500 years. Possibly in other eras, others developed as well. These exercises are refined by each teacher.

One method is what is called 'bare attention' or 'choiceless awareness'. It is a form of mindfulness that involves complete openness to the present moment, without an underlying object such as the breath. Anything is allowed to enter the mind or the heart – anger, jealousy, irritation, love, aversion, memories of the past, hopes for the future, pain, longing. Nothing is judged good or bad. Even if a strong urge to kill someone arises, it is not judged bad. Nothing is clung to, either. Thoughts and feelings are watched, noted and allowed to pass. They are not pushed away in an attempt to control but any proliferation through conscious willing is also avoided. Godwin Samararatne:

> Bare attention is a practice where there is no object. This means that whatever happens when one is meditating, whether one is experiencing a thought, a sensation, an emotion or hearing a sound, one just has bare attention to what is happening. So it is a technique which enables one to see things just as they are. Or to put it in another way, it involves being with what is.
>
> In focusing on an object, there is an element of control. When thoughts arise, one has to control them. In bare attention, a very important aspect is that you learn not to control but to allow. And then, when things arise, what is expected is just to note, to be aware of what is happening without controlling. So I would suggest that in the beginning there has to be an element of control when meditating on an object, but then when the mind is stable, when the mind is calm, then the need to control may not arise.

In choiceless awareness, the mind and heart are watched in a completely non-judgemental way. Each meditation session, in its sheer
openness, can then be a voyage of discovery into one's thoughts and
feelings. What arises can sometimes appear purely superficial: a
sense of aversion to a persistent noise or a nagging pain in the knee;
the constant replaying in one's mind of an argument. Yet much
deeper things can force themselves into consciousness: a feeling of
red-hot anger or painful loss, long repressed; faces of people forgotten years ago. Whether what arises relates to immediate stimuli or
to deeper levels of repressed feeling and experience, watching oneself in this way leads to knowledge of self or, at the very least, to a
growing awareness of how the mind and feelings work, above all,
how they have been conditioned to respond since childhood. The
practice is not for the faint-hearted. Helen Jandamit:

> It is an amazing process of discovery, finding out who you are. I
> mean really who you are. You have to be very courageous because
> much of what you discover is unpleasant, surprising, frightening.
> And you have to stay with it and, by staying with it in awareness,
> a cleansing process takes place. Purification happens of itself. It's
> not something which you determine – today I'm going to purify
> greed. It doesn't work like that. But just through being open to the
> moment and to your real experience of it with awareness, the
> purification happens.

Aloysius Pieris, speaking as a Christian, sees it as release from a
drugged state into clarity:

> Mindfulness is a key word in Buddhism, as in most spiritualities
> outside Buddhism. In Buddhism, the state from which one has to
> be delivered is a state of sleep, of being drugged, of being doped.
> Greed or selfishness is a form of drug by which we get ourselves
> completely mindless. Therefore, the situation from which the
> teaching of the Buddha would like to deliver us is precisely this
> drugged situation. Therefore, mindfulness is the opposite. It is to
> be completely aware at every moment of what is happening within
> us. Not to be programmed – that's the ideal. From birth we are
> programmed and it is so that we can deprogramme ourselves and
> be constantly aware of various forces which make us slaves that
> mindfulness is important. It is the process by which we awaken
> ourselves and keep awake constantly. It is a process of constant
> discernment, constant awareness of what is happening within so
> that we are not out of control of ourselves. The key word of the

Dhammapada, the little manual of spirituality in Buddhism, is *appamādo*. It means vigilance, not being doped, getting detoxified, total awareness.

Moha, another key word used by the Buddha to describe this situation, is to be completely de-mented [literally, in a state of utter delusion]. Ninety per cent of us are de-mented. And so *amoha*, the opposite, is again a word for *nibbāna*. Mindfulness is the process of deliverance that is available to anyone who wants it. It is not something from outside. It is something you can do and it is to be done continuously so that it becomes a permanent state.

Deprogramming is a concept very much used by Godwin Samararatne. He speaks of working from a situation where the mind is reactive or conditioned towards a state where the mind is unconditioned, where it is able to perceive and respond without being weighed down by a legacy of responses built up since childhood, often through greed, hatred and ignorance:

In the context of mindfulness, a conditioned mind reacts mechanically, habitually and one may neither know it nor be conscious of it. Human beings are conditioned by their culture, by childhood experiences, by the teachings they have been exposed to. With such a reactive mind, as it is said in the *Dhamma*, the result is the experience of suffering. So, in the context of meditation, it is really important to realize and come to know these conditionings, in whatever form they arise. The first step is to acknowledge them, to know how one is conditioned and how a conditioned mind functions and then, through that understanding, to develop insight, and through insight, gradually, one may be in a position to get a glimpse of what can be described as a mind that is unconditioned.

Godwin also commented on the question of repressed feelings arising:

People generally control, repress and deny things. They push away what they consider unpleasant. So in meditation, these things arise. When they arise, the practice of bare attention is extremely helpful because, if I may use psychological terms, this enables one to make one's unconscious conscious. This enables meditators to handle whatever they have been burying in their unconscious minds.

'Making one's demons one's friends' is another way of seeing it.

Vipassanā meditation is most often practised in a sitting posture, but the development of mindfulness is also helped by walking meditation. Many meditators alternate the two. From the outside, walking meditation can seem strange, almost ludicrous, so different is it from the walking we do every day. Every movement is slowed, relaxed, sometimes exaggerated. The same piece of earth or floor is repetitively traversed in silence. Helen Jandamit, each weekend, in Bangkok, holds meditation sessions in her *Dhamma* centre. Meditators leave their shoes outside and sit on cushions on the floor in front of a shrine stretching across one wall of the room. At one point in the session, the cushions are pushed to the side and walking meditation begins. The aim is to develop awareness of movement and why we move. Helen Jandamit:

> As you move, why do you move? Immediately you feel something uncomfortable, you will move. When caught in a car in a traffic jam, if you watch people standing at a bus stop, you see an amazing dance. They're moving all the time, scratching, putting hands in pockets, taking them out – wiping off the sweat in Thailand. There's non-stop movement. But it's totally without awareness.
>
> Now when you're practising walking meditation, you notice the impetus that starts your movement. What is it? What is the intention? What is the feeling that prompted you to move? Or in some cases, it's not a feeling. I moved my hand then for a reason but it wasn't exactly a feeling. It was because of my patterns of communication. Normally we're not aware of why we move. We do it automatically. So, in walking meditation, the intention to move is one of the things we always notice.
>
> When we're doing walking meditation in Thailand, at each point we stop and say, 'intending to, intending to walk'. Walking meditation is walking but knowing that you're doing it. At the beginning you just become aware of your body standing. So you stand very still with your hands in a suitable position, usually with one hand touching the other to keep the energy flow moving within the body rather than flowing out. And you make mental acknowledgements of your body standing and of any tensions within it, any feelings that you have. There will be thoughts which come up as well and you notice those. But you're really trying to be aware of the position of the body standing. Then you become aware of this intention to walk and you can feel the body changing as you're aware of this intention. The whole balance shifts. The distribution of the weight changes. The tensions will move to different parts of the body and you notice this as you say, 'intending'. Then, as you move, you put your attention on the foot that is moving and again make acknowledgements of that movement as it is happening. And within the Mahāsi Sayadaw[2] tradition, there are

six different steps. Each one gradually builds up greater and greater awareness of each foot movement. There are lots of ways of practising. You can either do a long walk or a short walk but practically speaking most people don't have space to do a long walk. So they have to turn and walk back. Again you acknowledge turning and you do it in a very specific and itemized way, which keeps your attention there. The mind doesn't go outside because you've got so much to attend to in the simple act of turning. You're making, in the first exercise, four pairs of foot movements as you turn. If you're attending to that, the mind doesn't have a chance to go outside.

Not all walking meditation is as structured as that practised in Thailand at Helen's centre. Some meditation centres allow meditators to find their own pace on their own patch of ground among the trees or grasses in the open air. Yet each form involves developing complete awareness of the present moment and of the mental processes underpinning action, especially volition, which, in Buddhism, is considered a form of action.

Being able to catch the mind before intention or volition becomes external action is one fruit of the process and this can be extremely useful when applied in everyday life. It is the ability to see conditioned responses rising in the mind and to choose not to go along with them, not to be enslaved by them, in Dr Pieris's terminology. If an angry response arises, it need not be acted on if caught quickly enough. Conflict-causing words and actions that would usually be thrown immediately into the world can be stopped in their tracks if the moment of volition is noticed. This kind of mindfulness involves cutting through the web of responses we have built up from childhood and which prevent objective perception. It opens a path to eradicate responses based on craving (taṇhā) or greed and hatred (lobha, dosa). Insight into the nature of our minds and our hearts can result.

Many Buddhists, however, would claim that meditation goes further than insight into the nature of their own minds and hearts. What they seek through meditation is insight into the nature of reality as a whole, in other words the death of ignorance and delusion and the birth of wisdom. This is how one woman meditator in Sri Lanka put it:

> The goal of meditation is to realize what life is, to see things as they really should be seen. I want to realize the truth that the

Buddha has spoken about, to see the sort of life we should live so
that we reach the ultimate goal where we're not born again.

Mithra Wettimuny's description of *vipassanā* was different from
that of Helen Jandamit or Godwin Samararatne, in that he saw it as
retaining one object, but the goal he gave would be shared by all:

> Serenity of mind is one fruit of meditation. But the bigger fruit is in
> the other path – the path that leads to wisdom. Now, that practice
> is called insight meditation. Here what we do is to take any object
> and establish our mindfulness on that object and then try to see
> the true nature of that object. Wisdom is to know and see the true
> nature of things. So, for example, we take the breath and try to
> understand the true nature of this breathing. If you come to know
> and see the true nature of one thing in this world, you'll come to
> see and know the true nature of all things in the world.

Life, according to Buddhist doctrine, is marked by *anicca, dukkha,
anatta*. Chapter 2 made clear that to see into the nature of reality is
to see into the heart of these. All Buddhist traditions agree that
meditation is one of the finest gateways to this, for what is true for
the individual mind and heart is true within the whole of life. For
instance, as the mind is watched in meditation, the impermanence
of thoughts and sensations is seen. Thoughts arise in the mind and
leave. Feelings of anger can emerge with such strength that they
make the body flush, but they pass. Sensations can pulse through
knees unaccustomed to being bent for so long but, without any
change of position, they diminish. It is the same for facial itches and
nerve pains. All that our bodies throw up is impermanent, without
constancy. Mahāyāna Buddhists would say that all is emptiness.
Watching the mind, the breath or the feelings with awareness,
therefore, can be a direct window onto impermanence. It can also
be a window into the meaning of *anatta*. Here, the key question is
whether we can control what comes into our minds. Most people
practising *samatha* meditation, where the aim is to bring the mind
back to one object, find that, however much they strive to remain
concentrated, thoughts push themselves in. Where then is control?
Where then is the self? Where then is static personhood?

The Zen tradition, an important form of Buddhism in Japan,
places silent meditation at the very centre of all its practice, even
more so than do other groups. Beth Goldering is an American who
was brought to Zen Buddhism after leaving Judaism and exploring
other spiritual paths, as well as psychotherapy. She became a

Buddhist in 1986 and was ordained a Zen priest in 1995. She described vividly 'sitting Zen', in other words meditation in Zen:

In Zen, what you do is literally sit. There are two cushions, a round one on top of a square one. You're allowed to arrange your legs in one of four or five ways and if you really have trouble you can sit on a chair. The essential matter in terms of posture is that your spine should be absolutely straight. Now by straight we don't mean flat, because the curve at the base of your spine has to remain slightly rounded so that you sit on the front part of your pelvic bones. And then your knees, depending on whether you're sitting full lotus or half lotus or Burmese, together with the base of your pelvic bones, become a triangle, a three-pointed space, which is the source of your stability. Then, your left hand is on top of your right hand and your thumbs are just touching and you put them just below your belly button where your stomach swells and you breathe from the diaphragm. And you don't try to control your breathing, to make it long or short or see how long it is or how short it is. You let your breathing be what it is from that space, with your eyes open but not exactly focused about five feet ahead of you, so that your lids are half-way down. Your tongue is against the top of the back of your teeth which keeps your mouth from salivating too much. Your mouth is closed. Some practices suggest that you smile.

And then you simply sit there and you do not move. And when your nose itches you don't scratch it and when your legs fall off, you let them fall off. And then after a while, thirty, thirty-five or forty minutes, a bell rings. You get up. You bow and you walk four, five or ten minutes, either very slowly in Soto Zen or faster in Rinzai Zen, with your hands in a specific position and your back straight, keeping your concentration until it is time to go back to your cushion and sit again. So when we're talking about sitting meditation we really are talking quite literally.

When sitting, everything in the whole universe is going on in your mind. Traditionally in Zen we start with counting our breaths and we count to ten. You bring the number and the breathing together. When you've done that for a while your teacher will give you something else. In classic Soto Zen it's following your breathing. In Rinzai Zen you get the famous *kōans* – 'What is the sound of one hand clapping?' – that kind of thing. They are puzzles for your mind that cannot be resolved by the mind. They can only be resolved by wearing out the mind's processes of defence until something else can emerge.

In a retreat, we might sit from 6 to 8 in the morning, then from 9 to 12, then 2 to 5 p.m., then 6.30 to 9.30 p.m. You will see your teacher once or twice during that period and you'll also have a lecture. You will keep silent all day. You'll go to sleep. You'll get up. You'll do that for five or six or seven days.

During the first couple of days, you get tired. Your legs hurt. About the third day, the silence in a good place becomes like clean water and it's like sitting by a waterfall in the rocky mountains in the summer. So what happens is that, as you practise, your mind does everything. It figures out what's wrong with how you tie your shoe laces. It solves some problem in physics. It writes the great novel. All the time it's doing that, you are not interfering with it, but you're also not co-operating. We say it's like a ball. If, when a ball bounces, you hit the ball, it keeps bouncing. If you don't hit the ball, it loses its energy. So the practice – the counting, the breathing, the *kōan* – is the way you keep your hands from bouncing the ball. So the mind will do what it does. What it does depends on your personal history, on your temperament, on all kinds of things. Eventually, the mind will get tired of all that and the ball will stop bouncing and when the ball stops bouncing then the universe can come in and then you find the universe has been there all along.

DEVELOPING COMPASSION

Several speakers have mentioned creating the circumstances for something else to enter the mind. The arising of wisdom is the ultimate goal, yet several meditation practices also seek to develop qualities linked with wisdom, such as compassion and loving kindness. Gaining insight into how the mind functions when conditioned by such things as greed and hatred is most important, as is glimpsing *anicca* and *anatta* through seeing how impermanent thoughts and feelings are. Both lie at the heart of *vipassanā*. Yet replacing greed and hatred with their opposites is also important for all schools of Buddhism, although methods vary.

In the Theravāda tradition, a much loved practice is the *mettā* meditation – meditation on loving kindness. In an early Pāli text, the *Sutta Nipāta*, these words are found:

> Just as a mother would protect her only child at the risk of her own life, even so, let him cultivate a boundless heart towards all beings.

Let thoughts of boundless love pervade the whole world: above, below and across without any obstruction, without any hatred, without any enmity.

(*Sutta Nipāta*, verses 149–50, trans. H. Saddhatissa [London: Curzon, 1985], p.16)

They have become the basis of a practice which involves spreading loving kindness to the whole universe, beginning with oneself. There are many variations to it. One traditional form takes these words as its core: 'May all beings be free from hatred, suffering and anxiety. May all beings be happy.' First, they are applied to the meditator. Sitting in quietness, the meditator surrounds herself with loving kindness, wishing herself happiness, well-being and health. Then, the words are gradually pushed outwards to embrace others in an ever-widening circle. To picture a loved teacher is often the next step and the meditator thinks, 'May he or she be happy and free from suffering.' Next could come a parent or a dear friend and then a person towards whom one feels neutral. Finally, the words are used to embrace an enemy. Alternatively, instead of bringing to consciousness individuals, groups of people can be pictured, beginning with those in the same building, room or organization and moving out to one's neighbourhood, town, country and planet. Ranjani de Silva described a possible progression:

First think of yourself and say, 'May I be happy. May I be happy.' Then say of your dearest ones, 'May my mother be happy, may my father be happy, may my family members be happy. May my closest friends be happy.' You go on like that to your neighbours, to anyone. You can go to people who are suffering in hospitals, army camps and refugee camps. You can think of them all and say, 'May they be happy.' And your heart should go with the words.

Whatever the practice, loving kindness, like a stream of light or warmth, is radiated outwards.

Traditionally, the *mettā* meditation is seen as an antidote for hatred and ill-will (*dosa*). Many Buddhists practise it daily, placing it at the beginning or end of *samatha* or *vipassanā* practice. In Theravāda Buddhism *mettā* is the first *brahmavihāra* or divine abiding. As stressed in the last chapter, there are four. Compassion is the next and some Theravāda Buddhists use compassion within meditation in a similar way. Ven. Bhikkhu Sumedha, about whom more will be said later, is a German monk who now lives as a hermit in a cave in Sri Lanka. When asked how compassion is practised, he replied:

To begin with, one should think about the horror and terror of the opposite of compassion. That will foster knowledge and motivate compassionate thoughts. And of course, sitting in such a body, compassion can be understood from direct knowledge of one's own problems. We should be compassionate towards our own problems first. Then we can form a strategy. For instance, it is good to direct compassionate thoughts always to the nearest point where they are needed. That includes ourselves first. But then it is the next one. So out of this compassion, together with wise reflections, we may be able, in our way, to be a blessing to the next being who is in need of our compassionate action. For, it is not enough to say, 'Oh the poor dog' – you have to go into the kitchen and get a biscuit.

VISUALIZATION

Compassion in Buddhism is an active quality. Meditation on compassion should lead to compassionate action. A form of meditation used in the Tibetan tradition is visualization or deity yoga. Here, beings that embody positive states such as compassion are visualized and honoured in order that the qualities they represent are born in oneself. Ringu Tulku:

> In Vajrayāna Buddhism there are many deities. We all have too much attachment to our own way of seeing things. We solidify what we see and say, 'This is this. This is the truth.' So we are very caught in our own concepts and assumptions. In order to get out of this, in order to see differently, deity yoga is used. It is like using the result as the path. While we are still in this not-so-enlightened state, we take the enlightened state of another being or ourselves and imagine that we are already in that state. And we try to look, feel and think as if we were in that state. That's the practice. Suppose you want to train yourself as a doctor or an actor, you can first imagine yourself as a doctor or an actor and ask yourself how you would walk or talk if you were either of these. This can help you to become what you want to be more easily.
>
> The deities are not like individuals. They are principles and concepts. The meditation is a method of exercising your mind. There are countless deities and you can make them up also. So therefore they are not individuals. Sometimes you have very wrathful, ugly-looking, ferocious deities with lots of heads; sometimes they are very peaceful and beautiful, very seductive. It's all a means of trying to work on your own state of mind and your emotions, negative emotions especially.

Some of these deities are seen as *bodhisattvas*, as beings capable of generating compassion for the help of humankind. Yet, through this method, meditators come to realize that the qualities visualized in the deities are within themselves. By imagining these qualities in all their embodied force within another celestial being, it is believed that they will grow in oneself or will be discovered within oneself. Compassion is one of the most important qualities visualized.

MANTRAS

In Tibetan Buddhism and some forms of Japanese Buddhism, mantras have a place in meditation. Theravāda Buddhism usually avoids the use of words in meditation except when a word such as *Buddho* is used to concentrate the mind or loving kindness is practised. Yet, in the Japanese Soka Gakkai movement, which gains its inspiration from the Nichiren[3] tradition, the chanting of the invocation to the Lotus Sutra is central to meditation: *Nam-myōhō-renge-kyō*. This means, 'I take refuge in the Lotus of the Wonderful Law Sutra.' The words are believed to carry enough power to lead an individual to enlightenment. In meditation practice they are repeated over and over again so that they permeate the psyche and lead the mind and heart into the compassionate message of the Lotus Sutra.

In Tibetan Buddhism, the words which carry supreme importance are: *om-mani-padme-hum*. Ringu Tulku explained:

> This is the mantra of Avalokiteśvara. Avalokiteśvara is a *bodhisattva*, the most courageous *bodhisattva*, who has made a commitment not to enter into buddhahood until he has seen all sentient beings become Buddha. Therefore, Avalokiteśvara is regarded as the embodiment of compassion. So therefore the Chenrezi practice – and 'Chenrezi' is the Tibetan word for Avalokiteśvara – is seen as the strong way of developing compassion.
>
> *Om* is the syllable or the sound which is believed to be the source of all sounds, because it is a sound which can be made without making any movements of your tongue or lips. *Mani* in Sanskrit means the wish-fulfilling jewel and *padme* is the lotus flower. The wish-fulfilling jewel is the representation of compassion, for it is said that compassion is the one thing from which you get nothing but benefits for yourself as well as others. It is therefore the wish-fulfilling gem, the legendary object which gives you all you wish for. *Padme*, the lotus flower, is usually regarded as a symbol of purity, unstained. In India, lotus flowers are grown in

very muddy ponds everywhere but, even if they grow in dirty
places, no speck of dust or stains can be seen on the petals.
Therefore, this represents wisdom, which is a state where all negative things, all defilements, all ignorance just go away, as sunshine
drives away darkness. *Hum* is a word which means 'I am' – I am
compassion and wisdom.

   Om-mani-padme-hum is the name of Chenrezi. The mantra is a
reminder. It is a slogan. You think on it. You meditate on it. You
see your true nature in it.

In Tibet, the mantra is painted in bright colours on rocks leading to
temples. It is also placed inside containers, popularly known as
prayer wheels. These can be seen turning in the wind in the Tibetan
countryside. They are also used in temple ritual. With a small wrist
movement, the 'wheel' can be set in motion at the end of its shaft,
revolving with a rhythmic, flowing energy. Ani Kunzang, a Western
nun trained in the Tibetan tradition, explained its significance:

   Inside the prayer wheel are many small *om-mani-padme-hums* and
   so it's called a *mani* wheel. Other mantras are used as well sometimes. The wheel is turned in a clockwise direction. The turning of
   the wheel many, many times embodies the idea of multiplication.
   It's like one person saying the mantra but many many times. It has
   the idea of multiplication and getting much more benefit from the
   mantra.

Whether it is meditation on the quality of compassion or on an epitome of compassion such as Chenrezi, or the turning of the *mani*
wheel in the coolness of the Tibetan mountain air, the aim is the
realization of compassion within oneself or, as Mahāyāna
Buddhists would term it, the realization of *bodhicitta*.

OBSTACLES AND BENEFITS

Obstacles in the path of the meditator are many. Godwin
Samararatne mentioned a few he had noticed as encountered by the
Westerners who came to Nilambe:

   One hardship is in relation to expectations. When meditators have
   expectations in relation to what they want to achieve and when
   they are not fulfilled, naturally they're frustrated and disappoint-
   ed. Another area where people have problems is in trying too hard.
   There can be two extremes – trying too hard and not trying at all.
   When you try too hard, the general result is restlessness, tension,

agitation and doubt and, if you're not trying at all, the result is sluggishness. What can be described as effortless effort or right effort must then be discovered. Meditators also experience physical pain and discomfort because of the sitting posture, and even the practice of silence can be hard.

Among those who have not had the occasion to be introspective or to be alone with themselves, another hardship is the experience of unpleasant memories from the past – I call them psychological wounds, wounds in relation to what they have done to others or what others have done to them. Guilt, remorse, hatred and ill-will result. Then, some meditators find it extremely hard to be friendly to themselves. When the meditation on loving kindness is introduced, they find it difficult to make the switch from hating oneself to being friendly to oneself.

Overcoming such obstacles can take a long time. Meditators who come to Nilambe often stay continuously for several months and then return year after year. Yet as these hindrances are faced and overcome, what are the practical fruits, seen by others and experienced within? The gaining of wisdom, through insight into the nature of reality, has already been stressed; so has the ultimate goal of greedlessness. Yet, for many Buddhists these goals are like a distant field pulsing with light, to be worked towards rather than to be experienced daily. None of the people we interviewed claimed to be enlightened! So, what are the immediate benefits seen in everyday life? Mithra Wettimuny voiced the most traditional description of the results of *samatha*:

> If you practise the path of concentration you will acquire a very calm, tranquil and serene mind. This is very valuable because there is a happiness, a pleasant feeling, a serene joy, a joy which is free of material, which arises with this serenity of mind. Now if you take this practice to its highest levels you can reach those states called absorptions.[4] These are merely very advanced states of concentration. If I were to give a simile, it is like sharpening a knife. When you have gone into such realms of concentration your mind is very sharp, as a knife must be sharp to be effective. However, serenity is what is most important.

Helen Jandamit stressed similar qualities:

> One very superficial one is that you learn how to relax. It's superficial but very valuable. Also, you build up concentration skills. If you have good concentration skills, well, of course, you can apply

them to any aspect of your daily life, whether you're working in an
office or whether you're bringing up young children. Whatever
you're doing, if you're really concentrated, and I don't mean force-
fully concentrated but naturally concentrated, there isn't an element of tension involved. It is a very natural attention. There is
some effort involved but it is not to the extent that you build up
tension across your shoulders or develop headaches. It's quite the
opposite. And, if you have good concentration, then whatever task
you're doing gets done efficiently, quickly. You don't make mistakes. You don't have to go back over things, checking whether
you've done them or not, because you did them in awareness. A
task of work that may have taken two days before, with good concentration, will take maybe one day.

Your mind becomes more concentrated, cool and calm. You're
not swayed by emotions in the same way as you used to be. It
doesn't mean that you don't feel. It doesn't mean you don't have
emotions. I hope a lot of people don't misunderstand this. You
don't suddenly blank out your feeling ability. But you're not
swayed by your feelings. You're not controlled by them.
Consequently, when you work, you can do a better job. When you
interact with people, you do it without being hit around like a
ping-pong ball from one emotional reaction to another. There is
feeling, but you're aware of it and you can choose to react or not
to react. There is a freedom there. And in daily life I think that is
of great benefit.

Also, people who practise at any deep level will automatically
avoid those actions that cloud or disturb the mind. Usually such
actions are ones that harm you or harm another person. Someone
who is clear minded will not chose to do that.

Ven. Santikaro, an American monk trained in the Thai Forest
Tradition, also stressed calm but went further:

I'm more relaxed through the kind of meditation I do, which is
based in the breathing. It's a very simple and natural way to calm
yourself. That gives me more energy for work. Another thing I've
learnt from meditation is that the whole structure of self is very
much centred on control. That means controlling ourselves and
controlling other people and it includes all the systems of domination in the world such as ongoing imperialism, class domination
or gender domination. And Buddhism is my way of getting free
of that.

Other responses included:

> I am less angry and listen more and practise more. When friends
> have some difficulties and come to me, I am ready to share, ready
> to listen to them patiently. (Niramon Prudtatorn, Thailand)

> Meditation has made me a different person. I have been able to
> curb my temper. I am more patient. It has given me a different out-
> look. (Woman meditator in Sri Lanka)

> Meditation means you are able to retain calm and quietness in your
> heart, not just while you close your eyes and meditate but also
> when you live your life, when you make connection with others.
> (Dr Chatsumarn Kabilsingh)

CREATING A DISCIPLINE

Where and for how long Buddhists practise sitting or walking meditation varies. There is no one model to follow, which is hardly surprising given Buddhism's internal variety. There are also, quite
naturally, different patterns for lay and ordained people. For
laypeople, practice has usually to be integrated within family
responsibilities, employment and travel. It therefore demands discipline, even sacrifice, to find time for it. Yet, countless Buddhists
do just this. This was Mithra Wettimuny's advice:

> You should practise every day, preferably at a set time, and you
> must also gradually increase the time span of your practice. The
> ideal time span for one session is one and a half hours. Now, no
> beginner can get there straight away. Therefore, I suggest that a
> beginner starts with fifteen or twenty minutes. Time your practice.
> Always resolve when you start the extent of time you're going to
> practise and do not stop halfway under any conditions. Gradually
> increase the time span of your practice. In the first week, you
> could practise twenty minutes. In the second week you could
> practise, let's say, thirty minutes. Once you come to an hour, that's
> a critical point. Stabilize that hour. It may take you even a month
> or two do so. True concentration will only dawn when you have
> stabilized that hour. Do not expect any rapid results until you get
> to an hour and stabilize that hour.

For one woman meditator we spoke to in Sri Lanka, the night was
the best time:

> I find the best time is in the night. Whenever I wake up in the night
> – sometimes it's about 12 o'clock, sometimes it's 1.30 – I get up

and I wash myself. I drink a little water and I sit down to meditate. I find that at that time, everything is quiet and my mind is clearer.

Others prefer the early morning, before breakfast. This is probably the most popular time. Meditation days or retreats can also be injected into lay life as a chance for intensive practice. Nilambe Meditation Centre, mentioned earlier, is high up among tea plantations near Galaha in the central highlands of Sri Lanka. Mountains stretch out on all sides and punctuate the horizon. No public transport reaches it. It is an hour's upward walk from the main road. Shortcuts exist for those who know. For those who don't, the twists of the track can seem endless. There is no electricity and the nights can be cold. Men and women meditate together but sleep in different buildings. The whole place is wrapped in outstanding beauty. Just to watch the sky is to see the truth of impermanence – now blue, now grey; now with white or purple clouds which themselves seem like mountains; now shot through with the golds of sunset; now black, lit only by the brilliance of stars and planets.

There is no time limit on visits to Nilambe. Some come for several months at a time. Others stay only a weekend. Except for special groups that occasionally book in, the timetable is the same each day. Godwin Samararatne:

> A gong goes at 4.45 in the morning to wake you up. From 5 to 6 a.m. there is group meditation in the hall and we practise three postures: sitting, standing and walking. At 6 o' clock, there's a break for tea. Then, from 6 to 6.30 a.m. – a beautiful time of the day – you are encouraged to develop a sensitivity to nature (and for this there must be a degree of mindfulness), to notice a tree, a flower, the clouds, the distant hills. From 6.30 to 7.30 a.m. there is yoga, to develop awareness in relation to your body.
>
> Breakfast comes at 7.30 a.m. It is emphasized that you must eat in complete silence. The idea is to be aware while you are eating. Then after breakfast we have working meditation, which allows you to see how far you can work in a mindful way, how far you can see work as something not different from meditation, whether in the kitchen, washing the toilet, helping in the garden. From 9.30 to 11.00 a.m. there is group meditation, followed by individual and outdoor meditation from 11.00 to noon.
>
> At noon there is lunch. Here again the meditators are encouraged to eat in silence and to eat with awareness. There is a break from 12.30 to 1.30 p.m. – a period of rest. Then I meet the meditators individually to find out whether they have any problems or

difficulties in their practice. From 2.30 to 4.00 p.m. there's another session of group meditation in the hall. And at 4 o'clock there is a tea break. During this we encourage the meditators to speak to others so that they will learn how to speak with awareness as far as possible.

Then there's more yoga. From 5.30 to 6.30 p.m. the meditators are on their own. And sometimes it's a beautiful time of the day with a sunset. At 6.30 p.m. there is chanting, followed by a sitting from 7 to 7.30 p.m. After that, there's a snack and then a discussion from 8 to 9 p.m. We end the day with meditation on loving kindness.

Meditators are not compelled to attend all sessions. Yoga, for instance, is not a widespread practice amongst Sri Lankan Buddhists and is therefore more popular with the foreigners at Nilambe than the locals. There is also a small library of books and tapes.

Throughout Asia and now increasingly in the West, meditation centres with a similar schedule to Nilambe flourish. Techniques and timings vary according to the tradition. Less silence and more chanting might be found in a Tibetan centre and longer periods in the meditation hall within Zen practice. But what is important is that meditation within Buddhism is increasingly becoming part of lay practice. This has not always been so. The traditional understanding, in many Buddhist countries, has been that the deeper levels of meditation were for the one who was ordained alone.

Yet, for those who are ordained, too, meditation practice can involve carving out time from a busy schedule. Many monks and nuns live in a community, in close proximity to towns and villages. They therefore find themselves with a teaching and counselling role. This schedule of a nunnery in Cambodia can be duplicated across Asia, especially in rural areas where there is poverty and lack of resources. So Mouy, a Cambodian nun who has established her own nunnery:

Like most of the temples in Cambodia, we wake up at 4 o' clock in the morning. We then chant and pray and practise meditation. Then, around 7 o' clock we have breakfast. Then, we start work. For us, in our temple, this means work in our garden, helping to grow the vegetables for our food. Then, we teach and work with the children in the school near the temple.

Then we have lunch and a rest and in the afternoon we study for ourselves, for our own education and practice. We study meditation. We study *Dhamma* and then in the later part of the afternoon, we do a clean up around the temple and the areas surrounding the temple.

The villagers near our temple are very poor. So they provide some food but not all, not enough. So we cook for ourselves. We, the nuns, prepare our own food. Sometimes they add to what we have but we are responsible for sustaining ourselves.

In such a situation, finding time for meditation does not come easily. It is the result of discipline and effort, as it is for laypeople. Living in close proximity to villages means that the monks and nuns become involved in the life of the community.

Another pattern of monastic life can be seen in the Forest Tradition of Thailand. Even within this one tradition, practices vary but central to all forms is closeness to nature, strict adherence to the monastic code of discipline and meditation. Ven. Santikaro, who was drawn to the monastic life after working in Thailand as a Peace Corps volunteer, lives within a dynamic but perhaps somewhat unrepresentative community within the Thai Forest Tradition at Wat Suan Mok, in the south of Thailand. He gave an explanation:

> The Forest Tradition is inspired by the fact that the Buddha spent not one night in a city, according to the texts. At best, he was in a park or a grove on the edges of cities. But he did spend a lot of time on hills or in a forest. And the original lifestyle of a *bhikkhu* was one of wandering and spending a lot of time close to nature.
>
> The Forest Tradition at Suan Mok has an emphasis on living close to nature. One of the ways we translate the word *Dhamma* is 'nature, the Law of Nature', and we feel by living close to nature we can get more in touch with this. When we're with people, we tend to be pushing each other's buttons all the time, stirring up each other's egos, each other's worries, each other's fears. But when you're with trees, ego stories do not come up and so it's much easier to see what is going on in your own mind and to develop a practice of mindfulness.
>
> Also, the forest is not as competitive as human society. Although neo-Darwinists have seen it as very competitive, you can see a lot of co-operation in the forest and impermanence. By living in the forest, you don't so much receive this intellectually but you become familiar with it through experience. The Buddha's teaching becomes not just something in books but part of your life.

It's also a more simple life. Many forest *wats* [temples] don't
have electricity. Where I live we only have electricity in our main
building. Our huts in the forest do not have it. We eat once a day.
We tend to be more strict about the monastic discipline. Many forest monks do not touch or use money, although at my monastery,
that's not the case.

On a typical day for our small community, which is near a
large one founded by Ven. Buddhadāsa, my teacher, we wake up
at 3.30 a.m. At four we have a chanting service where we chant
some of the Buddha's teaching in the Pāli language with English
translation. Then we meditate for an hour. At 6 a.m., just after
dawn, we go on our alms round. We come back and eat together
at 8.30 a.m. using our begging bowls. Then, after we have cleaned
up, people are free to meditate, study or do work projects. At 3
p.m. we have another group meditation for one hour. At 5 p.m.
we have tea together and discuss life or the Buddha's teaching – or
just chat. At 7.30 p.m. we have another group meditation till 9
p.m. Then, some go to sleep, some stay up. Some days, I give a
talk, as senior monk, or I give translations from our teacher. We
have various visitors and sometimes host workshops and then the
schedule gets turned upside down.

Ven. Professor Dhammavihari, whose story has already been mentioned in chapter 2, became a monk after retiring from an academic
career as Director of the Postgraduate Institute of Pāli and Buddhist
Studies of the University of Kelaniya in Sri Lanka. He now lives in
an urban situation but he was first placed in a forest community in
Sri Lanka and even now goes out of the city on retreat frequently.
He was asked what he gained from this; what follows here is only a
small portion of his reply:

It was enhancing – adding more and more to my detachment and
seeing more and more joy through living so close to nature. I had a
little cell, a little dwelling, which was located on the slope of a hill,
facing the west. And every evening, as the sun set and I sat on the
verandah, all the big trees would cast their shadows on my wall
like a cinema screen. And I would look out and see the massive orb
setting in the western sky. You develop such a rapport with all
that is around you. I tell you honestly, when I used to return after
our regular discussion about 7 or 8 p.m. at night, with a fairly
powerful torch and a little stick or umbrella rolled up, I would
sometimes see a beautiful, creepy, shiny snake across the road. I
would know it was a poisonous one but I would just put a stick

under it and pick it up. It would curl up and look at me. I would talk to it and put it down.

When I live in the jungle, I truly live within it so that all the inmates of the jungle, including the massive trees, the creepers and the flowers are all part of my life. I talk to them as it were, live with them. Because in accordance with the aspirations of monks in the Buddha's day, we have to cultivate an attitude of mind which asks whether there is such a difference between the branches of the oak tree, gnarled and years old, and the limbs of our body. Earth to earth and dust to dust as it were. You realize that you're not different from the world you live in. The ego is reduced.

Where I was, the lifestyle and routine of a forest-dwelling monk began at about 4.30 in the morning when you came down from your private little cell to the central hall, the Buddha Hall, to do your regular worship. Then you would take your bowl and robe at about 5 or 5.15 a.m. and start your begging round, with a torch, because it is still dark in the hills there. After a half an hour's descent from the hills, you come to the villages and for another half hour you go from door to door collecting a little food, which the people are prepared to give you because they know you come. For half an hour you walk through the lanes, crossing over fields and over a little stream. It's delightful to start the day while the birds sing in the trees and the air is fresh. In another half hour you come back to the monastery and you surrender your bowl of food. It is not your property. It is *Sangha* property and it is put onto a tray and anyone can take anything. Then you go back to your cell and find leaves fallen. So you take a broom, clean it up and in the process of sweeping you can learn many things. The fall of leaves in the night has made the place untidy. So it is with you. Greed, hatred and delusion must be swept away. Living in the jungle there are many lessons that one learns.

In Tibetan Buddhist monasteries and nunneries, monks and nuns are sometimes sent away from the main community for a long retreat, for a form of practice much more intensive than the normal life of the community could allow. One traditional retreat lasts three years, three months, three weeks, three days. It has a specific pattern, a progression of practices laid down in a set order by previous retreat masters. Ani Kunzang, a British nun trained in the Tibetan tradition, described what the discipline was like:

You don't see anybody from outside but you have a caretaker. The ladies have a caretaker and the men's retreat has a caretaker. The two are separate. The caretaker will bring you food. The caretaker is not allowed to bring you news from outside except letters that you can receive from your family once a month. These shouldn't give all the gossip that's on the television. The point is to be in an undistracted environment so that you can do your practice in a fairly intense way.

The retreat I did was a four-year retreat. The three-year, three-month, three-week, three-day is the traditional one but we did a few extra practices so it took four years.

The time gives you a chance to get to know yourself quite well and to know your limitations. Within the retreat you have many different practices. Over the three or four years we change practice every two months, three months or six months. There is one practice which lasts for six months. Some practices may be more difficult for some people than for others. Every person is different. So each individual experiences the retreat in a different way. In one particular practice, you don't talk for six months and during that time you don't receive any letters and you're not allowed to write or pick up a pen. Some people find that difficult but others really like it because it gives them a chance to practise completely undistracted.

THE TEACHER

In the Tibetan tradition, the role of the master, teacher or guru is central to meditation practice. Discernment is used at first in making the choice of a teacher but then, once this is done, his or her word is often trusted implicitly. Ringu Tulku:

We believe that the teacher–pupil relationship is very important because what we are talking about in Buddhist practice is not information. It's an experience. Therefore, it's very difficult to communicate – but the only possibility is communicating. It's therefore important to get a qualified teacher, a genuine teacher. If you don't get the right teacher then you can be completely misled. From the Tibetan Buddhist point of view, examining the teacher is one of the most important things for the student. The first step is to find a genuine teacher. If you find a genuine teacher through examination and all the tests, then you can trust. Trust is very important. If you don't trust, then you don't open up.

Geshe Lhudup Sopa, again speaking for the Tibetan tradition, said, 'The teacher is the one who is leading you from an impure world to a pure world. The religious teacher is the one who shows the way, the path.'

In the Theravāda tradition, the teacher–pupil relationship is also very strong, particularly for those who have renounced home and family to become monks. Ven. Bhikkhu Bodhi:

> The Buddha did not conceive of the *Saṅgha* just as a loosely knit order of those striving for their own individual salvation. One can see that he set up very clear-cut principles to ensure that the *Saṅgha* became a means by which the teaching would be preserved in a continuum from generation to generation. According to the rules of the Order, when a novice is ordained as a *bhikkhu* he has to remain five years under the guidance of his teacher and the purpose of this is to ensure that the newly ordained monk is able to learn all the essential principles of the training and of the doctrine. The Buddha also taught that the teacher should look after his pupils just the way a father looks after his children and the pupils are to look after a teacher just like a child looks after a parent.

Dr Aloysius Pieris gave a moving example of this:

> The relationship is one of great respect, reverence and openness to the teacher as one who knows, one from whom you get the maximum and one on whom you depend for your future knowledge. Everyone knows the case of the Peliyagoda monastery [just outside Colombo in Sri Lanka] where there was a famous scholar-monk, Ven. Yakkaduwa Paññarāma. His pupil was Ven. Kusaladhamma Thero, a friend of mine. What struck me was that up to the moment of death, for this pupil, the old monk was his master and he attended as a personal nurse to him in his last days, cleaning him and caring. Even when the sick monk threw up, he put out his hands and took the matter. This love and devotion is something unique between pupil and teacher in most monasteries. It is something I've not witnessed elsewhere.
>
> Monks are considered brothers in the monastic order, always in terms of having one master. The tradition is passed on from teacher to pupil. It's an honour to say, 'I am from the lineage of this monk or that monk.' But sometimes the word 'lineage' is also used to show the unbroken line of tradition going up to the Buddha.

Traditionally, for lay Theravāda Buddhists, the monks in the local temple were their teachers and a close relationship between the two existed. Now, with socio-economic change fracturing traditional relationships, the situation is not so clear-cut. Many Theravāda lay Buddhists go to several teachers. They use their discernment to choose who are worthy but will not feel tied to one or another of them. Greater individual autonomy has come about. Yet, although great importance is placed in Buddhism on individual effort and choice in meditation, in all traditions, the role of the teacher is central. Neither the authority of the texts nor the internal authority of individual conscience is enough. The Buddhist is guided in his or her meditation practice, at least in the early years of learning, by another.

THE HERMIT TRADITION

Once meditation practice is established, one option which has, from an early stage, been open for those who have renounced is solitary meditation practice – the life of a hermit or recluse. An early Pāli text, the *Khaggavisāna Sutta* of the *Sutta Nipāta*, suggests that it was an important practice in the early centuries. It contains forty one verses and each one ends with the same refrain: 'Let us live alone like a Unicorn's horn.' So, for example:

> Having given up the characteristics of a layman like the Kovilara tree which has cast off its leaves, having broken the fetters of the household life, the courageous one lives alone like a unicorn's horn. (*Sutta Nipāta*, verse 44, trans. H. Saddhatissa [London: Curzon, 1985], p. 5)

Although most Buddhist monks live as a community, there have always been some who have sought complete solitude in the forest for intensive meditation. In Sri Lanka, there is a strong tradition of solitary practice. Caves were often set aside for this. Some are still in use today – one such lies a little outside Kandy in the centre of the country. To reach it one drives alongside the Mahaweli River and then away from it, along a narrow road. From the road, the cave is about ninety-nine steps upwards. A huge boulder-like ledge of rock overhangs the platform outside the cave and a curtain of bamboo has been allowed to grow in front. On the platform are always several chairs, a low table and several cushions covered in dark orange cloth. It is not completely quiet. Noise from the road, amplified chants from a nearby temple and, of course, insects, birds and animals can all be heard. It is no idyll. When rain comes, the cave can partially flood.

Brahmi script on the rock implies the cave has been used by Buddhist recluses for more than two thousand years, maybe in uninterrupted succession. Today the occupant is Ven. Bhikkhu

Sumedha. Born in 1932 in Switzerland, he trained as an artist at the
École des Beaux Arts in Geneva and Paris. He then lived and painted
in Zurich and later London. In 1970, he came to Sri Lanka. The cave
has been his home for the last seventeen years. When he was asked
to speak about the environment of the cave, he had this to say:

> Complete silence is like a metaphor. But I would say when the
> silence is such that you can hear your heart beat, your breath and
> an ant walking on a piece of paper, then it is quite silent. There is
> definitely that silence when you can hear your own thoughts. As
> for the bamboo, I planted them by not doing anything. They have
> been let grow. It is a wonderful curtain, because it is teaching
> something. We all know that the inside of the bamboo is empty.
> That alone is preaching something. Also the bamboo has its own
> noise in the wind by which we are reminded of old age.
>
> The whole physical environment with time becomes a preacher,
> a teacher, a piece of art. Whatever we see, it turns into a thought
> regarding *Dhamma*. If we see roots growing over, we see craving;
> if we see falling leaves and the decay, we see impermanence and
> the tenacity of impermanence despite the fact that things grow
> again and again and again. Things are teachers in so far as we are
> aware that we are looking, aware that we can easily fall into the
> trap of seeing the world in the hallucination of stability and
> ownership and happiness.

What was the task to be achieved in the forest?

> It is very simple. To gain the ability to remove agitation, to remove
> anger and to make the heart more mellow so that how things real-
> ly are can be see in more depth than when the mind is agitated.
> Here already, with this, we are moving to the goal – that wisdom
> cannot be without compassion and compassion alone is very little
> without wisdom. Knowledge without compassion is nothing at all.

But what had he gained by being alone that he could not have
gained by living within a community of monks?

> Fewer problems and a more bearable existence and more time for
> a contemplative life. So the comfort which comes with this, that
> little comfort, gives me more power to think. We don't like to talk
> much about what we have gained because this can be misunder-
> stood. It can be taken for attainments. It has become bearable and
> for me that is better than good. If you have learnt to bear it, that is
> a little bit of what we call happiness, something which in Pāli is
> called *sukha*, which is really the super-ability to bear the ups and

downs. If we gain that, then we have gained the condition for liberation.

But could it be said that there was any joy?

> Joy is already a product of having a foothold in confidence, having trust in the method. This alone is reason for joy. I think these things are like the small satisfaction of a man who drinks a cool glass of water in the shade after walking in the heat. You see how things come and go and enjoy the possibility of the consequences of this vision, which is the marvel and beauty of dis-enchantment. This leads to the removal of what we call self and *rāga* [lust]. When this is temporarily established then we can see freedom.

Trust in the method. Trust that becoming aware of how things are will lead to the gradual removal of selfish craving, true compassion and a glimpse of liberation. In one sense, Ven. Sumedha is not alone. There are other monks who live as hermits in Sri Lanka. Some come down to a town only once a year. Laypeople support them but their lives are far from easy. Some have been social activists but each, in the present, has chosen to seek the end of suffering, the end of rebirth, in solitude. Nyanasiri has also made this choice. When she first became a nun, she spent much of her time promoting the welfare of the other nuns, enlisting laywomen to help with their ongoing education. She went to the extent of organizing three conferences for them. Now, she feels impelled towards solitude:

> Now I will just do an occasional piece of work. But in general I do not do any more work. I have been eliminating and eliminating. It's time now for a bit more isolation. It feels right. I'm goal-directed towards solitude.

For Nyanasiri, this solitude is for meditation practice.

Whether a Buddhist is lay or ordained, a disciplined meditator or someone who finds little space for such practice, few Buddhists would deny that silent meditation is necessary for progress along the religious path and that it is transformative. One Buddhist monk who once taught me said:

> Meditation is the ultimate practice of non-violence. Suffering, pain and feelings of anger are not suppressed, but faced, confronted and transformed. To face anger, to recognize and accept it, may mean that it's changed into something like compassion.

It is compassion that the next chapter will study.

NOTES

1. The number of Buddhist monks left in 1979 is not certain. Some sources give as many as 3,000 (e.g. Mahā Ghosānanda, *Step by Step*, eds. Jane Sharada Mahony and Philip Edmonds [Berkeley: Parallax, 1992], p. 12). Other sources place the number much lower, at 100 or less, e.g. Ian Harris, 'Buddhism in Extremis: The Case of Cambodia', in *Governing the Buddhaland: Buddhism and Politics in the Twentieth Century*, ed. Ian Harris (London: Cassell, 1998). The number that we were given by some of those we talked to in Cambodia was 2,000.
2. Mahāsi Sayadaw (1904–82) was a Burmese meditation master whose methods have been widely adopted throughout Asia and the West.
3. Nichiren (1222–82) was a Japanese Buddhist monk. He became an outspoken critic of the Buddhism of his day and encouraged a form of Buddhism which placed the Lotus Sutra at the centre of devotion and practice. His life contained the experience of arrest, exile and pardon. A large number of contemporary Japanese Buddhist groups take their inspiration from his life and writings. These embrace both traditional groups and new religious movements such as Soka Gakkai and Rissho Koseikai.
4. In Pāli, these 'absorptions' are termed *jhāna*. They are achieved through the practice of intense concentration and are marked by alertness and lucidity, although the fivefold sense activity temporarily ceases. Traditionally, there are four *jhānas*. The first two are marked by tranquillity and joy, the last two by equanimity, a state beyond both pleasure and pain.

4

BUDDHISM AND
SOCIAL ENGAGEMENT

'The term "engaged Buddhism" is problematic. It implies Buddhism is normally disengaged from society.' This is one response to what has come to be known as 'engaged' or 'socially engaged' Buddhism. It is a response that sees the very term playing into the hands of one Western misunderstanding of Buddhism – that Buddhism by its very nature encourages individualism and non-involvement. As the previous chapter suggested, even the image of the Buddha can appear to some to radiate indifference rather than active concern for humanity. The facial expression can seem distant and inward-looking. The body can appear almost too perfect, too peaceful to have anything to say to the stresses, the untidiness, the imperfection of modern life. Meditation itself can appear a self-centred activity aimed only at feel-good sensations.

Chapter 3 forthrightly challenged these stereotypes by looking at the practice of meditation itself. This chapter challenges them from the standpoint of Buddhists who see themselves as socially engaged. It takes further the story of the social activists mentioned at the beginning of chapter 3, asking what principles they draw on from within Buddhism and then looking at what is actually being done in several different contexts to put these principles into practice. For, however problematic, the term 'socially engaged Buddhism' is being used by many Buddhists throughout the world to describe what they see as an often overlooked but nevertheless central aspect of Buddhism.

PRINCIPLES FOR SOCIAL ENGAGEMENT

Sulak Sivaraksa was one of the activists mentioned in the last chapter. Born in 1933 in Thailand, which he prefers to call Siam, he gained his higher education in the West and qualified for the Bar. However, when he returned to Thailand in 1962, rather than enter the legal system, he became involved with grassroots development organizations and emerged as a critic of Thai society. Eventually, he helped to found the International Network of Socially Engaged Buddhists. For over thirty years he has challenged Buddhists in Thailand and worldwide to take a critical attitude to contemporary society, especially the patterns of oppression and domination which make the rich richer and the poor poorer. The challenges he has posed to his own government have led to exile and arrest. His inspiration comes from the heart of Buddhism. He explained it in this way:

> The Network of Engaged Buddhists is an organization which tries to alert Buddhists to the fact that the Four Noble Truths are the most essential part of Buddhism – that is, the truth of suffering, the cause of suffering, the elimination of suffering and the way to overcome the suffering through the Noble Eightfold Path. These are the essentials that Buddhists tend to forget. This means Buddhists must sometimes make governments feel uncomfortable because suffering is now the result of the social structure, which is unjust and violent and promotes consumerism. The Buddha says the causes of suffering are greed, hatred and illusion. Consumerism is the personification of greed and hatred is connected to power, weapons, militarism, big organizations and multinational corporations. Buddhism can offer some help here, if Buddhists are aware that practising Buddhism is not only for personal transformation but also for social transformation.

If the Buddhist path aims to eradicate greed, hatred and delusion and these are found not only in individuals but in social structures, then Buddhists, according to Sivaraksa, must work for social and political change as well as for personal change. When Sivaraksa was in Britain as a student, the message he heard from the Buddhist Society there was that Buddhism was about personal transformation only. He disagreed. 'I felt that was escapism, not Buddhism or certainly not the whole of Buddhism,' he declared. When he found the same attitude in America and other places, the International Network of Engaged Buddhists was well on the way to being born. Together with the Four Noble Truths, the Five Precepts also have a social imperative for him:

> In today's society, to observe the Precept not to harm living beings must involve challenging the arms trade, the army and the navy. All of them are breaking the second Precept also. The money used on arms is stolen from the taxpayer's money, which should be used for such things as health care.

As shown in chapter 3, Sivaraksa is adamant that meditation must not be forgotten, that personal transformation must go alongside social action. Yet, he sounds a note of warning:

> *Vipassanā*, insight meditation, can give one great strength and endurance but if critical self-awareness is not linked with critical awareness of society, one will accept oppression. The meditation masters of this country are wonderful but they have not said a word against consumerism. This is why the practice of *samādhi* must be linked with developing critical analysis.

Sivaraksa's approach is supported by Ven. Santikaro, the former Peace Corps volunteer from America who now lives at a monastery within the Thai Forest Tradition. He also sees the Buddha's teaching as reaching beyond personal transformation to the structures of society:

> To me, the main thrust of Buddhism is an approach to life that aims at ending suffering, and suffering the way the Buddha presented it was never modified by pronouns like 'my' suffering or 'our' suffering. He just talked about the reality of suffering in the world and analysed its causes and proposed responses that intelligent, committed people of good will could put into practice. He never limited it to just *my* suffering. I think many Buddhists have made a mistake of interpreting the teachings very personally. That's of course part of it, but there's suffering everywhere. Buddhism needs to be a vehicle for individuals and groups and if possible even societies to understand, confront, and dismantle the structures that create suffering, whether it's an inner personal ego structure or a structure in society such as capitalism, consumerism or patriarchy. It's not just what goes on in *me*. That may be the key to ending suffering. But there are also things going on structurally in society and, if we don't work on these together, we're just going to keep perpetuating tremendous injustice, tremendous pain.

Humans should take responsibility for the elimination of unjust patterns within human relationships and should seek to alleviate suffering, not only within the individual person but in society. That is the main emphasis of Sulak Sivaraksa and Ven. Santikaro, and they draw their inspiration from what they see as the core of the *Dhamma*.

This is also true for Raja Dharmapala, Director of the Dhammavedi Institute in Sri Lanka, which seeks to encourage Buddhist monks and laypeople to apply their awareness of Buddhism to social issues and social development. In his youth, Raja spent over a decade as a Buddhist monk. After disrobing, he joined the religious programmes unit of the Sri Lanka Broadcasting Corporation. This brought him face to face with the other religions of Sri Lanka – Christianity, Hinduism and Islam – and the critical social and political problems facing the country. The result was that he eventually left broadcasting to found an institute which would reach out to members of the ordained *Saṅgha* with a message often overlooked. 'I realized there was an urgent necessity to enthrone the basic tenets of Buddhism and apply them to social issues,' he declared.

When asked what basic tenets of Buddhism he considered most important in his situation, he immediately replied:

> The most fundamental principle is the concept of equality. The Buddha did not recognize distinctions with respect to caste, colour, race or status. This is fundamental to Buddhism. But in our society we see caste divisions everywhere – in education, in religious institutions – and also divisions according to race. People have been manipulated to place nationality above everything else and to define identities in terms of ethnicity or nationality. But Buddhism does not segregate people according to these categories. There is a universality to being human and so we must restore and enthrone this principle of equality.

For Raja, it was the gap between what the Buddha taught and what he saw in society that impelled him into social action. Throughout his life, he has not been able to remain silent in the face of what he has seen as denials of the Buddha's message.

Dr Asanga Tilakaratne is also concerned that Buddhists in Sri Lanka should take issues of human rights seriously. He simply stressed what he saw as the heart of the Buddhist path:

> Buddhism always thinks about the person in the context of society. The Eightfold Path begins with morality or *sīla*. *Sīla* makes sense only in the context of society. When you say, 'Don't kill,' it assumes a society. *Sīla* is the foundation. Without *sīla* you cannot go to *samādhi*. Without *samādhi*, you cannot go to *paññā*. So, therefore, the very foundation of Buddhism is very much social. Of course, social behaviour moulds your own character. That is inevitable. But the path for moulding your own character is through social behaviour, social action. So, therefore, although ultimate realization of *nirvāṇa* is personal, the path is in the context of society. It has a highly significant social aspect.

For many, the motivation for social action is simply compassion. As every chapter has stressed, compassion lies at the very heart of Buddhism and it is an active compassion. Lack of it is a stigma, as an old Pāli text makes clear:

> Whoever in this world harms living beings, once-born or twice-born, in whom there is no compassion for living beings – know him as an outcast. (*Sutta Nipāta*, verse 117, trans. H. Saddhatissa [London: Curzon, 1985], p.117)

'Without compassion there can be no Buddhism,' was how one Sri Lankan monk once put it to me. He might have been thinking of the Buddha himself. The Buddha left his home out of compassion. He taught others out of compassion and, according to the Theravāda tradition, sent out his first followers to preach the *Dhamma* 'out of compassion for the world, for the good, benefit and happiness of gods and humans' (*Vinaya*, i, 20). According to all traditions, an enlightened person is the epitome of both wisdom and compassion.

Few people understand how compassion arises better than Ven. Mahā Ghosānanda, who has long been a witness to the agony of Cambodia:

> Compassion comes from suffering. If you have seen suffering, you become a compassionate person. Compassion must be active and must be balanced with wisdom otherwise you walk only with one leg. The two things have to go together just like a bird which flies in the sky must have two wings.

He went on to speak of human relationships:

> In Buddhism we say, 'All living beings are our mother.' Therefore, we have to help all living beings. We have to respect them, to help them, to love them, to serve them, even when they are our enemy.

The Mahāyāna Buddhist emphasis on interdependence is also relevant here. This was made clear when both Professor Gunapala Dharmasiri of Peradeniya University in Sri Lanka and Ringu Tulku, both Mahāyāna Buddhists, turned to interpersonal relationships and social action. Professor Dharmasiri spoke with particular reference to the Hua Yen School of Mahāyāna Buddhism:

> In Theravāda Buddhism the word *paṭiccasamuppāda* is translated as 'dependent origination'. Hua Yen developed this so that it meant interdependent. Everything is interdependent. Everything is part of a sophisticated web of interdependent relations – everything into

everything. This implies another form of voidness. Because if everything is interrelated then there is no 'thing' – no one thing, no place for any principle of individuation. If there is no 'thing', that means nothing, therefore nothingness. This contains an extremely sophisticated theory of morality. If you are related to others, that means you have obligations to everything else. Your existence is dependent on everything else in the universe. Therefore, everything in nature becomes your parent. You exist because of them and therefore you have this incredible moral obligation, gratitude and respect towards everything. For example, Hua Yen teaches a most sophisticated form of ecological thinking. We could start with our bodies. Our bodies are not ours. They are made up of water, plants, animals. They are part of the world. If there were no oxygen in this room for ten minutes, we would be dead, such is the level of interdependence. Therefore, according to Hua Yen, we owe this incredible debt of gratitude to nature. Nature is our parent. An incredible morality develops out of this.

According to Dharmasiri, to experience the truth of this, in the heart rather than in the head, is another entry into compassion, 'Experientially speaking, when a person really starts understanding, experiencing this voidness, an incredible amount of compassion starts welling up from him, because you see and feel this relationship.'

Ringu Tulku also commented on what happens when one begins to see oneself as dependent on everything else:

If we see ourselves in this way, then our strong sense of separateness from all other things, our strong sense of ego-centredness, becomes less strong. Then we can understand the problems of others because everything is interrelated and this has consequences for action. Let us take the example of having hatred in the mind, having the desire to harm someone. If we seek to push someone down and pull ourselves up, we sometimes think that this will help us. He will be down and I will be up! But if we understand this philosophy more deeply then we will know that this will not happen. If we seemingly work for our own benefit, then it will not be for our benefit. If we work for the benefit of others, we will be working for ourselves too, because we are included in the action. One cannot work for one's own benefit and neglect all others.

Buddhism, therefore, offers much to motivate social action: whether it is awareness of greed, hatred and delusion at the heart of social structures or the implications of the Five Precepts and the centrality of *sila*, morality; whether it is compassion flowering when the depths of human suffering are known or the awareness that we are enmeshed within patterns of interdependence with all else that lives.

There is also another pragmatic consideration present in the earliest texts. This is that physical well-being and freedom from intense hardship and oppression are essential if the *Dhamma* is to be heard and acted on. Although it is true that an experience of suffering, *dukkha*, can make a person see the truth of the Buddha's teachings in a particularly clear way, continual hardship, poverty or fear for life strips away the energy needed for religious practice. If one does not know where the next meal is going to come from, how can there be space to act on the Buddha's teachings! Many Buddhists would say that the gift of the *Dhamma* is the greatest gift possible, but would add that a certain level of physical security and comfort is necessary if it is to be welcomed. Early Buddhism placed responsibility for seeing that everyone had enough to hold life together on the king or the state. If this was not honoured, then ordinary citizens had a duty to act.

When these principles are applied to the present world structure, the language becomes surprisingly contemporary. Ven. Mahā Ghosānanda was asked what message he gave to refugees and then about Human Rights Day:

> If you give the *Dhamma*, you give everything because everything is supported by the *Dhamma*, the Truth. We tell people that if they follow Human Rights Day, they follow the *Dhamma* and if they follow the *Dhamma*, they are free from all suffering.

At this stage, some might want to interject, 'But doesn't Buddhism also encourage detachment? Isn't there a limit to social action within Buddhism?' The questions are important. Buddhism does praise and foster detachment. Yet, as both Dr Aloysius Pieris and Ven. Paisan Wisalo stressed, it is not a detachment that seeks non-action or withdrawal from concern for the world. On the contrary, they would argue, it is the form of detachment that is essential for effective action:

> There are two aspects of the Buddha's teaching. The first is to act intelligently, the exterior act. The second is to enlighten your mind. To be detached means to be free from hatred, greed and delusion. It doesn't mean that we should refrain from action, that we shouldn't do anything. The Buddha emphasized that we have to work hard, to be diligent, to accomplish what should be done. This is the aspect of exterior behaviour that is accomplished by

our body. It is social work. But at the same time it has to be done together with mental work and the mental work is to be detached. To be detached without working, without doing anything, is not the Buddha's teaching. Both aspects have to go together, to work socially and to work spiritually. Detachment implies spiritual work. (Ven. Paisan Wisalo)

The word 'detachment' can be misunderstood. There *can* be a withdrawing type of person in Buddhism. That has to be accepted. But the teaching of the Buddha and his own example is that detachment is simply an attitude of freedom to get involved. To take personal freedom, one can use the example of a bee who gets stuck in the honey. The honey, which usually is a source of life for the bee, is supposed to kill the bee if it becomes trapped through over-indulgence. The bee that is detached takes just what is needed and nothing more and therefore remains free. That is the theory of Buddhism – not giving up everything and having a suicidal approach to life, but just taking what is necessary for life and enjoying it, gaining freedom. But this freedom is not for yourself only. It's to be shared. It's to be given. Therefore you've got to be involved in society. It's interesting that the Buddha was one of the religious leaders who spoke about economics. He entered into social life in spelling out a model of management, political and economic, based on greedlessness or detachment. Detachment is not withdrawal. It is a healthy way to get involved without killing yourself and others. (Aloysius Pieris)

Ven. Paisan Wisalo stressed that detachment is freedom from greed, hatred and delusion; Dr Pieris that it is greedlessness. The Pāli and Sanskrit word usually translated as 'detachment' means just this. The word is *virāga* and it literally means without (*vi*) lust (*rāga*). It therefore has nothing to do with absence of compassion or concern for the world, but means absence of destructive qualities such as greed, hatred, competitiveness, anger and jealousy. Dr Pieris and Ven. Wisalo were stating that far from being inimical to social involvement, detachment as defined by Buddhism is essential to it: in other words, the absence of negative qualities such as greed and hatred, attachment and aversion is a prerequisite for effective social action. To look at it from another angle, withdrawal as defined by Buddhism is a withdrawal from selfishness. If it is a withdrawal from society, it is a withdrawal from the values that usually govern society and cause havoc within it, not a withdrawal from active concern for human need.

Socially engaged Buddhists also draw strength from the doctrine of *kamma* (Skt *karma*). It is a doctrine that some Buddhists over the centuries have interpreted fatalistically. They have believed that whatever happens to them is due to actions in a past life, and that not much can be done, therefore, to change their present situation. The interpretation that activist Buddhists prefer is completely different. They insist that the doctrine is hopeful and positive because it is linked with dependent origination or *paṭiccasamuppāda*. In other words, they insist, with the speakers in chapter 2, that the doctrine of *kamma* is about the possibility of change, for, according to the principle of dependent origination, if the causes of ill are identified and eradicated, a better future can be created, starting in the present moment. When applied to ill in society, it affirms that if the causes of injustice are isolated, then injustice can be challenged and perhaps eradicated. When the fatalistic interpretation of the doctrine was mentioned to Pracha Hutanawatr, this was his response, against a background of birdsong at Wongsanit Ashram:

> The teaching of *kamma* is proactive not reactive. It is the understanding that you are the one who determines your own fate, your own life. Yet this depends on how you interpret the word *kamma*, because the social structure is also part of the collective *kamma* and that also causes poverty. But, if you look at the concept of *kamma* carefully it is far too simplified to say that you are poor because you have done something bad in the past. I don't agree with that. The doctrine of *kamma* gives you the courage to work and change society and change your life. If you take the doctrine fatalistically, that is not Buddhism. It is one of the wrong views.

Is the message coming from people such as Sulak Sivaraksa, Pracha Hutanawatr and Raja Dharmapala new? In that it is firmly rooted in awareness of today's global conflicts and injustices, it is. Yet both concern for the welfare of others and awareness of the importance of political management has been present in Buddhism from the beginning, as this and other chapters have suggested. The Pāli texts, for instance, contain some striking mythological narratives stressing the need for rulers to heed the advice of religious advisers. In one, anarchy and bestiality engulf the people because the king does not heed the advice that resources should be given to the poor.[1] In another, a ruler seeking the perfect sacrifice to bring prosperity back to his land is advised to create a situation of economic justice first.[2] It is known that the Buddha himself advised kings and others with political power. Stories which show him as peacemaker and mediator between competing power blocs have helped to form popular biographies. Historical tradition developed this model. In countries such as Thailand and Sri Lanka the ruler has traditionally been both protector of the monastic *Saṅgha* and protected by its advice. Historical chronicles such as the Sri Lankan *Mahāvaṃsa* show the strength of the link.[3] Even today, monks in Sri Lanka are regularly seen at political meetings. Within the Tibetan tradition, the very fact that the Dalai Lama is both a political and a religious leader is another expression of the importance Buddhism has always placed on the role of the *Dhamma* in public life.

In the relationship between temple and village in numerous Asian countries, the social and the religious has also been combined. Ven. Paisan Wisalo explained what he saw as the traditional role of Buddhist monks in Thailand:

> From the point of view of monks in the north-east of Thailand, it is part of our tradition for monks to be involved in social work. Especially in the north-east, monks and temples have had a social role for many centuries. As social institutions, temples or monasteries were the centre of the community and monks were involved in many activities outside the border of spiritual practice. Temples were the centre of the community in the sense that they provided such things as education, health care and information about herbs for the villagers. Many aspects of village life were dominated by the temples. In that sense, Buddhist monks were already involved in the social dimension of the community.

Mr Chheng Ponn suggested that the situation in Cambodia was similar, except during the disruption of the Pol Pot era:

> The pagoda is the school for the villager and the monks are the pillar of the building. They are the people whom the villager can believe and trust in. The pagoda and the monk have two duties: to lighten the physical suffering of the people and to lighten mental suffering. A human being needs something for the mind and something for the body. There are also two illnesses, one of the body and one of the mind. So the pagoda and the monk are the two elements to lighten the physical and the spiritual suffering of the people.

The schedule described by So Mouy in chapter 3 confirms this. Traditionally, in many Asian countries, all education was linked to the temple. Monks, nuns and villagers were interdependent. The monk and nuns depended on the villagers for material goods. The

villager depended on the monks and nuns for teaching, moral guidance and, often, practical advice and help. When the people starved,
so did the monks and nuns. When the people were prosperous, so
were the monks. True to the spirit of Buddhism, when the monks
helped the villagers to prosper, they helped themselves. When they
betrayed their role through negligence or corruption, they were the
eventual losers.

Now, throughout the world, Buddhists are reaffirming this heritage
with language appropriate to the twentieth and twenty-first centuries.
They are involved in conflict resolution, human rights, the promotion
of democracy, the protection of the environment, caring for the needy
and creating new patterns of community. In a chapter such as this,
only a few cameos can be given.

WAR AND VIOLENCE

Two of the countries visited for the radio programmes were caught
in war situations: Sri Lanka and Cambodia. In both, we found
Buddhists tirelessly working for peace, sometimes at great personal
risk to themselves. Several quoted these words:

> For not by hatred are hatreds ever quenched here, but they are
> quenched by non-hatred. This is the ancient rule. (*Dhammapada*,
> verse 5)

SRI LANKA

In Sri Lanka, the root causes of the present conflict are mainly political
and economic rather than religious. The country is a meeting point for
four religions and two main ethnic groups, Sinhala (74%) and Tamil
(18%). Buddhists make up about 69.5% of the population and
Hindus 15%. With only a few exceptions, all Buddhists are Sinhala
and all Hindus are Tamils. The north and east of the country are predominantly Tamil. Of all religions in the country only Christianity
spans both ethnic groups. Sri Lanka gained independence from its last
colonial power, Britain, in 1948. In the first Cabinet, all ethnic groups
were represented. However, the centralized majoritarian parliamentary model inherited from the British was not really suitable for a
multi-ethnic country since it meant that the centre of the country could
not be other than Sinhala-dominated.

In the 1950s, a Sinhala nationalist movement grew in the south
of the country. It was a protest against the post-colonial hegemony
of English and what was seen as a disproportionately high presence

of Tamil people in top positions. In 1956, this led to a massive electoral victory for a party that appealed to Sinhala language and ethnicity. One of the first acts of the government was to introduce a bill that made Sinhala the national language. The result was that the Tamil-speaking quarter of the population – many Muslims, who make up 7.5% of the population, also speak Tamil – was immediately linguistically crippled. This was a turning point. In retrospect, it can be seen as a mistake. An understandable movement to challenge the power of the elite led to acts that alienated the minority Tamil population.

In the years that followed, there were further actions by the Sinhala-dominated government which alienated the Tamils. Pacts which would have given some regional autonomy to the north and east were signed in 1957 and 1966 but, in each case, the pact was abrogated because of pressure from Sinhala groups. In the 1970s, legislation to restrict entrance to university according to a quota system was seen by Tamil youth as a personal attack on them. Opposition to the government by Tamils was more or less constitutional until about 1970. Devolution along federal lines was pressed for, but with non-violent strategies. Gradually, though, the Tamil youth became tired of the methods of their elders. The result was the growth of numerous militant youth groups demanding a separate state in the north and east.

Conflict with the Sri Lankan military then began. There is no space here to enter into the complexity of the years that followed or all the atrocities that flowed from the conflict, perpetrated by all sides – the attack, for instance, on Tamils in the south in 1983, which left thousands without homes and many dead, or the numerous murderous forays by Tamil militants into Sinhala border villages. Eventually, by liquidating dissent, the Liberation Tigers of Tamil Eelam (LTTE) became the most powerful Tamil group. Several phases of war can be identified, punctuated by abortive peace talks. As this book is written, what Sri Lankans are calling Eelam War Three is in process, with the military and the LTTE locked in combat in the north and east.

No community in Sri Lanka has remained untouched by the war. Colombo, the capital, has frequently been hit by terrorist bombs. Some have targeted one individual. Some have caused indiscriminate civilian deaths, such as when the Central Bank in the commercial heart of Colombo was bombed on a busy weekday morning. Jaffna, the main town in the north, has been bombed or shelled so many

times that few buildings remain unscathed. At the heart of the conflict is the clash of two extreme nationalisms and the failure of a
parliamentary democracy to recognize the grievances and meet the
aspirations of its minorities. The Sinhala nationalist position is that
Sri Lanka is a Sinhala Buddhist country and any form of federalism
would be a betrayal of this ideal. The Tamil nationalist position is
that the Tamils form a separate nation in Sri Lanka and should have
the right of self-determination.

Distrust between Sinhala and Tamil people is deep. Many, but
not all, Buddhist monks place themselves on the side of the Sinhala
nationalists. Some have consistently sought, through words and
actions, to build bridges of understanding with Tamils. Two of
these were interviewed for the programmes. Both had worked in the
north where the Tamils are in the majority. Both had found themselves in the middle of the war helping non-Buddhists, at some risk
to themselves. Ven. Delgalle Padumasiri spent fourteen years on the
Jaffna peninsula at Kankasanturai from 1973. He built his own
Buddhist temple, Tissa Vihāraya, although there were very few
Buddhists there, and found that the Tamil people eventually started
to come to him:

> In the beginning, the Tamil people would not generally have any-
> thing to do with the Buddhist temple. But over time, many Tamils
> started to come, much in the same way a patient would seek assis-
> tance from a doctor. A doctor ministers to patients whether they
> are Tamil, Muslim or Sinhala, irrespective of community and this
> is the same way we monks treated the people. Eventually, there
> were about one thousand Tamil people who had relationships
> with the Buddhist temple, which included participating in some of
> the religious processions.

It was through painstaking, sensitive, trust-building that Ven.
Padumasiri gained the trust and friendship of the people. When
work on his temple began, in March 1973, some Tamils harassed
him. A mayor even tried to cut off the drinking water. Ven.
Padumasiri earned trust by showing that he treated Tamil and
Sinhala alike. He pressed the government to build new housing for
the poor, began a multi-ethnic pre-school and built up relationships
with the Hindu priests. In this way, Tissa Vihāraya became a place
of reconciliation. Tamils came there when there were disputes or
when they experienced obvious injustice at the hands of government
officers. Employment and difficulty in accessing government services
were the two major problems at first but, as the years passed, the

conflict between the militant groups and the government, with civilians caught in between, came to dominate everything else. Until 1987, when Ven. Padumasiri was forced to leave, the temple was a sign that there could be understanding between Sinhala Buddhist monks and the Tamil population. That it did not last is witness to the gravity of the present war.

Vavuniya, the home of Ven. Wimalasara Thero, is at the point in the island where the Sinhala-dominated south meets the Tamil-dominated north. It has been the frontier, separating the war zone from the south, for many years. As such, it has often been a tinderbox of tensions. Ven. Wimalasara:

> The need of the Tamil people to have a relationship with the Buddhist temple came about due to the war. The Tamil people have suffered many losses. When someone from their community was arrested, they were often afraid to go the police or the security forces, so they would come to the temple and ask us to go along with them, or at least to help them gain access to those who had been arrested. For example, in the south, in Boosa detention camp,[4] there are thousands of Tamil prisoners. But the people were afraid to go down there to visit them. So we would arrange for them to go with security. We also used the temple to provide a safe sanctuary where Tamils could meet, or at least send messages to loved ones in prison in the south.

Such involvement has brought risk and life-threatening situations to both monks. Ven. Delgalle Padumasiri:

> I have faced death at least four times. Once a T56 weapon was held to my chest but I have never had the fear of death. I have confronted death but I don't know the fear of death.

Ven. Vavuniya Wimalasara:

> There have been many instances where I have been able to intervene effectively. During the negotiations in Thimpu,[5] there was a major confrontation between the security forces and the armed militants. Many people were involved and there was severe loss of life. At this time, I was able to intervene and save lives. I brought Tamil people to the temple and protected them. Then, in 1985, I came to know of a plan to set fire to Vavuniya so I alerted the security forces and was able to stop this act of violence.
>
> Also, when the security forces are exposed to attack and suffer casualties, there are often reprisals against civilians. At such times

the people are defenceless. Here, I have also been in a position to save people. Once, when sixteen people were being attacked by a militant group of thugs, I was able to intervene and save their lives.

What made both Buddhist monks such effective channels of reconciliation and peacemaking was that they built up relationships of trust both with the people and with the government agents and security forces. This was why they were able to intervene and save lives. Yet, what motivated and strengthened such monks? Both were asked what Buddhism said about war and what the roots of Sri Lanka's present conflict were:

> According to the teachings of Buddhism, it is never possible to win people through war. War can only win territory. On principal, Buddhism rejects war as a means of achieving anything. Buddhism should certainly challenge the kind of ethnic conflict going on here. Buddhism does not make distinctions between people in terms of their ethnicity. Among the animal world and in nature, there are so many species, but Buddhism looks at people as one species and does not recognize ethnicity, caste or any other social division as a basis for conflict or discrimination. This can be seen clearly in the *Vāseṭṭha Sutta*.[6] (Ven. Vavuniya Wimalasara)

> Two of the Lord Buddha's visits to Sri Lanka were precisely to end war and bring peace, once to Mahiyangana and once to Nagadipa.[7] This practice of peacemaking is basic to Buddhism. The taking of life for any purpose is considered against the *Dhamma*. One has only to look at the Five Precepts. War brings about destruction. It can never bring about anything constructive.

> The solutions are crystal clear in Buddhism. The first step is to ask what caused the war in the north and east. Why did the young people take up arms? The same thing happened in the south.[8] The key to the solution is rooted in this basic question. We must tackle the causes.

> Now that the conflict in the north and east has spread, we must apply the teachings of Buddhism and other religions as well. The basic message is that war is destructive and the people know this. It is the ordinary people who suffer in war and they want peace. So we must work for it. There is no alternative.

> Before the black July of 1983, whatever differences there were, the Tamil and Sinhala peoples more or less lived in harmony. There were conflicts but basically there was no question of separate identities. But after 1983, things changed. Why? We must analyse

the causes. Before 1983, the Tamils in Jaffna would come to the
Buddhist temple on 1 January and have what we call the *pirit* thread
tied around their wrists. It is a sanctified thread.[9] They would come
to the Buddhist temple to observe this rite. That showed how much
we were in harmony. (Ven. Delgalle Padumasiri)

CAMBODIA

War has also wracked Cambodia and resolution seems as distant as
in Sri Lanka. Cambodia gained its independence from the French in
1953 after a century of colonial rule. For a decade afterwards, the
country enjoyed relative prosperity. Then, it became caught in the
conflict between America and North Vietnam. Prince Sihanouk, the
head of state, accused America of making incursions into Cambodia
and severed economic and military relations. America did not desist
but began bombing the Cambodian countryside to destroy North
Vietnamese military bases and supply lines. This led to a coup and
the ousting of Prince Sihanouk in favour of someone more
pro-American. As in Sri Lanka, the build-up of the conflict was a
complex process. As the Cambodian government's alliance with
America grew, so did a counter-movement, the communist-inspired
Khmer Rouge, eventually supported by Prince Sihanouk. Cambodia
was plunged into a vicious civil war and by 1975 was on the verge
of famine.

On 17 April 1975, Phnom Penh fell to the Khmer Rouge under
Solath Sar or Pol Pot, an authoritarian ideologue committed to a
radical reconstruction of society along collectivist lines. The Khmer
Rouge was welcomed into the capital because people assumed their
entry marked the end of fighting. But the day after their entry, all
inhabitants of the city were forcibly marched towards the countryside to work as peasants. Those who dared to take possessions with
them were either shot or eventually had to jettison everything. Some
who were not forced to march – the elite of society, the leaders and
professionals – were incarcerated in Tuol Svay Prey High School,
where the living conditions until inevitable death were so hellish
that barbed wire had to be placed on balconies so that the prisoners
could not commit suicide.

Pol Pot's vision was of a utopian, classless, self-reliant, agricultural
society untouched by the West. During the four years in which Pol
Pot had power, everything that evoked Cambodia's former cultural
foundations or its colonial past under the French was outlawed or

destroyed. People with any status in the previous regime were killed. Acres of mass graves eventually spread across the country. Even owning a pair of spectacles was seen as a sign of westernization and could be a death warrant. Although the Khmer Rouge before victory had seemed to praise Buddhism, organized religion in Cambodia was systematically dismantled. The traditional rural community structure with the Buddhist temple and the family at its heart was replaced by centralized planning governed by local Pol Pot agents who dictated the terms of life down to the last detail. Non-compliance with them could mean death, even if it was gathering an extra handful of rice to alleviate hunger. Families were often separated and lost contact with each other.

Almost all Buddhist temples were destroyed. Buddhist monks were seen as parasites and were either killed or given degrading labour. Libraries containing priceless documents and manuscripts were gutted. The Buddhist Institute in Phnom Penh had forty thousand documents. All were destroyed. Training centres and places of academic excellence shared the same fate.

The Pol Pot economic experiment was a monumental failure. Collectivization did not bring an end to famine and disease, it increased it. Hospitals, banks, and industries were allowed to fall into ruin. When the Vietnamese defeated Pol Pot in 1979, the country was in ruins. However, war did not end in 1979. Pol Pot was defeated but the Khmer Rouge still had areas of influence and conflict between the Vietnamese-backed state and the Khmer Rouge continued. Other factions also arose. To simplify a long story, a UN-brokered peace treaty in 1991 brought four of the factions together. An interim government was appointed and UN-supervised elections took place in 1993, but complete peace still eludes the country, since there are still independent Khmer Rouge strongholds and conflicts at the heart of government.

One person who has worked tirelessly for peace in Cambodia is Ven. Mahā Ghosānanda. He was born in 1929 and became a monk in his youth. As a young monk, he had an outstanding academic career. When the Khmer Rouge took over, he was living in a forest monastery in Thailand and so escaped immediate threat. In 1978, he began working with refugees. Later he returned to Cambodia. His words have been quoted in earlier pages. Put simply, his message is this, 'We have to put wisdom, compassion and charity into practice.'

His name is closely linked with a series of annual Peace Marches or Dhammayietras which began in 1992 and continue today. Each has ventured into a different area of conflict. Each has been a remarkable witness for peace. Liz Bernstein came to South-East Asia from America in 1987 and at first worked in refugee camps among Cambodians in Thailand. Two years later she and a friend started the Coalition for Peace and Reconciliation, which sought to create links of understanding between different groups of Cambodians. In 1992, she began to work with Mahā Ghosānanda:

> When I started to work with Mahā Ghosānanda, he had long held a dream of a Dhammayietra or a Pilgrimage of Truth, a walk for peace, and we had also been thinking independently of this. When the Peace Accord was signed in 1991, it seemed to be the right time for a walk. So, in 1992, we had the first Dhammayietra. We started from the Thai border with about a hundred Cambodian refugees. For many, it was their first time home after ten or twelve years. Some of them wept as they crossed the border and touched the Cambodian soil. As we continued walking, every day there were emotional reunions all along the way as people met mothers, children, grandmothers and uncles, long lost. It was moving, as was the response of the villagers along the way. Buckets of water were laid out by the road and people brought us food. Having had no idea how the walk would be received, we were overwhelmed. It touched something in the hearts of people – the Buddhist monks, nuns and laypeople, walking through the country for peace.
>
> That proved to us that there was a call for a peace movement and a return to Buddhism in the country.

The first Dhammayietra took place before all the refugees from Thailand had been repatriated. By the elections of 1993, all had come back. After this, the Coalition for Peace and Reconciliation moved to Phnom Penh and Ven. Mahā Ghosānanda became an active part of it. The second Dhammayietra came in 1993. Liz Bernstein:

> The second walk came on the eve of the UN-brokered elections. The UN had come to the country with twenty thousand peace-keepers, yet the situation still remained very unstable. Fear was very widespread. There were political assassinations and much conflict. There was still a fear that elections wouldn't happen or that people wouldn't dare to vote.
>
> The walk began from Angkor Wat[10] and went through one of the heaviest areas of conflict to Phnom Penh. On the eve of the

walk there was a firefight between the Khmer Rouge and the government soldiers right in the grounds of the temple. As everyone huddled
in the temple and rockets and grenades were flying, one grenade
came into the temple where three or four hundred people were
huddled and landed next to the Buddha image. It didn't explode.

Afterwards, the walkers decided to continue. There had been
two or three walkers injured and they sent messages from their
hospital beds that the walk must continue. So the walk left Siem
Reap and went through areas where the UN peacekeepers were
stationed but where they did not leave their bases. They didn't
walk five hundred metres from their bases because of the conflict
between the government and the Khmer Rouge. So, people along
the road saw that even where the peacekeepers wouldn't go, here
was this line of five hundred monks and nuns walking for peace.
Again we had an incredible welcome from the people. They said,
'We have never seen peace. We have heard on the radio that they
have signed a peace accord but we are lying in our bunkers at
night. We have never seen peace until we have seen this walk.' At
the bridges the soldiers who were guarding laid down their
weapons and came to Mahā Ghosānanda and said, 'Give us a
blessing so that our bullets don't hit anyone and so that their
bullets don't hit us.'

So the walk went on. When we were about to arrive in Phnom
Penh it was just the day before elections and the city was very
tense with fear. The UN had ordered their staff to send their families abroad because the situation was unstable. They were expect-
ing attacks from the government or the Khmer Rouge and people
were very, very frightened. When the walk entered the city, tens of
thousands joined the walk and just kept walking around Phnom
Penh calming people down, stopping at monuments and temples
to meditate in silence for fifteen minutes. We then appealed for
peace and for calm.

We continued to walk for three days. Everyone came out to
vote – ninety-five per cent of the electorate – and many people
have credited the walk with helping to calm people down so that
they dared to vote. Afterwards, there was a feeling of tension and
because things continued politically unstable, the walkers continued to walk, for two weeks. At this point, they were joined by students, women's groups, human rights groups. All sectors of society
joined the walk to pray and meditate for peace.

After the second walk, the Dhammayietra Centre for Peace and
Non-Violence was formed, to enable co-operation between groups

in such things as training for non-violence. A people's movement was in the making. Monks, nuns and members of non-governmental organizations united and the walk was a catalyst. In the following year, 1994, still there was no peace. This time the Dhammayietra walked to Pailin in the extreme north-west. Liz Bernstein again:

> Pailin was at that time a stronghold of the Khmer Rouge. So the theme of the walk was walking in compassion towards our enemy, to make our enemy our friend. It was an attempt to cross areas controlled by both the government and the Khmer Rouge. Just before the walk, which was in April and May, there had been a government offensive which took Pailin for a few weeks, after which the Khmer Rouge took it back. So it was an area of intense fighting.
>
> Eight or nine hundred people showed up in Battambang, the city in the north-west where the walk was planning to begin. Before starting, there were training sessions and daily we made pleas and press releases calling for a ceasefire and both sides to negotiate. When the walk started towards Pailin, government troops were firing over our heads. In the end, the walk was not allowed to pass through so it turned around to seek another route and then encountered crossfire between the government and Khmer Rouge again. Walkers were injured. A few of us were taken by the Khmer Rouge for a few hours and then released, but the walk went on. People continued to walk because the war continued. One of the men who was injured by the fighting encouraged the walk to go on, saying that if we just struck back then it would be an endless cycle of violence. So, the walk did continue on until its end.

There were walks in 1995, 1996 and 1997. Cambodia is becoming accustomed to the sight of orange-robed monks, white-robed nuns and laypeople braving the threat of bullets, raising the dust of ill-kept roads with hundreds of pairs of rubber sandals, carrying yellow banners proclaiming the need for peace and non-violence, snaking their way through villages where mines have created colonies of the crippled. In 1995, the walk was part of an international pilgrimage from Auschwitz to Hiroshima to mark the fiftieth anniversary of the ending of the Second World War. Thirty international walkers joined eight hundred to a thousand Cambodians. Along the roads, thousands came out to greet it.

The training given to the walkers is almost as important as the walk itself. Between walks, workshops on non-violence and peacemaking are held at various levels, and the teaching given is rooted in

Buddhist practice. Kim Leng, a Cambodian woman who works at the Dhammayietra Centre for Peace and Non-Violence and who has recently received an Honour Award from Peacefund Canada, described what she saw as the heart of it:

> First the Dhammayietra teaches its own participants, the walkers, to have *Dhamma*, to walk in a spirit of meditation and to have peace within our own selves first before we can make peace outside. So, when we are walking, we are mindful at every moment, not allowing our thoughts to go in different directions. We are walking in mindfulness the entire time.
>
> We teach all participants about non-violence, so that even if we enter dangerous areas we will not be afraid. We will know that even if we are risking our lives, we are risking our lives for peace. It is also important to teach participants how to deal with their own fear, how to deal with any danger that they might encounter so that they do not wait for others to solve problems for them. Each person takes responsibility for his or her own life and can help deal non-violently with any problem we might encounter.
>
> Another important function of the Dhammayietra is teaching the villagers. Mahā Ghosānanda gives *Dhamma* talks and teaches the important lesson that hatred is never overcome by hatred but only by love, and that we must have love and respect for one another. Another lesson is that conflicts do not come from anywhere else except the hatred, greed and delusion within ourselves. So we teach the villagers how to reduce hatred, greed and delusion.

SOCIAL DEVELOPMENT AND ECOLOGICAL AWARENESS

Dhammayietra walkers risk their lives for peace, convinced that they must witness to an alternative to violence rather than collaborate through silence with the forces opposed to peace. However, this is not the only level at which Buddhists are socially active within Cambodia. War has created crushing economic problems in the country. Poverty as well as war grinds the people down. Ven. Yos Hut Khemacaro was another Buddhist monk who escaped the Pol Pot holocaust. In 1975, he was studying in France. He returned to Cambodia in 1989 and has become very involved in human rights, development work and training for non-violence. He is acutely aware that unwholesome actions have become the norm in Cambodia; that in a situation where many of the young people have only known violence, there is little possibility of them seeing an alternative without proactive strategies:

Because of the lack of education, ignorance, and the generations who have only lived in a situation of war and violence, people are used to acting from violence. Many are living in difficult circumstances, experiencing great suffering. All they see around them is violence, so they repeat the acts of violence they have experienced themselves. Evil actions have become the norm and so now it is our job to change this.

We have held seminars in Phnom Penh and the provinces. We teach people about living together in peace, respecting one another and being honest. We teach the values of Buddhism and the values of development – planting trees and protecting the environment, digging wells, providing safe water-sources for people, improving irrigation patterns, building schools so that children may have access to education. There are also monks who have started rice banks and credit schemes to help villagers borrow money without high interest.

When asked why monks should be involved in this way, he was quick to claim that this was not the principle role of the monk but that the circumstances demanded it, because of the suffering of the people:

I have often said in training and seminars that this development work, this economic work, should not necessarily be the role of monks. If the government was fulfilling all of its role and helping development and the social needs of the people, we should be able to fulfil our true role as leaders and spiritual guides in ethics, culture and religion. This is our true calling. But the needs are so great, that as long as they remain and the government and other institutions are unable to fulfil these roles, we must complement and help where we can.

Liz Bernstein confirmed that some of the young monks in Battambang in the north-west were involved in rice banks, credit schemes, teaching health and showing villagers how to raise chickens. She added that it was as though the monks had said, 'The people are suffering, we are suffering, we depend on the people and we have to respond to their suffering where it is, right now.'

Monks in Cambodia are not alone in making this response to the economic suffering of the people. In Thailand, Ven. Paisan Wisalo and a few others like him also see a decline in the well-being of rural areas. They are aware of an increase in poverty, a breakdown of community values and ecological erosion. Their response has been an activist one rooted in concern for the people. Ven. Paisan Wisalo admitted that many monks did not see beyond giving sermons from the temples, but he saw this as a betrayal of their traditional role:

> What some of us try to do is restore the self-confidence of the people and the social and ecological well-being of the community. It is not an easy task. The livelihood of the people depends on water, the forest, food and the animals in the surrounding areas. We try to conserve this environment with the co-operation of the villagers. First, we try to protect the forest. Then, we try to introduce a new way of agriculture. The modern way is monoculture and this has destroyed the environment. It has destroyed the soil and the water and it is the cause of forest encroachment. When the villagers change to organic or integrated methods, it helps reduce environmental problems and also assists them financially, because they do not need to invest so much in fertilizer and machinery. Most of my own work now centres on the environmental issues connected to agriculture and on such things as how to raise income without destroying the forest.

This is what he added about his motivation:

> The Buddha emphasized the role of compassion, the role of *dāna* [generosity]. *Dāna* is not only to give or to offer money. As monks, we don't have property to offer to the villagers but we have time, intellect and good will to offer to them. Compassion is the ground on which all of our activities are based. Also, since we are part of a social and traditional institution, we have a role to help the villagers as leaders of the community.

Ecological awareness is also present among many Buddhists in Sri Lanka. Ven. Gnanapala, of the prestigious Vajirārāma Temple in Colombo, has long called on the Sri Lankan state to halt deforestation and environmental pollution. Unlike Ven. Paisan Wisalo, he feels that the role of the monk is to advise and encourage, rather than to become involved as an activist. Therefore he saw his role as stimulating interest through sermons and speeches, rather than going out into threatened rural areas. He called attention to two texts that he had mentioned in articles he had written:

> The forest with its unlimited kindness and benevolence does not demand for its sustenance and extends generously its produce during its lifetime. It gives protection to all beings even to the axeman who destroys it. (Pāli Canon)

> O great King, the birds of the air and the beasts have an equal right to live and move about in any part of the land as the land

belongs to the people and all other beings. Thou art only the guardian of it. The time has come for us to live in harmony with birds and bees but also with the earth's resources, the air, the land, the water on which our very existence depends. (Words traditionally thought to have been said by Ven. Mahinda to King Devanampiyatissa when he came as a missionary to Sri Lanka in the third century BCE)

This is a message that Dr Nihal Karunaratne has also taken to heart. Similar quotations are placed outside his surgery door in Kandy, a town surrounded by green hills in the central highlands of the island. Since 1959 he has been interested in environmental conservation. When asked why Buddhism should be committed to conservation, he replied:

> Being a Buddhist, it is not very difficult to be involved in conservation. If you take the first precept – 'I shall abstain from taking life' – that is something I'm very involved in. For one thing, I'm a doctor and my duty is to save life. The other thing is that I've been very involved with wildlife conservation. Long ago I realized that we were going to get into ecological trouble with the dwindling forests. A few friends and I started various programmes on ecology and preservation of forests and habitats. Today, there is one bird, the thick-billed flowerpecker, which is on the brink of extinction. Way back in 1959, I did an eight millimetre movie on this little bird and its nesting habits. That gave me a lot of happiness, getting into the forest, being with nature – the peace, the quietness, the tranquillity. I then imparted all this by teaching my patients.

Above Kandy, there is a green sanctuary, an ancient forest, with a history stretching back hundreds of years. Deep inside its winding paths is the hermitage that is now home to Ven. Bhikkhu Bodhi. Once, it was a royal forest, patronized by the kings of Kandy before the Kandyan kingdom fell to British control in 1815. The fact that it remains a forest is in no small part due to Dr Karunaratne:

> Another thing I did took me nearly thirty years. There is a forest here called Udawattekele, meaning 'the forest above the palace'. I found that the forest was dwindling. There was land-hunger because of an ever-increasing population. Each government which came into power wanted land for housing schemes and they took it from the palace. In order to prevent the forest being destroyed and to save its scenic beauty and aesthetic value, I worked with schoolchildren. I went to schools and showed two films. One was

called *The Peace Game*. It was shot in Kruger National Park and showed how animals could live in ecological harmony. The other, *Elephant Poachers*, showed elephants being brutally hacked to death. Using those two principles, I showed the two films in forty schools around the central region and I invited children to join me in saving this forest.

The first group happened to be my son's group. This was way back in 1974. The children came every Saturday morning and worked from 7 a.m. till 11.30 a.m. I gave them only a cup of tea. First they planted trees around the perimeter. Then, they collected firewood from the forest and left it along the roadside. Then, they went to the neighbouring houses and villages and told the people, 'Don't go into the forest to pick the firewood. We have brought it for you.' So the necessity to go into the forest to cut trees was diminished. Then we put a wire fence around the whole forest of 252 acres. Working every Saturday, it took two and a half years, with schoolchildren. And today it's an emerald island in this beautiful city.

In the West also, Buddhism and ecological awareness go together. Martine Batchelor, who has co-edited a book called *Buddhism and Ecology*,[11] shared this:

A lot of the principle tenets of Buddhism encourage an ecological awareness. The first two precepts encourage harmlessness and not acquiring things, not stealing things. Harmlessness leads to respecting all life. And that is what is beautiful in Buddhism. It's not only humans that you are not supposed to harm. It's grass. It's animals. It's anything. So you try to harm as little as you can. For me, that's a very ecological view.

The second precept is not to take what is not given. This leads one to think, 'How much do I need in this world in terms of material possession?' Our economic system is unfortunate. We have to consume in order for people to work, in order to produce so that we can consume. But the Buddha only named four requisites for monks and nuns: shelter, clothes, medicine and food as alms.

Meditation can also be helpful here. It helps you to be more contented and if you're more contented you need fewer things from the outside to make you happy. Then, in connection with the wisdom aspect of Buddhism, and the three characteristics, if you contemplate impermanence you realize the resources are finite. If you contemplate suffering, then you are led to ask what the cause of people's suffering is and whether you can do anything about it. And the third characteristic is not-self or interdependence. If you are aware that everything is connected to everything else, then you try not to harm. So, within the very tenets of Buddhism, there is ecological awareness.

HOLY ISLAND: AN ECOLOGICAL EXPERIMENT

Kagyu Samye Ling Tibetan Centre in Scotland is the largest Tibetan centre in Europe. Set in the Scottish border country, close to a river, it is surrounded by beauty, sometimes calm and tranquil, sometimes turbulent. It is headed by Dr Akong Tulku Rinpoché. Forced to flee Tibet in 1959 when the Chinese invaded, he came to Britain. Although in Tibet he had been the Abbot of a Buddhist temple, recognized as the reincarnation of a lama, in Britain he was forced to work as a hospital orderly. Yet, people began to come to him for meditation. He realized there was a need in the West for the kind of teaching he could give. In response, Samye Ling arose under his guidance. Chapter 3 gave the voices of some meditators there. Samye Ling is much more than a meditation and teaching centre, though. It supports educational, health, cultural and environmental programmes in many countries, and has also bought an island off the west coast of Scotland. Ecological awareness is written into every part of the planning of 'Holy Island'. Thom McCarthy, an American Buddhist, works with the chaplain of Samye Ling, Lama Yeshe Losal, on the project:

> Holy Island is in the Firth of Clyde one mile east of the Isle of Arran. It's two and a quarter miles long and three-quarters of a mile at its widest point. It rises to a height of 140 feet and is massive rock, with a little arable farmland at the north and south ends. Ninety per cent of the island is rough grazing with a lot of heather and a lot of stones. It's got a great deal of character, actually. There's a very famous saint's cave which is right in the middle of the island on the west side, facing Arran. In the sixth century, it was used by a Celtic saint called St Molaise just after the time of St Colomba.
>
> The direction of the project is under Lama Yeshe. His vision has several levels. Firstly, it's a place for all people. We are preserving one of the sacred sites of the planet. So, an ecumenical or inter-denominational retreat facility will be at the north end of the island, open to those of all faiths. Then, there will be a Buddhist retreat facility on the south end of the island. In October 1995, planning permission came through for the interdenominational retreat facility and the Buddhist retreat facility has been given a grant from the Department of the Environment for research into such things as energy efficiency.

In its connection with humans, the island is specifically for retreat. All the other aspects of the project are related to environmental awareness. We've planted thirty thousand hardwood trees, sponsored by people all over the world at five pounds each. To date [May 1996], we've planted fifteen per cent of the island. It has been fenced off because there's also a population of animals – goats, sheep and Eriskay ponies – which was introduced previous to our taking ownership.

HUMANITARIAN AID

Also connected with Samye Ling is the Rokpa Trust, a charitable institution. Ani Rinchen Khandro, a British Buddhist nun trained at the Centre, explained:

Rokpa is the Tibetan word for 'help'. It's an umbrella term for all the charitable activities which emanate from Samye Ling. Dr Akong Tulku Rinpoché was the founder and, because of him, these activities are almost limitless. He really is the epitome of wisdom and compassion in action. He's a very practical man and everything he does ripples out into the world to help people spiritually and practically.

Rokpa started as a charity to help Tibetan refugees, predominantly in India at Dharamsala and Nepal. But it has mushroomed now so that it helps people all over the world. What is most astonishing is the work in Tibet itself. Rinpoché has actually started seventy-six projects in Tibet. They are very practical and all fall into the categories of health, education, cultural preservation and environmental and wildlife protection. In Tibet, Rokpa has, of course, to remain completely apolitical. It's concerned not with who is running Tibet but with how to help the people who are there. And all the projects there are undertaken in response to people's needs. It's not a case of experts coming in and saying, 'This will be good for you.' If the people need a school or a clinic, Rinpoché is able to provide that. He works with the local authorities and Rokpa has its own representatives in different areas.

As for Nepal, the work is predominantly under the leadership of Lea Wila. She is a Swiss–German actress who started Rokpa with Rinpoché about twenty years ago. It began with a soup kitchen in the coldest months of the year and that still goes on, near the Great Stupa in Kathmandu. It's now staffed by volunteers from all over the world. People apply to come and help. From that soup kitchen, the whole project has grown. We've rescued about forty street children who were in a pretty desperate situation.

Now, they're at school and doing well. The problem was then how
to provide a loving home. So, just recently, we've managed to rent
a house. The long-term plan is to buy a centre to be a focus for this
and all Rokpa activities in Nepal, Kathmandu particularly. We
also help women who are destitute or homeless. We've started several small businesses so that they can learn handicrafts and traditional Tibetan and Nepali skills. They're now exporting. We sell
some of their goods here and hope it will spread further afield so
that the women become independent through self-sustaining
export businesses.

Dr Akong Tulku Rinpoché, in a short interview, added this:

> In charitable work, we try to do many things. If we want to change
> other people's lives, health and education would seem to be the
> two most important things. So, in Tibet, we train teachers. One
> group of forty finished training last year and they are now in forty
> village schools.
>
> But we also work in Britain in city projects. We do soup kitchens
> in London, Birmingham and Glasgow. There is also one in Brussels
> and we hope one will soon start in Holland and maybe Moscow.

Another charitable organisation that has grown out of a Buddhist
movement or institution is the Karunā Trust, started by the Friends of
the Western Buddhist Order, which was founded in 1967 in England
by Dennis Lingwood, who had taken the name Sangharakshita when
ordained as a novice monk in India. The word *karunā*, of course,
means compassion. The Karunā Trust is an organization that works
among Buddhists in India, many of whom converted to Buddhism
under the influence of Bhimrao Ram Ambedkar. Ambedkar was born
an 'untouchable' but rose to an influential position in the Indian polity
whilst continuously campaigning for the rights of his people. In 1956
he converted to Buddhism, since he believed it to be the best option
for untouchables. Mass conversions followed. He died soon afterwards. In the years since his death, some of the converts reverted to
Hinduism but sizeable communities of Buddhists still exist in India.
One leading woman in the Western Buddhist Order is
Dhammacarini Sanghadevi. She explained the background to this:

> The Order was drawn into this work because of Sangharakshita's
> personal contact with Dr Ambedkar, who was a leader of the
> untouchable community in India. Ambedkar was an untouchable
> who became a politician. He looked into how he could free his
> people from the constraints of untouchability and at first he tried

to do it through political means. He actually helped to draw up the constitution of the new independent India. Yet, he came to realize that a political solution was not the answer. So he actually researched all the different world religions and came to the conclusion that Buddhism offered the best prospects to further the hopes of his people. This was because Buddhism emphasized the value of individual responsibility. He believed that if the 'untouchables' gained more confidence in themselves, they would have the courage to stand up against the oppression and prejudice they still received from caste Hindus. So he took the step of becoming a Buddhist and it was during that process that he was in dialogue with Saṅgharakshita, asking Saṅgharakshita's advice on certain texts and so on. Then there were mass conversions in the 1950s. After Ambedkar's death, Saṅgharakshita stepped in and taught the converts for the next fifteen years whilst he was in India. After he came back to the West and founded the Western Buddhist Order, he asked some of his disciples to go back to India and carry on the teaching work. And it has continued in the form of an organization named Trailokya Bauddha Mahasangha Sahayak Gana.

The Western Buddhist Order has always considered *Dhamma* education to be a priority, yet social work came to play an important part, simply because of the level of humanitarian need in India. This is why the Karunā Trust was born. Saṅghadevi continued to describe the current work in India:

> The work consists of social projects under Karunā and *Dhamma* projects under Trailokya Bauddha Mahasaṅgha Sahayak Gana to help ex-untouchable Buddhist communities not only to practise and learn the *Dhamma* but also to improve the quality of life of the people in their community. The aim is that the projects will become self-financing. We don't want to perpetuate a dependency syndrome. The social work has arisen because we have realized that we will be hampered in teaching the *Dhamma* if we're not also helping people on the social level. People are much worse off than in England in terms of such things as health and education. If people are still fighting to live into adulthood or to become literate, then the benefit they will gain from *Dhamma* practice is limited. So, social work and teaching the *Dhamma* are interlinked.

WOMEN

Political engagement, challenging structures of power and influence, working with ordinary people to create a better quality of life, protecting the environment, reaching out a hand of compassion to those in need and offering help in emergencies – all this is on the agenda of Buddhists throughout the world. Of particular significance to some is the position of women. The Rokpa Trust has found that it is often women who are the most downtrodden and in need of help, especially in countries such as Nepal. In Thailand, the same has been discovered by Maeji Khunying Kanitha and other Buddhist women. Thailand has become known for prostitution. There could be between seven hundred thousand and one million Thai prostitutes. Some are voluntary prostitutes but many are involuntary, forced into such 'service' because of poverty. The problem is immense. Buddhist women such as Dr Chatsumarn Kabilsingh and Maeji Khunying Kanitha have been active both in pressing the Thai government not to use prostitution as a way of boosting tourism or the economy and in reaching out to women caught in prostitution. Maeji Khunying Kanitha, before she took on the robes of a nun, began an emergency home for women, not only for prostitutes but for any woman threatened with violence:

> I got the idea for an emergency home from other countries in Europe, the USA and Canada. It was not only for battered wives but also for rape victims and prostitutes who had run away from the brothels. When I started it, I used my own house, barehanded. But I wrote letters to women's organizations and embassies selling a project to build a shelter to help women. I called it 'an emergency home to help women and children in distress'. Many donations came. I raised about three million baht in the first year so we built our first shelter. At that time I was a member of the Women Lawyers' Association of Thailand. I served as their president for four years. The first shelter was built on top of the Women Lawyers' Association building. That was sixteen years ago.
>
> When I was using my home, I also wrote to all the police stations and hospitals in Bangkok telling them to send any woman needing a temporary home because of distress. I will always remember the first time an ambulance came to my house. It happened to be a woman who was drunk. She had been unconscious on the roadside with a five- or six-month old baby crawling on her body. The police had not known what to do with her. One eventually remembered, 'Oh, there was one lady who offered her house!' So they brought her to me and I cleaned her with cool water and things like that. We helped her.
>
> Many men come to Bangkok from rural areas to work on building sites. These workers send the money to their family or ask

their family to come and collect the pay. This woman had come several times to one construction site but, that particular month, the construction work had finished and everyone had moved away. So, she didn't know what to do. She told me, 'I was so frightened. I got lost. I had no money – only three baht.' And she had used that money to buy alcohol. This is the kind of thing that happens to many women. The men leave the family behind and they find other women in the big city.

I have helped many kinds of women. One other case was an elderly woman who had several children. She told me she could not live with any one of them. They had made it obvious they did not want her. So she had to leave their homes and someone recommended she come to us. She was the first woman to move from my house to the new shelter.

The experience of Maeji Kanitha is that women are often disadvantaged in Thailand. Her social engagement has been directed towards them. But is this true of women within Buddhism in general? This is what the next chapter will look at.

NOTES

1. *Cakkavatti-Sīhanāda Sutta*, *Dīgha Nikāya*, iii, 58ff. In this story a king does not take seriously the words of his spiritual advisors that he should give resources to the poor and destitute. The downward spiral begins with a growth in theft, which is followed by an increase in murder, lying, evil-speaking, adultery, incest and lack of religious piety. All moral sense leaves the society until it reaches a point where there is a 'sword period' of seven days when people look on one another as wild beasts and kill each other.

2. *Kūtadanta Sutta*, *Dīgha Nikāya*, i, 127ff. Here, a kingdom is harassed by crime. The king wants to organize a huge sacrifice. Yet the solution to the crime suggested by a Brahmin is that food and seedcorn should be given to farmers, capital to traders, and wages and food to government servants. Crime ceases when this is done.

3. The *Mahāvaṃsa* (The Great Chronicle) is one of several Pāli Buddhist chronicles of Sinhala history. It begins with the time of the Buddha and reaches well into the Common Era. The main part of it was composed in the fifth century CE by the Mahāvihāra, an influential fraternity of monks in Sri Lanka. The Chronicle tends to evaluate rulers by their adherence to Buddhist principles and the support they give to the monastic *Saṅgha*.

4. In the 1980s, Boosa detention camp, on the southern coastal belt between Dodanduwa and Galle, became notorious for its detention of both Sinhala and Tamil youth suspected of terrorist activities.

5. In 1984, peace talks were held in Thimpu, Bhutan, between Tamil leaders and the Sri Lankan government, under pressure from India. The

first round broke down after six days because the government representatives had rejected the four proposals put forward by the Tamil groups:
recognition of the Tamils as a nation; recognition of an identified homeland for the Tamils; recognition of the right of self-determination for
the Tamil nation; the right of citizenship for all Tamils in Sri Lanka. As
the talks were to begin again, a landmine devastated a police jeep in
Vavuniya and severe reprisals were inflicted by the security forces. This
was followed by further disturbance at Vavuniya, which cost the lives of
civilians. The second round ended with the Tamil representatives walking out of the talks. See M. R. Narayan Swamy, *Tigers of Lanka: From
Boys to Guerrillas* (Delhi: Konark Publishers, 1994), pp. 152–8.

6. The *Vāseṭṭha Sutta* (*Majjhima Nikāya*, ii, 196ff.). Two Brahmin youths
    come to the Buddha because they cannot agree whether virtue or birth
    determines a person's worth. The Buddha convinces them that human
    beings are biologically equal and that it is such things as morality and
    freedom from greed, hatred and delusion that mark human worthiness.

7. The *Mahāvaṃsa* (see note 3) describes three visits made by the Buddha
    to Sri Lanka during his lifetime; to Mahiyangana in the centre of the
    island; Nāgadipa in the north and Kelaniya in the south. Although
    there is no corroborative material to support the historicity of these
    visits, they hold an important place in the hearts of Sri Lankan
    Buddhists. See *Mahāvaṃsa*, i, verses 1–84.

8. In the late 1980s, the south of Sri Lanka was rocked by an uprising of
    militant youth who were disenchanted by the state's record on job provi-
    sion, poverty alleviation, etc. The JVP or Janatha Vimukti Peramuna
    (People's Liberation Front) used violent means to eliminate 'traitors' and
    sought to bring the country to the point of economic collapse through
    strikes backed by death threats. The uprising was viciously crushed by
    state extra-judicial killings.

9. At a *pirit* ceremony, members of the monastic *Sangha* chant a series of
    Pāli texts believed to have the power to bless, heal and protect. During
    the chanting, participants are linked together by a ritual thread, which
    passes around a clay pot full of water. At the end, each participant
    receives drops of the purified water and a piece of the thread is tied
    around the right wrist.

10. Angkor Wat, in the north-west of Cambodia, was the centre of a vast
    Khmer empire between the ninth and the fourteenth centuries CE. It
    eventually stretched north to Laos, west to Burma, south to the Malay
    peninsula and east to the South China Sea. Today, the extensive
    remains at Angkor form Cambodia's major tourist attraction, but the
    area has been and still is within a potential war zone.

11. *Buddhism and Ecology*, ed. M. Batchelor and K. Brown (London:
    Cassells, 1992).

5

WOMEN IN BUDDHISM

In many Buddhist communities in Asia, there are now more women devotees than men in the temples. In Thailand, they place pieces of gold leaf on certain images of the Buddha and offer flowers. In Sri Lanka, they light wicks in black, cup-like lamps filled with coconut oil and place flowers, on ledges, in front of Buddha images. On Poya Days (full-moon days), in the urban areas of Sri Lanka, more laywomen than men take eight precepts and stay the whole day, dressed in white, to meditate and listen to sermons. Buddhist women are visible in Asia, not only as givers and listeners but also as teachers and nuns. Yet how does Buddhist text and tradition present women? At a time when religion throughout the world is being criticized for being patriarchal, how does Buddhism stand up? What kind of strength and encouragement is Buddhism giving to women as women now?

WOMEN IN THE TEXTS: A LIBERATING MESSAGE?

One place from which to start a study of what Buddhism offers to women or says about women is with the Buddha and how his words about women are recorded in the texts. Yet this is not a straightforward task. On the question of women, a plurality of voices emerge in the texts, from the unequivocally positive to what some feminists would call androcentric, if not misogynist. These voices can seem to contradict one another. Yet, as far as the texts go, the positive outweighs the negative. Dr Lorna Devaraja is a Professor of History and has made the position of women in Buddhism a special study throughout her life. She is convinced that the Buddha was a pioneer in the area of gender equality:

> When you read the teachings, you realize that the Buddha did not distinguish between men and women. There is no gender difference in many things that he said. For instance, in connection with

the main tenets of Buddhism, when he says that salvation has to be achieved by one's effort, it presupposes the spiritual and intellectual equality of men and women. So there was no need to give a special address to women and when he spoke to his flock, very often he said *bhikkhu, bhikkhunī, upāsaka, upāsikā,* which means monks and nuns, male lay devotees and female lay devotees. So, he addressed all four sections of the gathering and whatever he said was meant for everybody. I personally feel that there is no gender difference in the path to salvation. Men and women can achieve the objective of Buddhism, which is *nibbāna,* by following the same path.

The ideal of the Fourfold Society consisting of monks, nuns, male lay followers and female lay followers was mentioned in chapter 1. In support of Dr Devaraja, texts can be quoted from the Pāli Canon in which the Buddha uses the same commendatory adjectives to describe people within all four categories if they live according to the *Dhamma*:

> Monks, these four who are accomplished in wisdom, disciplined, confident, deeply learned, *Dhamma*-bearers, who live according to *Dhamma* – these four illuminate the Order. (*Aṅguttara Nikāya*, ii, 8)

No gender discrimination can be detected here.

ORDAINED WOMEN

When the Buddha first began to invite people to leave their homes to embrace homelessness, women were not included though, as chapter 1 pointed out. But women were not content with this. According to Buddhist tradition, it was the Buddha's aunt and foster mother who spearheaded the resistance. Not satisfied with a pious lay life, she and a group of other women came to the Buddha, barefooted, to ask for equal opportunities. The story says that the Buddha at first refused. Dr Chatsumarn Kabilsingh:

> The Buddha was the one who gave ordination to women. The person who actually asked for ordination was his own aunt and stepmother, Queen Mahāpajāpatī. She, together with five hundred women from the court asked for ordination. In the beginning the Buddha hesitated, and some have interpreted this as meaning that the Buddha never wanted women to join the Order. But this needs to be looked at again to see what was in his mind. Maybe at that time it was not really appropriate for women to become ordained because they had to live in the forest. They had to live a very hard

life. Therefore, he hesitated. But finally he gave ordination to women for the reason that women are equal to men in their potential to become enlightened. That's the highlight for women's issues.

Dr Kabilsingh's explanation for the Buddha's initial hesitancy is that he was aware of inhibiting social factors, rather than that he doubted the spiritual capabilities of women. After all, the life of renunciation was hard. The wider society might not have respected the decision. The possibility of scandal within the whole Order would increase. It is a plausible explanation: if the Buddha hesitated, it was probably because of social factors, for there is no doubt that Buddhism insists that, when the mind and heart is set on liberation, it does not matter whether one is a man or a woman. 'Buddhism says the meditative mind has no gender. Therefore, women are equally as able to reach enlightenment as men,' was how Nyanasiri put it.

With the ordination of these women, a *Bhikkhuṇī* (Skt *Bhikṣunī*) Order, or Order of Nuns, began. According to the texts, however, the Buddha not only hesitated to grant ordination but set down a number of rules for the new women recruits which placed them below the monks in terms of this-worldly hierarchy. For instance, they were to pay homage to monks regardless of seniority.[1] This meant that a *bhikkhuṇī* of forty years' standing had to bow down to a *bhikkhu* ordained but a day. Again, social restraints might have made this necessary. Such rules might have been the only way of gaining recognition for the Order in a patriarchal society. The other explanation that has been put across by some Buddhists is that the rules were not the Buddha's at all, but were added later through the process of oral transmission.

In terms of spiritual hierarchy, there seems to have been little difference between men and women in the early years. In the texts, the early *bhikkhuṇīs* appear as strong, liberated women. Within the Pāli Canon, a whole volume is devoted to their poems. Dr Lorna Devaraja:

> Many women flocked to join the Order of Nuns. The expressions of the nuns and their sayings are given in a book called the *Therīgāthā* [verses of the sisters]. It is supposed to be the earliest literary work compiled by women anywhere. In the *Therīgāthā* we find capable women of great intellectual ability, women who left the chores of household life and domestic drudgery, joined the *Bhikkhuṇī* Order and gained emancipation not only from the shackles of society but also from the shackles of existence, of *saṃsāra*, and they gave joyous utterances of their feelings.

Nyanasiri almost echoed Dr Devaraja's words:

> The *Therīgāthā* is an entire book of women who became enlight-
> ened. One was Dhammadinnā, who was able to give difficult
> explanations of doctrine which the Buddha said were absolutely
> correct. They came from every section of society. Several nuns were
> former prostitutes who realized that their lives weren't getting any-
> where. One was a very old woman who had given her property
> away, very much like King Lear, and then had been abandoned by
> her children. But she became enlightened. So they came from many
> walks of life and many became completely liberated.

The *Therīgāthā* is part of the *Khuddaka Nikāya* within the *Sutta
Piṭaka* of the Pāli Canon. These extracts give an idea of their variety:

> I sought delight in decking out myself
> With gems and ornaments and tricks of art.
> By baths and unguents, massage, I ministered
> Unto this body, spurred by lusts of sense.
>
> Then found I faith, and forth from home
> I went into the homeless life, for I
> Had seen the body as it really is,
> And never more could lusts of sense return.
>
> All the long line of lives were snapped in two
> Aye, every wish and yearning for it gone.
> All that had tied me hand and foot was loosed,
> Peace had I won, peace throned in my heart.
> > (Bhikkhuṇī Nanduttarā, *Therīgathā*, verses 89–91)
>
> How should a woman's nature hinder us?
> Whose hearts are firmly set, who ever move
> With growing knowledge onward on the Path?
> What can signify to one in whom
> Insight does truly comprehend the Norm?
> > (Bhikkhuṇī Somā, *Therīgāthā*, verse 61)
>
> O woman well set free! how free am I,
> How thoroughly free from kitchen drudgery!
> Me stained and squalid 'mong my cooking pots
> My brutal husband ranked as even less
> Than the sunshades he sits and weaves alway.
> > (A *bhikkhuṇī* named 'Sumangala's mother', *Therīgāthā*, verse 23)

That there was gender equality at a spiritual level between monks and nuns is expressed in several ways in other parts of the Pāli Canon as well. Ven. Dhammadinnā, the nun already mentioned by Nyanasiri, provides one example. One of her most famous sermons was given to her husband, Visākhā. She takes the role of spiritual director rather than wife and the Buddha is recorded as saying afterwards, 'If you had asked me, Visākhā, about this matter, I too would have answered exactly as the nun Dhammadinnā answered' (*Majjhima Nikāya*, i, 304–5, *Cullavedalla Sutta*). In other words, her sermon is sealed as *Buddha vacana*, word of the Buddha. This is not an isolated incident. One way in which the words of the early nuns were authenticated was to declare them to be at one with the teaching of the Buddha himself. Also found in the Pāli texts are nuns who openly assume spiritual equality with their male counterparts. For instance, Ven. Bhaddā compares herself with Ven. Kassapa, one of the foremost monks surrounding the Buddha:

> We both have seen, both he and I, the woe
> And pity of the world, and have gone forth
> We both are *arahants* with selves well tamed
> Cool are we both, ours is *Nibbāna* now!
>
> (*Therīgāthā*, verse 66)

The *Bhikkhunī* Order spread out from India just as its counterpart, the Order of *Bhikkhus*. Dr Chatsumarn Kabilsingh:

> The *Bhikkhunī* lineage travelled from India to Sri Lanka at the time of King Aśoka, that's about the third century BCE. A group of fully ordained nuns from India was invited by royal invitation to go to Sri Lanka and they established the lineage there. So, Sri Lanka was the very first country outside India to have received the lineage. Then, a group of nuns from Sri Lanka were invited to China to give ordination to Chinese women.[2] At the very first ordination in China, three hundred women were ordained. So that was how the *Bhikkhunī Saṅgha* of fully ordained nuns in China was formed and of course, later on, it spread to Japan, Korea and the rest of the Mahāyāna countries.

LAYWOMEN

Buddhist literature speaks of many strong, spiritual laywomen. For instance, there is a remarkable commentarial story connected with one of the verses in the *Dhammapada*. Sumana, the youngest daughter of Anāthapindika, a rich benefactor of the Buddha,

addresses her father as 'younger brother' and dies. Anāthapindika is
horrified at such seeming irreverence. Society was, after all, patriarchal. When he mentions the incident to the Buddha, the Buddha
tells him that his daughter had been totally justified in speaking in
the way she did because she had reached a higher spiritual stage
than her father.[3]

This story challenges the assumption that those older in years are
older in spiritual awareness, as well as having a message for women.
Theravāda Buddhism also possesses texts which chart a new pattern
in marital relationships by challenging models of wife–husband
relationships that demand complete submission from the wife.
Dr Lorna Devaraja:

> We can give the example of the *Sigālovāda Sutta* [*Dīgha Nikāya*,
> iii, 180ff.] where the Buddha discussed the relationship between
> the husband and the wife as one of several examples – parents and
> children, servants and masters, employers and employees. All
> those lay relationships are mentioned in the *Sigālovāda Sutta*.
> Regarding the relationship between the husband and the wife,
> there is nothing specifically Buddhist in it. It can be applied even
> today in any society. The husband is told he should treat the wife
> like this: he should buy her clothes; he should entrust all his wealth
> to her; he should treat her with respect and he should be faithful to
> her. And the wife too has similar obligations to the husband. Now
> the great thing in this relationship is that it is reciprocal. In many
> of the contemporary teachings, the man only had rights and privi-
> leges; the wife only had duties and obligations – for example, the
> Laws of Manu or the Code of Confucius. But the Buddha advocat-
> ed a mutually reciprocal relationship.

WOMEN IN HISTORICAL TRADITION

Just to take the Pāli textual tradition of Theravāda Buddhism, therefore, reveals much which is liberative to women. A similar study
could be made of the Mahāyāna texts.[4] Yet the crucial question is
whether these practices and principles remained strong in the ongoing
historical tradition. Some Buddhist women answer with a resounding
'yes'. Dr Devaraja, speaking from the perspective of her historical
research into Sri Lankan history, is one of them:

> I think these [the positive principles seen in the text] were all practi-
> cally seen in most Buddhist societies, especially Sri Lanka, Thailand
> and Burma but also Tibet. In all Buddhist societies, there is no

segregation of the sexes. That is what distinguishes Buddhist societies from other societies in Asia. In many world religions today women are not admitted to the priesthood and in some societies they are not even admitted to places of worship. There are other societies where women are admitted but are behind a curtain or on a separate side. In Buddhist societies women were given permission to do all this over two thousand years ago. Even today, especially in Sri Lanka, if you go to a Buddhist temple for any function, ninety per cent of the devotees are women, in both the urban and rural areas. And women don't participate just in making tea and washing the dishes. They are doing all the important organizational work. Even the monks can speak to the ladies – of course they are celibate – but conversation is not debarred. So these liberal ideas which the Buddha expressed are practically seen in Buddhist societies.

Going back into Sri Lankan history, regarding which I can speak with authority, the women were in the forefront of all the main economic activity. The main activity was rice cultivation and women participated with the men, not only as helpmates. They had their own duties to perform. Except for ploughing and sowing, most of the agricultural work was done by women. Then women were foremost in religious activities, going back even to 300 BCE when Buddhism came to Sri Lanka. This is proved in literary sources, archaeological sources and even inscriptional evidence.

Women also had more legal rights than in many Western countries. We have a book called the *Niti Nighaṇḍuwa* which gives the laws prevalent in the Kandyan kingdom before the time when British came.[5] It is very clear that women could own property, inherit property, and bequeath their property to anyone they wished without let or hindrance from their husbands. Even in married life, whatever wealth the woman brought to the married household was hers. There was no communal ownership of property between husband and wife. Whatever they earned after their marriage belonged to both of them. If they chanced to separate she took back her property and he took back his property and anything earned together was divided into two. That is very clear in Sri Lankan law books. Women also had the right to divorce and remarry after divorce. Widows also had the right to remarry and there was no discrimination against widows.

Lorna Devaraja is convinced that the liberality of the laws in the Kandyan kingdom in Sri Lanka before it was taken over by the British in 1815 was due to the influence of Buddhism. Embodied in the *Niti Nighaṇḍuwa* she sees the spirit of the *Sigālovāda Sutta*. She had to admit that much of this had been lost under the British, yet not all was lost, as Nyanasiri was keen to stress, speaking from Sri Lanka, although American by birth:

> What Buddhism does for women is very important. Education for girls must be equal to education for boys. In a country like Sri Lanka, if a girl is firstborn, that's considered a great piece of good luck for the family, and the girl is called very often the 'second mother' or the 'little mother' because she will take the mother's place if the family is large and the mother dies. In this country, there are more women at law school than men. The universities have at least fifty per cent women. Women are in every field. So, for day-to-day living women have done very well with Buddhism. There are cultural overlays but the actual teaching of Buddhism has done more for liberating women than most things, and in this country women are very confused about women's lib. or women's movements. They don't understand what women want because they have it all.

PATRIARCHAL ELEMENTS?

There is much evidence to suggest, therefore, that Buddhism has a liberating message for women. But is this the whole story? Has Buddhism escaped the male-dominated patterns that have become part of many other religions? Has it been unaffected by patriarchy? Lorna Devaraja and Nyanasiri would say 'yes' or 'almost' and would know that they were not alone. Yet the experience of others is less positive. Even within the same country or school of Buddhism, there can be a plurality of voices. For instance, Ven. Dr Somchai Kusalacitto's words in Thailand about the education of girls were very different from Nyanasiri's:

> One thing about Thai tradition and perhaps other traditions is that we believe that the girl children should study only housework – how to look after the house, how to look after her father and mother, how to be skilful in preparing food – not to know much about other subjects. Many believe it should be for the man to study and not for the girl. We do have opportunities for girls to study but not enough at present.

Martine Batchelor also sees elements of patriarchy in Buddhism today and feels the problem partly arose because of the patriarchal nature of the societies Buddhism entered:

The texts say that men and women are equal. Yet Eastern society was patriarchal so Buddhism had to fit within that. Therefore, although the Buddha said men and women are equal and that they could both be enlightened, within the practical consideration of that there was a certain difference between men and women.

To take Buddhist nuns first; in Korea, nuns take their place beside monks, as equals, in official functions. In Taiwan, there are more Buddhist nuns than monks and their status is good. Yet in Theravāda Buddhist countries the situation is very different, as Martine Batchelor found out during the ten years she was a nun in the Korean tradition:

> I would put the position of Asian nuns in the whole Buddhist context in this way. The Korean nuns are ninety-five per cent equal. Japanese are seventy-five per cent equal. Taiwanese are eighty-five per cent equal. And Theravāda, they are ten per cent equal. So somebody in Korea said to me, 'Monks and nuns, they are the same. They're just like two wings of a bird. If you just have one wing, the bird can't fly.' So for them it was very obvious that there was no difference at a certain level – the level of practice and teaching. It was the same in Taiwan. They were all doing things together and there was no difference between the monks and the nuns. But that is not true in Theravāda countries.

Although the Buddha himself gave higher ordination to women, no Theravāda country officially offers that option today. Women can gain higher ordination in the Mahāyāna countries of Taiwan, Korea, Vietnam and China but not in Theravāda Burma, Cambodia, Sri Lanka or Thailand. In the Tibetan tradition, women can go no further than the position of novice, śrāmanerika (P. samanerī). Dr Chatsumarn Kabilsingh:

> The English word 'nun' is very problematic today because people tend to understand it in a Christian context. In Buddhism, we have the word bhikkhunī in Pāli and bhiksunī in Sanskrit, meaning 'fully ordained nuns'. So we always have to use the phrase 'fully ordained nuns'. Yet, in many countries, especially Theravāda countries like Thailand, Sri Lanka, Myanmar, Laos, Cambodia, we have 'contemporary nuns' only. Contemporary nuns are not fully ordained. They just observe eight precepts or ten precepts.
>
> The reason for the lack of fully ordained nuns in Theravāda countries is that according to the Buddhist texts, in order for a woman to be ordained, she must at first receive her ordination from at least five

nuns. Then, the nun who actually is her preceptor or the one who gives ordination must have at least twelve years' standing as a fully ordained nun. Now, logically, when you do not have nuns in a particular country, you could not possibly start the Order. First a woman has to be ordained by five nuns and then by at least five monks.

It has already been pointed out that a *Bhikkhuṇī* Order was brought to Sri Lanka from India in the third century BCE. It flourished for at least a thousand years and took ordination to China during that time. Yet, in the tenth or eleventh century CE, the Sri Lankan order lost its capacity to ordain new nuns, simply because there were not enough existing nuns to confer ordination. War and political upheaval were the probable causes. The order was not reinstated from any other country, it was simply allowed to die. The same did not happen when, in the eighteenth century, the Order of *Bhikkhus* lapsed. In that case, higher ordination for men was brought from Thailand.

For Sri Lankan women now, there is only an Order of *Dasasil Mātās* (ten-precept mothers). They wear robes but only follow ten rules of discipline rather than the three hundred plus rules of the *Bhikkhuṇī Pātimokkha* (Skt *Prātimokṣa*).[6] To use Dr Kabilsingh's terminology, they are 'contemporary nuns'. A similar order exists in Burma. Indeed, it was from Burma that a Sri Lankan woman gained the ten-precept ordination that founded the Order of *Dasasil Mātās* at the beginning of the twentieth century. Thailand never received a higher ordination for women, nor a ten-precept ordination. Thai women who renounce wear white, the colour of the lay devotee, and follow eight rules. Nuns in Cambodia are also white-clad.

'Contemporary nuns' hover perilously between the lay and ordained states. In Sri Lanka, for instance, it is possible for nuns, sitting in rows at an official function, to be ignored completely in a speaker's opening remarks. Only the presence of monks will be recognized. The situation is worse in Thailand. There the nuns have had no official standing whatsoever. Maeji Khunying Kanitha became a *maeji,* a Thai nun, in 1993, after a full professional and married life:

> *Maejis* are women who wear white and shave their heads and their eyebrows. There have been women wearing white in Thailand for at least seven hundred years – men also. In the Bangkok period of Thai history, over two hundred years ago, records show that in

many Buddhist temples, there were sections where women could become nuns and could come and live, serving the monastery. As part of Thai law, we have *Saṅgha* law, the law of the Buddhist monks. But this does not mention women religious. So the word *maeji* does not exist in Thai law at all. The *maejis* are illegal, they have no legal status, and on our identification cards, they don't call us nun or sister; they call us Miss or Mrs according to our civil status.

Written into the structures of Buddhism in Theravāda countries, therefore, there is discrimination against women who wish to renounce. Attitudes of women towards this differ. At one end of the spectrum, some 'contemporary nuns' disclaim interest in higher ordination because they feel it might bring them less freedom, not more. A discipline of over three hundred rules is not to be taken lightly, as Martine Batchelor found out when interviewing nuns for a book on women in Buddhism:[7]

> If we look at the Theravāda nuns as Westerners, we say, 'This is not logical, this is not nice.' But I met one nun and she told me, 'We have ten rules, isn't that enough? Who wants over three hundred rules!' I think it's a good point.

Other 'contemporary nuns' stress that serious religious practice is not dependent on *bhikkhuṇī* status. If higher ordination were available they might take it, but it is practice rather than structural equality which is important for them. Martine Batchelor, drawing again on her research:

> But what was interesting was that in Thailand, where I would have thought the nuns would have mentioned the disparity of status, they, on the contrary, spoke not about wanting to be Buddhist women but about wanting to be Buddhist human beings. The Buddhist path was about transcendence for them. It was not about trying to be equal, not about having status. They were looking at things from the other side. They were saying, 'Of course, it's good if nuns have better opportunities to study', for they knew that having less status meant less opportunity for study. But being good Buddhist human beings was more important. Nothing stopped their practice. They were great teachers, they were very respected. Although the circumstances might be difficult it doesn't stop women shining through them. But, no doubt, if the situation was easier, there might be more nuns.

Yet there are some 'contemporary nuns' who do yearn to follow the complete *bhikkhuṇī* rule of discipline. They see entry into higher ordination as something to be desired, personally and institutionally. For them, an ordained *Saṅgha* without the presence of women is a *Saṅgha* diminished, a *Saṅgha* which denies the Buddha's vision of a fourfold society.

Some Buddhist women also claim that the lack of higher ordination in Theravāda countries is a symptom of a wider context of discrimination in Buddhism that embraces lay life also. The words of Ven. Dr Somchai Kusalacitto about education for girls have already hinted at this. Evidence to suggest that women in some Buddhist communities have been encouraged to internalize negative images of themselves was not wanting in the interviews. Niramon Prudtatorn rejected Buddhism when young because she felt discriminated against:

> I was brought up in the Theravāda tradition where women have very little role as spiritual leaders. I found that very difficult to understand. I was told, 'Women can't do this; women can't do that.' The monk could do all the important religious things but we, as women, were taught in such a very strict way that I didn't feel comfortable as a human being. I felt it was not fair. I could only see that men could be ordained, and that women had no position. They could only be a white-dressed nun and most of their duties even then were in the kitchen, cleaning and serving the monks. The monks could give orders and the women could only take orders. For the men, education, shelter and respect was possible through ordination, even though they were poor. But for women there was nothing. Once I wrote an article about this and suggested that my readers should imagine what would happen if all the brothels in Thailand were closed and turned into temples for the girls and the girls were given everything that was given to the boys. Some of my readers got angry.
>
> Once I went to Chiang Mai and saw a sign on the pagoda, 'Women are not allowed.' When I asked the monk why, the monk couldn't give me an answer. I felt angry. Why was it that women, who gave so much in the way of food to the monks, were not allowed – surely this was superstition!

Niramon was eventually brought back to Buddhism through Sulak Sivaraksa and the International Network of Engaged Buddhists mentioned in chapter 4. In Sulak, she found an ally who was sympathetic

to her perspective on women in Buddhism. In Sri Lanka, too, village
women are often locked in attitudes which inhibit rather than pro-
mote freedom. Monica Ruwanpathirana, development worker and
poet, has, over many years, worked with Buddhist women in some
of Sri Lanka's more remote villages. Here she speaks about
women's views on *kamma*:

> As a development worker, I sometimes have to be critical but I'm
> positive also. Usually, our women, the poorest, believe they are
> poor because of sin in a previous birth; in other words, they
> believe that the reason why they have not got many things in this
> life is that they were bad in their last birth. Sometimes this is a bar-
> rier and I have to criticize. But I don't criticize Buddhism. I want to
> open their thinking. I repeat to them that I'm not criticizing their
> beliefs, otherwise they wouldn't listen to me.

How these negative images appeared in Buddhism is not completely
clear. The Pāli Buddhist texts recognize that a woman's life in
Indian society at the time the texts were formulated was hard, with
the risks of childbirth and the strain of leaving parents and family to
wait upon a man. There is a realistic attitude to the pressures
women face as women. One of the nuns in the *Therīgāthā* is seen to
exclaim:

> Woeful is a woman's lot! has he declared,
> Tamer and driver of the hearts of men:
> Woeful when sharing home with hostile wives,
> Woeful when giving birth in bitter pain,
> Some seeking death before they suffer twice...
> (Bhikkhunī Kisāgotamī, *Therīgātha*, verses 215–16)

This very realism could have led to the internalization of negative
images, for it is only a short step from this to conclude that women
have been born women because of unwholesome actions in the past.
It is as though, over the centuries, women in Buddhist countries
have thought or have been encouraged to think: 'Well, if my life is
so hard as a woman, I must have done something wrong in a previous life to be born a woman!' Religious verses exist, recited by
women, which express the aspiration that they will be reborn as
men in their next lives. In the narrative tradition of all Buddhist
schools, there are stories which imply that a woman cannot become
a Buddha, but must change gender at some stage. Then, sprinkled
among the more philosophical Pāli texts are verses that seem to

denigrate women as intellectually inferior to men and sexually uncontrolled:

> Women are uncontrolled, Ānanda. Women are envious, Ānanda. Women are greedy, Ānanda. Women are weak in wisdom, Ānanda.
>
> (*Aṅguttara Nikāya*, ii, 80)

> Monks, if ever one would rightly say: it is wholly a snare of Māra [the principle of evil or the unwholesome] truly, speaking rightly, one may say of womanhood: it is a snare of Māra.
>
> (*Aṅguttara Nikāya*, iii, 67)

> Monks, women end their life unsatiated and unreplete with two things. What two? Sexual intercourse and childbirth. These are the two things.
>
> (*Aṅguttara Nikāya*, i, 77)

Similar attitudes can be found in some Mahāyāna stories. No Buddhist academic would say that either these negative textual quotations or the popular attitudes given above are a reliable indicator of official doctrine. Even the view that a woman is what she is because of a previous birth does not stand up to analysis. Although the law of *karma* does imply that one's birth is affected by action in one's previous birth, it denies that previous action is the only reason for what humans experience, and certainly challenges any form of fatalism.[8]

CHALLENGING PATRIARCHY

The evidence of our interviews showed that, all over the world, Buddhist women are no longer willing to accept discrimination. They are involved in peacemaking and meditation movements. They are establishing training institutions for women and quietly but efficiently working to bring back the *Bhikkhuṇī* Order in Theravāda countries. They are working for changes in attitudes at many levels.

ENCOURAGING NUNS

To take the *Bhikkhuṇī* Order first, one challenge to monks who say that higher ordination has been lost forever in Theravāda countries is to stress that the nuns in China, a Mahāyāna country, still follow a Theravāda rule of discipline, since it was a Theravāda country, Sri Lanka, that took ordination there in the first place. Dr Chatsumarn Kabilsingh:

Theravāda monks usually argue that existing nuns belong to the
Mahāyāna tradition and therefore are different. It is like Catholic
and Protestant. They don't take lineage from each other. But then
the lineage of ordination is very much Theravāda, even though the
fully ordained nuns are Mahāyāna, because the lineage went from
Sri Lanka to China. The lineage of ordination, which is the
Vinaya, the monastic code, is very much Theravāda. So, that argument is not valid. The rules which Mahāyāna nuns are following
are more or less the same as those which Theravāda nuns are pre-
scribed to follow.

No Theravāda country has yet agreed with this argument officially.
Not one has asked China to send fully ordained nuns to ordain its
own nuns, although at least one has made investigations. Yet, in a
quiet but revolutionary way, laywomen in Theravāda countries
have been at work. Women in Sri Lanka have been particularly
active and this is now showing results. There are quite a few Sri
Lankan *dasasil mātās* who can now be called *bhikkhunīs* because
they have received higher ordination. They have done so, not by
going to a Mahāyāna Buddhist country but by attending an ordination ceremony in a non-Buddhist country such as America or India.
In 1988, a pioneering ceremony was held in Los Angeles. Dr
Kabilsingh:

> The movement to bring back the *Bhikkhunī* Order is stronger in
> Sri Lanka than Thailand, partly because there are more learned
> Buddhist scholars. Articles have been written for and against high-
> er ordination for women. And the government has gone further
> than the Thai government in the sense that they have actually sent
> some people at government level to go to China to find out the
> way to re-establish fully ordained nuns in Sri Lanka again. But
> they have not yet been able to follow this up.
>
> Then, ten Sri Lankan *dasasil mātās* actually went to Los
> Angeles in 1988 to receive to full ordination. Out of these, only
> five eventually received full ordination and returned to Sri Lanka.
> But they did not then stay in one particular place. They spread out
> and in that sense they were not able to share solidarity. They were
> not able to make the movement strong enough. Whereas in
> Thailand, there is no movement.

At the ceremony in Los Angeles, Theravāda and Mahāyāna women
received higher ordination from Mahāyāna nuns and Theravāda
and Mahāyāna monks, since there are a few Theravāda monks who

sympathize with the ordination of women. Yet, as Dr Kabilsingh suggests, the Sri Lankan nuns were not able to assert themselves on return. There was no aftercare. They were not even given Sinhala translations of the *Bhikkhuṇī Pātimokkha*.

More recent attempts to train and ordain Sri Lankan *dasasil mātās* have been more successful and have received coverage in the Sri Lankan press, some of it positive. On 20 December 1996 ten Sri Lankan nuns received higher ordination in Sarnath, India. The event was sponsored by the Korean World Buddhist Saṅgha Council but some sympathetic Theravāda monks were also involved. In contrast to the Los Angeles ordination, many months of preparatory training for the nuns preceded it. Then, from 15 to 23 February 1998, there was a further ordination at Bodh Gaya of fifty Theravāda nuns, twenty of whom were Sri Lankan. A larger number of Theravāda monks supported it. The women ordained on both occasions now follow the Dharmagupta *Vinaya* with 348 rules, which, as Dr Kabilsingh has pointed out, is close to the discipline of the Theravāda tradition. This has now led to a small ordination ceremony in Sri Lanka itself, but how wide the acceptance of this will be among the monastic *Saṅgha* there is uncertain.

For some contemporary nuns, however, education is more important than ordination, as Martine Batchelor has implied. Many are longing for better tools to equip them for the religious life, better access to education, better training facilities. In countries such as Thailand, Cambodia and Sri Lanka, where for centuries nuns have been treated as second-class monastics, this is vital. When I asked Dr Kabilsingh whether there was a movement in Thailand for the higher ordination of women, she quickly turned to education:

> In Thailand there is no movement for ordination. Maybe I'm the only one in this country who has been talking about ordination of women long enough to realize that I have started from the wrong end. I was talking about *x, y, z*. But people in Thailand were not ready for that yet. Maybe I should have started with *a, b, c, d*. So, my work now is going back to the roots to train women to understand more about Buddhism, to understand more about their role as Buddhist women. Then, maybe one day they will ask for ordination.

Maeji Khunying Kanitha, a close friend of Dr Kabilsingh, has written letters to the Thai Ministry of Education asking them to provide a budget for a nun's college. This is the kind of curriculum she would like:

We must have literacy courses. And of course the compulsory courses must be on the Buddha's life and Buddhist practice. Then we will have many other courses so that the nuns can help the community: English, typing, computer, teaching, accountancy. If we want the nuns to do things in the community, they must be educated and know how to manage.

Ven. Dr Somchai Kusalacitto is one of their male allies:

I personally work with many women's groups who fight for women's rights and work for the improving of woman's status in society. I have addressed many meetings. We should give more chances to women to study. Even at the Buddhist University here there is no objection to admitting ladies to be students. We think in the same way. But we do not have enough space or enough funds. If we had enough teachers, enough space and enough money, we would be willing to admit women.

So Mouy has similar concerns in Cambodia. During the Pol Pot period she lost her parents and many other relatives. In 1985, she became a nun and eventually started her own nunnery near Sihanoukville, where eight nuns now live. A typical day at this nunnery has already been described in chapter 3, and some of her concerns for peace in chapter 4. She is active in work with Mahā Ghosānanda. Now, a national organization for nuns is being formed:

We formed the organization after we had a national nuns' conference in May 1995. We have representatives from different provinces, a steering committee of sorts and assistance from the Heinrich Böll Foundation in Germany. We hope to find funding to build a place to ensure that teaching can continue for the nuns. Then, for developing a curriculum for the nuns we have Dr Hema Goonatilake[9] from Sri Lanka. She will help with research into Pāli and particularly into the *Vinaya*, the discipline for nuns, in the past and present. We will try to find good, young and eager nuns from the provinces, who could come to this centre to study and then go back to educate the other nuns in their own provinces.

One of the laywomen activists behind the ordinations in Sarnath and Bodh Gaya in 1996 and 1998 was Mrs Ranjani de Silva from Sri Lanka. She is also acutely conscious that education is a priority for the *dasasil mātās*. For several years she has run courses for them, on a low budget, in simple surroundings:

I take one district and select ten nuns at a time. Our facilities can't take more than that. Our aim is to motivate them and give them more confidence and awareness. We start the day's programme at 4 in the morning. There is meditation until 6 a.m. with a cup of tea in between. At 6.30 a.m. there is a meal. Afterwards, there is a *Dhamma* talk and more meditation. In the *Dhamma* talks we include the *Vinaya* rules. Although they are nuns, they don't know the rules sometimes. Since we don't have the *Bhikkhunī* Order here no proper code of discipline is established. Before noon they have their main meal.

In the afternoon, I have outside lecturers come in. The nuns are keen to learn English. So we do spoken English every day. Other lessons include leadership training, communication, counselling, first aid and how they should work with society to help the needy and the poor. I was very keen to teach them first aid. Some are in remote places away from doctors and hospitals. They will be recognized if they have knowledge of how to handle someone fallen from a tree, how to stop bleeding, how to deal with fainting or insect bites. Professionals come to teach them and give them notes and we make sure they have a first aid box in their nunneries. My whole purpose is to get these nuns recognized. With better recognition, they will have more confidence.

Since she spoke to us, a sympathetic monk, Ven. Dr Mapalagama Wipulasara, has given her a much better building for a training centre, within a temple complex south of Colombo. Nuns are taught *Dhamma* by the same people who teach the trainee monks, but at different times, and the classes in other skills are not forgotten.

CHALLENGING ATTITUDES IN THE FAMILY

Art, drama and poetry have also been used by some Buddhist women to change attitudes within society as a whole. It is not only the nuns in societies such as Sri Lanka who need to be recognized for what they contribute, but also laywomen. A pioneer in this is Monica Ruwanpathirana. Her poems, in Sinhala, have consistently highlighted the often unrecognized strength of laywomen and the self-sacrificial work that they do:

I divide my poems into the early ones and now. I started writing twenty years back. In the first days, I was very radical. To give an example, there is a *Jātaka*[10] called 'the rabbit story'. The people say that on the moon there is a picture of a rabbit because of it. There are three animals in the story and they are very hungry. One of them, the rabbit, makes a fire and throws himself on it to feed the others. After that, it is believed, the King of the Gods takes this rabbit and draws his picture on the moon so all people could see him. In the late 1970s, I wrote a poem, appealing to this same god, saying, 'So you have done this very big job. You have drawn this rabbit's picture on the moon. It's very nice; but there's another picture you have to draw on the moon. It's of a very little hut. Moonlight is coming through the holes of the roof. On the floor a woman is sleeping without having any food. She has given all the food she has to her children. The rabbit you drew died only once, quickly. This woman is dying gradually. So you have to give attention and draw her picture also on the moon.' That was my poem.

But now, my poems are more mature. My poems are popular among the people because I get all my thinking, my roots, from the major community. Another poem is like this. People used to introduce mothers here as buddhas-of-the-home, because the mother carries all the burdens of the home with compassion. Now, the Lord Buddha, in birth after birth after birth, practised how to give compassion, how to develop the *pāramitās*, perfections. So I say in the poem, 'Go and see – there is a buddha-at-home, a mother. She has a lot of injuries in her body. She's practising the *pāramitā*. She's going to become a Buddha because she has so many wounds on her body. Now somebody has done this to her – her husband or her son. She is sacrificing herself like a buddha-to-be, for buddhahood. She is in front of the doors of death and is meditating. Go and worship her.' The Buddha's many practices I apply to this character and I'm saying, 'Please go and worship her because she will become a Buddha.' Why I said this is because, according to Buddhist tradition here, women cannot become Buddhas. Before I can be a Buddha, I have to be a man.

In poems like these Monica has drawn attention to violence against women and the self-sacrifice practised by women in their everyday lives. She has turned over existing norms by saying that here, among poor Buddhist women, are the qualities that the Buddha spent many lifetimes perfecting. Here is spiritual attainment.

Monica Ruwanpathirana points to the strength of women not only in her poems but in her own life. Consistently, she has worked with and on behalf of village women. She has established a non-government organization for development alternatives. She is a positive symbol of what women can achieve. This can be said of all the women interviewed. Glimpses of their personal stories pepper these pages: Chatsumarn Kabilsingh, Ranjani de Silva, Maeji

Kanitha Wichiencharoen, Helen Jandamit, Nyanasiri. Another remarkable story that arose from the interviews was that of Renee Pan of Cambodia. In one way it is unique, but in another it can act as a pointer to the courage of many Buddhist women.

Renee escaped from Cambodia just five days before Pol Pot took over. Her husband had been deputy Prime Minister. She brought up three children in the United States alone, took an MA in Computer Studies and worked with South-East Asian refugees. In 1992, she returned to Cambodia:

> My story is very long. I left Cambodia on April 12th, 1975, the time when the US ambassador left the country. My husband, who was a government minister, was invited to leave by the US ambassador but he decided to stay. Since then I haven't seen him. We have three children and I raised them alone in the United States. They are now all grown up. The oldest one is married and he is a scientist with a company in Boston. My second son finished his Masters degree and he was a Peace Corps volunteer in Central Africa for three years. Now he continues his education for a doctorate. He came here last summer in order to find out what kind of research he could do to benefit the country. He told me before he left, 'Mum, I respect your path and I'm going to continue that path.'
>
> My girl, the youngest one in the family, she also has found her way to come back here. She left when she was only five years old. She vaguely remembers the face of her father, vaguely remembers Cambodia. The first time she came to Cambodia she asked me to take her to her house. So I took her and she remembered, 'Mum, this is my room, this is the place that I came early morning to visit your room.' That's what she remembered and she was also so embarrassed to be Cambodian and not to speak Cambodian fluently. After the trip here, she knew that she was Cambodian and she is trying to find ways to come back. She is working for her Masters degree in Public Relations.
>
> For myself, now that all of those children are grown up, what is left for me is to fulfil the path that my husband could not fulfil. He was a Minister of Education. He wanted so much for his people because he belonged to a poor family and being the son of a poor family he understood very well what life looked like. The first time when he was up there in power he tried to set up so many programmes, sending people out, finding scholarships, seeking to improve education in Cambodia. My role now is to provide education to the younger generation, especially through the introduction of the computer.

Her courage in returning to Cambodia had much to do with refind-
ing her faith:

> My ancestors were half French and half Cambodian. So, in the
> past, Christianity and Buddhism lived in harmony. Before the war
> everyone claimed to be Buddhist. If you went to the temple you
> were Buddhist. To overcome the loss of my husband I said to
> myself that this was maybe because of my *kamma*. I had to work
> hard, not to complain and to do something good to answer to that
> *kamma* in order to have a better life. But that doing good was not
> enough. The happiness I had during that time kept pouring out. It
> reached to the bottom of the glass where I had nothing to give
> away. That was when frustration came. Then, I found my faith –
> the faith that I can never put a price to. I became Buddhist. I found
> meditation. When I came back to Cambodia, I was prepared. I
> could cope with the suffering of the people. Many of my friends
> came back without equipping themselves, without having a fence
> to protect themselves. They became desperate and frustrated.
> Some of them went back to America.

BUDDHISM AND WOMEN IN THE WEST

During the twentieth century, Buddhism has put down strong roots
in the West. So it is worth asking how converts to Buddhism living
in the West regard the question of gender in Buddhism. The whole
issue of Buddhism in the West is covered more fully in chapter 6.
Only gender is the issue here. Generalizations are difficult to make
because of the great variety of expressions within Western
Buddhism. Some groups are very closely linked to specific Asian
traditions; others have sought to create a Buddhism that they see as
appropriate to the West. Yet Martine Batchelor was probably
speaking for many when she said that the way in which Buddhism
in Asia had, in some contexts, compromised with the patriarchy of
society was simply not acceptable in the West:

> There is no doubt that this can't be continued in the West. After a
> while it does not feel right. If you are told that you are a lesser
> birth, at first you might say, 'Who cares!' but after a while you
> say, 'No, I'm not a lesser birth. I'm of an equal birth.'

Western women who convert to Buddhism are certainly not willing to
internalize negative images of themselves and there is little evidence
that teachers of Buddhism in the West are hinting that they should.
One group that has consciously attempted to adapt Buddhism to the

West is the Western Buddhist Order. Dhammacarini Sanghadevi
has already been introduced as a leading woman member. When
asked to comment on gender awareness in the Order, she replied:

> In Theravāda Buddhism, women aren't able to become
> *bhikkhuṇīs*. Many women are very concerned about this. It is a
> technical problem rather than a spiritual problem. In our own
> order, women have the same opportunities as men. We're not
> caught up in technical hitches. There is the same ordination
> whether you're a man or a woman. In that way, it cuts right across
> the issues that many in the East are struggling with.

The Western Buddhist Order has set up a meditation centre especially
for women, Tārāloka. It is named after Tārā, a female *bodhisattva* in
the Mahāyāna tradition. Dhammacarini Sanghadevi:

> Tārāloka was founded in 1985 by myself and a few other women.
> It's a Buddhist retreat centre in North Wales. It was the first long-
> term project in our own movement which was set up totally for
> women by women. We run retreats the whole year round.
> Meditation retreats represent quite a large percentage, but we also do
> study retreats and devotional retreats. Maybe between six hundred
> and seven hundred women pass through the centre in a year, for any-
> thing from a weekend up to two weeks. It has a community of about
> ten women who live there full-time, meditating, studying, teaching
> and doing all the back-up work to run a facility like that. It has been
> a source of confidence and inspiration to many other women in the
> movement.

Kagyu Samye Ling Centre in Scotland has already been mentioned
in chapter 4. It seeks both to keep alive the Tibetan Buddhist tradition and to be sensitive to the needs of Western inquirers. Chapter 6
will explore this in more detail. The Abbot and retreat master,
Lama Yeshe Losal, for instance, allows Western women, and men,
to take on the robes of a Buddhist monastic for a trial period of just
one year. As in Tibet, the women who take on the maroon robes
cannot yet hope to become fully ordained within the Tibetan system
but they nevertheless spoke glowingly of the encouragement they
were receiving. Ani Tsewang Chödron came to Samye Ling for four
days originally but has now taken life vows as a nun:

> In Tibetan Buddhism from a woman's point of view, I haven't
> noticed any discrimination or anything which would make it
> appear that men and women or monks and nuns are treated any
> differently. There is a certain separateness, which under the

circumstances is wise. Some Westerners have a problem with the fact that it is very male-orientated as far as the teachers go. The teachers are men at the moment. But, having said that, they don't display any stereotypically manly characteristics. They have a perfect balance of all that makes up a nice human being and, from a woman's point of view, it is very encouraging. The teachers are saying, 'We need you; we need women to learn to be strong, to be independent, to be wise, to be compassionate and then you can teach.' That's what they're saying here. In the West, there are a lot of spaces to do that.

Already some Tibetan centres are being run by women. Ani Tsewang Chödron:

> Samye Ling has satellite centres in different parts of Europe and this country and many of them are run by women. Lama Yeshe pointed out to me that, as far as new centres in the south are concerned, I'm being sent down there and I'm a woman. If we are put into positions like that and we can do the job properly, there's no reason why this can't carry on to be the case. Who knows? Women may end up running Samye Ling. The space is being created for us if we want to do the job and we want to do it properly.

SAKYADHĪTĀ: DAUGHTERS OF THE BUDDHA

Of course, it's not only in the West that women are running Buddhist centres, and now there is much more contact between Buddhist women across the East–West divide. One point of contact is Sakyadhītā, an international association of Buddhist women. It was formed in 1987 at a conference on Buddhist nuns held at Bodh Gaya in India, the place where the Buddha gained enlightenment, now a place of pilgrimage filled with temples built by different Buddhist communities: China, Tibet, Korea. The conference was the brainchild of three Buddhist women: Dr Kabilsingh; the Ven. Karma Lekshe Tsomo, an American nun ordained in the Tibetan tradition and fully ordained in the Korean tradition; and the Ven. Ayya Khema, a German Theravāda nun who had taught in Germany, Australia and Sri Lanka. Dr Kabilsingh:

> The three of us started by corresponding with each other. Then, we realized that it was about time that we should come together. That was 1984. Ayya Khema started her international meditation centre in Sri Lanka.[11] I started my newsletter on international Buddhist women's activities in Thailand[12] and Ven. Karma Lekshe Tsomo was trying to start a nunnery in India. So the three of us cor-

responded and finally we agreed to organize the very first conference on Buddhist nuns in Bodh Gaya in 1987. Why Bodh Gaya? Because Bodh Gaya was the place where the Buddha became enlightened. So we took that as symbolic. After all, we were talking about the enlightenment of women! Many women joined that conference and Sakyadhītā, which means 'Daughters of the Buddha', was created. Now it is registered in the United States as a non-profit-making organization. The objective of Sakyadhītā is to support women in different countries to learn, to study, to practise and also to help women who want to become fully ordained nuns. So our conferences move around. At the first conference we had an audience with His Holiness the Dalai Lama and he suggested that we should go to countries where there are no fully ordained nuns yet.

We took his word seriously. The second conference was held in Bangkok in 1991. More than two hundred and forty laywomen and nuns from different parts of the world participated. Two issues from the Thai situation came to the forefront: education and opportunities for women to practise together. I picked up on that for my own local follow-up activities. The third one was in Sri Lanka in 1993. It generated quite a lot of interest about what Buddhist women could do in the world and also about the possibility of fully ordained nuns.

The next conference was in Ladakh. Ladakh was difficult because of the geographical setting. Maybe we were a bit crazy to make an attempt to hold the conference there, but it turned out very positively. The more hardship we went through together the more bonding there was. We gave exposure to Ladaki nuns who did not have any access to the outside world. All presentations were in English and Ladaki so that local Buddhist nuns and laywomen could benefit. The purpose is to bring awareness to each location we visit.

The conference following Ladakh was held in Cambodia from 29 December 1997 to 4 January 1998. Again, the venue was controversial, because of the uncertainty of the political situation. But it was a success. It attracted women from Australia, Bangladesh, Bhutan, Canada, England, Finland, France, Germany, India, Italy, Japan, Malaysia, Nepal, the Netherlands, Singapore, South Korea, Sri Lanka, Taiwan, Thailand, the USA and, of course, Cambodia itself. The pink, orange, maroon, grey and white robes of nuns from different traditions mingled with sarees, shalwar kameez and Western dress. 'Women in Buddhism: Unity and Diversity' was the theme. Academic papers took their place beside meditation sessions,

workshops and cultural performances. Practical issues for laywomen and nuns in different regions, such as training, ordination
and human rights were discussed. Workshops covered Buddhism
and the media, peace education, expressing Buddhism through the
arts, interfaith co-operation and strategies for transforming the role
of women. A trip to Angkor Wat at the end brought in the impres-
sive cultural heritage of Cambodia. Nepal was named as a possible
venue for the next conference – again a country where nuns face
considerable problems in education and training.

THE CONTRIBUTION OF WOMEN

Sakyadhītā believes that women have a specific and valuable contri-
bution to make to Buddhism in general and that, if Buddhism
dismisses its women, it will be to Buddhism's disadvantage. For a
study of women within Buddhism is not simply a question of what
women can extract from Buddhism but what they can contribute to
it. For instance, some aspiring *bhikkhuṇīs* in the Theravāda tradition
believe that a female presence in the monastic *Saṅgha* will irrevoca-
bly change it; that the very texture of Buddhism will be different as a
result, because women bring characteristics the *Bhikkhu Saṅgha*
needs. Martine Batchelor was one of those who mentioned this quite
specifically:

> Women and men are quite similar but women bring a more experi-
> ential and practical view of Buddhism, it seems to me. Three years
> ago I interviewed many women for a book and what was interest-
> ing to me was that they were slightly more experiential. I did not
> meet many women who were very philosophically inclined, trying
> to explain to me all the philosophy of Buddhism. What was impor-
> tant to them was how they lived it. That is very good – women
> bringing that very practical aspect, that Buddhism is not just in the
> mind but has to be applied.
>
> I interviewed Western Buddhists – American, German, French,
> English – and Asian Buddhists, because I really wanted to see as wide
> a range of women as possible to find out how Buddhism had
> changed their lives and how they were living it. So I went to Korea, to
> Japan, to Taiwan, to Thailand and I also interviewed some Tibetan
> women. It was fascinating and very inspiring. I had lots of fun.
>
> The common trend was mindfulness. All of them meditated but
> their practices were quite different, as techniques. And the colour
> of their robes and the way they wore them were different; so was
> their chanting and their organizational structure. But when you

talked to them about what they did, it was mindfulness and reflection. There was more unity. Their main practice was to be mindful. A lot of them had a practice of being reflective. At the beginning of the day they would set themselves a task – today I'll be generous; today I'll be kind – and at the end of the day they would review it.

Ranjani de Silva also stressed the practical effect of committed women. Her vision was of Buddhist women, rooted in the *Dhamma*, changing the world:

I feel that if we work like this as Buddhist women and if we have strong determination, we can change the whole world. Today there is violence everywhere. If all the mothers become conscious of the *Dhamma* in bringing up their children, it can bring a change to the younger generation who are going to be parents themselves. It can help to bring peace.

We try to start in a small way. In our own community, we have many societies, women's associations and Buddhist women's groups. We have our *Dhamma* circles, even in our own family and in our neighbourhoods. Even at our work, we encourage people to talk about *Dhamma* and we try to draw people's attention to life's priorities.

We are also making use of the nuns to spread the *Dhamma*. People are experiencing many material benefits but they are also beginning to know that material benefits are not the answer. In this country, there's a thirst for meditation at the moment and a lot of women are taking the lead.

When asked whether she had anything else to add at the end of her interview, Dr Kabilsingh said:

I am grateful for this opportunity to address women all over the world. When we are born women we should be very happy. We should use our potential as women for the best. We should not allow the fact that we are women to belittle us. I think women suffer through this throughout the world for no reason. I'm so happy to be a woman. It has not obstructed me in any of my activities.

NOTES

1. These rules are called *gurudhammas* (Skt *gurudharmas*). There are eight, which include the following: a nun should rise and venerate a monk even if she has had many years in the order and he is newly entered; a nun must not admonish a monk for offences but a monk can

admonish a nun; a nun should not receive food, lodging and other requisites before a monk; a nun must have a two-year probation period before higher ordination and must be ordained by both monks and nuns.

2. In 433 CE, a group of Chinese women requested help from the Order of *Bhikkhuṇīs* in Sri Lanka. A group of nuns went from Sri Lanka and ordained three hundred Chinese women. The lineage is still in existence today. The event is known through Chinese records, but is not recorded in Sri Lankan historical chronicles.

3. Each verse of the *Dhammapada* in the Pāli tradition has a story connected to it by way of commentary. The story contextualizes the verse by weaving a narrative around it. The story of Sumana and Anāthapindika illustrates verse 18: 'Here he delights, having passed away, he delights; the one who has done merit rejoices in both places; He delights [thinking] "I have done merit"; he rejoices all the more gone to a good rebirth.'

4. See Rita M. Gross, *Buddhism after Patriarchy* (New York: State University of New York Press, 1993); Diana Y. Paul, *Women in Buddhism: Images of the Feminine in Mahāyāna Buddhism* (Berkeley: University of California Press, 1985); Nancy Schuster, 'Changing the Female Body: Wise Women and the Bodhisattva Career in some Mahāratnakūṭsutras', *Journal of the International Association of Buddhist Studies* 4/1, 1981, pp. 24–69.

5. *Niti-Nighaṇḍuwa or The Vocabulary of Law as it Existed in the Last Days of the Kandyan Kingdom*, trans. C. J. R. Mesurier, Ceylon Civil Service and T. B. Panabokke, President of Dumbara, Kandy (Delhi and Colombo: Navrang, 1994; first published in 1880 by the Government Printer, Ceylon). Although collated well after the demise of the Kandyan kingdom, it is thought to be a fairly accurate record.

6. The *Pātimokkha* (Skt *Prātimokśa*) is the monastic rule of discipline itemized. It is traditionally recited by the monastic community on the day of the full moon and of the new moon. Three codes survive. The Theravāda code contains 227 rules for men and 311 for women; the Mula-Sarvastivadin 258 and 366, and the Dharmagupta 250 and 348.

7. Martine Batchelor, *Walking on Lotus Flowers: Buddhist Women Working, Loving and Meditating* (London: Thorsons/HarperCollins, 1996).

8. See *Aṅguttara Nikāya* i, 173, in which the Buddha itemizes three beliefs which inhibit the spiritual life and lead to inaction and fatalism: that all a person experiences is due to previous action; that all a person experiences is due to the action of a Supreme Deity; that all is due to chance, i.e. uncaused and unconditioned.

9. Dr Hema Goonatileka is a Sri Lankan academic committed to improving the situation of nuns. Following a visit to China in the mid-1980s, she was one of the first in Sri Lanka to point out that there were nuns in China who followed almost the same rule of discipline as Sri Lankan nuns. See *Sunday Observer* (Sri Lanka), 14 May 1986. As this book is written, she is working at the Buddhist Institute in Phnom Penh and

has been instrumental in inviting Sri Lankan monks to Cambodia to teach.

10. *Jātaka* no. 316. Traditionally, this involves a hare rather than a rabbit. The hare jumps into fire to feed another and his shape is impressed on the moon as a reward for his self-sacrificial generosity.

11. Ven. Ayya Khema had established Parappaduwa Nuns' Island on a small island in a lake near Dodanduwa in southern Sri Lanka as a meditation and retreat centre for foreign and local women meditators. Political instability in Sri Lanka forced her to leave it at the end of the 1980s. She eventually settled at Buddha Haus near Munich in Bavaria where she taught and gave spiritual guidance until her death on 2 November 1997.

12. Dr Kabilsingh's newsletter was called *Nibwa* at that stage. It continues as *Yasodhara: A Newsletter on International Buddhist Women's Activities*, published from Thailand.

6

CHALLENGING AND REINFORCING CULTURE

At the heart of Bangkok's congested roads and high-rise buildings is a Buddhist shrine with a golden image. It is next to one of Bangkok's busiest banks. High on the railings around the image are banks of crimson and orange garlands. On low platforms and tables offerings of food and drink lie alongside candles and incense sticks.

Fashionably dressed people come inside the railings in a continuous stream. They bow, kneel or squat on their heels to make their offerings. Vows are made, with hopes of success or simply the wish for peace of mind. The next stop is the bank, the shop or the office. The uncertainties and stresses of Bangkok's competitive commercialism seem to feed devotion. Commerce, competition and religion meet. Or do they? Has Buddhism adapted to the individualism of the market place? Is it succumbing to the pressures of a global economy?

This chapter focuses on what challenges Buddhists are giving both to traditionally Buddhist societies and to the West. It deals with values and meaning within the context of social change. Voices of Buddhists convinced that Buddhism has an urgent and relevant message for individuals and society have featured in all sections. Greedlessness, non-harming, compassion, mindfulness, peacemaking and social activism have all been highlighted. Buddhism has emerged not only as a system of beliefs but as a way of life. This chapter builds on this, through probing some of the energies at work in contemporary Buddhism as it comes face to face with war, economic change and modern searches for meaning. It takes as a starting point the fact that Buddhism is a global religion.

There is hardly a country in the world where Buddhists are not present. Asia was Buddhism's traditional preserve, yet in the last 150 years it has travelled west and east to become one of the fastest growing religions in Europe and America. Both Asia and the West are affected by this, just as both Asia and the West are affected by global economic patterns. So this chapter looks at models which

Buddhists are rejecting and those which they are adopting to challenge or revitalize the cultures of the world.

A MISSIONARY RELIGION?

One model adopted by some religions is the overtly missionary. Most religions of the world are missionary by nature; some religious people combine mission with, or even define mission as, proselytization, the making of converts. From the beginning, Buddhism was missionary in the sense that the Buddha decided both to preach what he had realized in meditation and to call others to follow his teaching. He then sent disciples out to teach others. The pattern continued in the following centuries. Buddhism became established in Sri Lanka because of the missionary activity of King Aśoka of India in the third century BCE. It travelled to Tibet because Indian Buddhists carried the message. Without missionary activity, Buddhism would have remained in India and perhaps died there, swallowed up into Hinduism or violently marginalized. At the heart of Buddhism is the conviction that to give the *Dhamma* is the greatest gift one can give.

Now, in Buddhist countries such as Thailand and Sri Lanka, there are training courses for monks and nuns who will staff Buddhist centres abroad. The word 'mission' is sometimes used for this. In Sri Lanka, media references to Buddhist monks going abroad as missionaries has been normal for many decades. Ven. Professor Dhammavihari in his interview for the programmes spoke very openly about the missionary tradition within the monastic *Saṅgha*. Ven. Gnanapala, whose voice featured in chapter 4, is part of the resident community of the Vajirārāma Temple in Colombo, which has long had a tradition of sending monks abroad. Monks have gone from the community to Britain, America, Scandinavia and Holland, to name but a few countries. The biography of one of its most famous monks, Ven. Piyadassi, is replete with foreign travel and the word 'mission' is used.[1] Yet, many contemporary Buddhists are unhappy with the word because it might link Buddhism with such things as coercion, manipulation or proselytization. Even Ven. Piyadassi, in later life, was to say he did not like the word because of this.[2] The subtitle of his biography is 'the wandering monk' not 'the missionary monk'. Ringu Tulku shed light on the subject from the Tibetan perspective:

> To decide whether Buddhism is missionary would depend on what you mean by missionary. Buddhism was started by teaching. The

Buddha didn't have anything else except his teachings and he taught. But he only taught people who were interested. The important thing is that we're not allowed, as Buddhist monks, to teach anyone who is not interested. We do not go out and just teach. We have to be requested. This is an understood code of conduct. There's not such a great emphasis on converting people. But of course the more we can help by sharing something the better. So you can call that mission if you like.

Thom MacCarthy, also a Buddhist within the Tibetan tradition, shared a similar perspective when asked whether Samye Ling would consider itself missionary because of its work in Moscow and elsewhere:

Particularly in this tradition, Buddhism is non-evangelical. It's definitely grassroots. The Buddhists in Russia have come to Lama Yeshe and asked for his help and he has agreed to become the abbot of their centre and to give them support and guidance. There's a need there and he was invited.

Buddhist reactions to the words 'evangelical' and 'mission' owe much to the way that Christian mission has been experienced and perceived. Sri Lankan Buddhists, for instance, in response to the methods of the Christian missionaries in the British colonial period (1796–1948) tended to co-opt Christian terms and practices for their own use, as humiliation at the hands of the missionaries turned to vigorous revival. The term 'mission' was one of them. In the West, on the contrary, there has been a turning away from the word because of its imperialistic and coercive connotations.

Whether the word is used or not, most Buddhists would resist the idea that one of the priorities of Buddhism in contemporary society is to gain converts in the sense of winning people over from other religions or ideologies by carefully planned strategic action. This is simply not part of the challenge Buddhism poses to the modern world. In fact, quite a number of the Buddhists interviewed stressed that a person need not be a Buddhist to follow the Buddhist teaching. Lorna Devaraja, for instance, agreed that Buddhism was missionary but was adamant that this did not mean stealing people from other religions:

One of the first messages of the Buddha was go forth and spread this teaching, the message of the Noble Eightfold Path. It was not that you had to be a Buddhist. You had only to give up evil and follow the correct path. I think it is made clear that the Buddha was not trying to win converts from other religions to Buddhism. He was only trying to teach people how to live a good life. Buddhism doesn't condemn other religions. Buddhism is not exclusive. It doesn't say this is the only truth. The purpose of Buddhist mission is to proclaim the Noble Eightfold Path, which can be followed by anyone. It can be followed by a person who is not a Buddhist.

When Sulak Sivaraksa was asked about the possibility of interfaith co-operation, he also expressed the non-exclusivity of Buddhism:

> The word 'Buddhist' was never used by the Buddha. We need not use the word 'Buddhist'. Those of us who practise the Buddha's teachings don't have the only truth. Non-violent paths can be practised by anyone. Everyone has the Buddha nature. I can quote the Buddha, 'The truth is there, the *Dhamma* is there, whether the Buddha is born or not.' The Buddha is anyone who transforms himself or herself from a selfish being to a selfless being. That is how one awakes. Once one awakes, knowledge becomes understanding and understanding becomes love. And I see that in all the great religious traditions.

Kagyu Samye Ling Centre in Scotland hosts many activities beneficial to body, mind and spirit, yet Ani Rinchen Khandro was quite clear that whether a practice was specifically Buddhist was not the most important thing for the Director, Dr Akong Tulku Rinpoché, 'Dr Akong Tulku Rinpoché is not concerned with labels – "This is Buddhist; this isn't Buddhist. This is Christian; this isn't Christian." That doesn't concern him very much. The point is whether it helps, whether it helps people.'

Of course, many Buddhists are thrilled when they hear of more people being drawn to Buddhism. But most would insist that the challenge they want to present to society is not a challenge to individuals to convert from one religion to another. If Buddhism grows, they insist, it will be because people choose to seek it. The challenge, according to many of those interviewed, had much more to do with the values that govern human communities than with labels of religious identity. The rest of the chapter bears this out.

THE CHALLENGE TO TRADITIONALLY BUDDHIST SOCIETIES

THE REVITALIZATION OF CULTURE: CAMBODIA

In Cambodia, traditional Buddhist culture was completely ruptured between 1975 and 1979, as previous chapters have illustrated. The centuries-old bond between village and temple was severed. Temples were razed and monks killed. Young and old were affected – but differently. Ven. Yos Hut Khemacaro, thinking particularly of the effect on the young:

> Externally, the things we lost were the great teachers and Buddhist masters, our *Dhamma* books and our documents, as well as the physical buildings, the monasteries, the temples and the libraries. Internally, we lost all of our great traditions and religion. People were taught to hate one another rather than respect one another and we lost our ethics. A new ideology was forced upon the people telling them that their own traditions, customs and religion were bad. Before the war, people lived together. They co-operated and helped one another, respected and trusted one another. Not like now.

In chapter 4, Ven. Yos Hut explained the vicious cycle he knows this has promoted – violence leading to the endless repetition of violence by those previously the victims. To the young, he stressed, the old village structure can only be known through the words of parents and grandparents and present efforts to revitalize what remains.

Yet for some older Cambodians, who were already mature in the 1950s and 1960s and who are therefore able to see recent history through eyes steeped in Buddhism, the experience is different. The horrific violence has almost served to reinforce the Buddha's teachings. Mr Chheng Ponn:

> The war damaged the outside but could not disturb anything inside. The external destruction should be a factor to us Cambodians to reinforce our belief inside. For example, when you see suffering, you see impermanence. Then you do not attach yourself to the impermanent. It can make our faith stronger. It can make truth emerge.

In other words, for some, personal experience of suffering has made the First Noble Truth, that of *dukkha*, stand out with a starkness impossible within a comfortable lifestyle, resulting in a renewed interest in religion. Renee Pan:

> I see in the people a wish for education in the Buddha's teaching. Do you know why? Because the Buddha selected the Middle Way. He experienced both the life of mortification and the life of luxury. Almost all of the Cambodian people have been through mortification to understand what suffering really means. They have not only watched and read. They have felt it through all six senses.[3] My

grandmother, when she was eighty years old, went to the temple
and sat in front of a corpse for ten days to see what life looked like
in the face of death. She imagined the body swollen and the worms
coming out of it. But almost all Cambodians have gone through
that in experience. There has been no need to imagine it.

So, in the years following the downfall of Pol Pot, Cambodia has
held within it both those who have never known anything except a
cycle of violence and hatred leading to more violence and hatred,
and those who are able to remember another ethic and therefore
have been drawn ever deeper into Buddhism because of the horror
they have experienced.

In this context, how have concerned Buddhists sought to revitalize
society? The first act of rebuilding after the defeat of Pol Pot was
restoration of the temples. 'It is amazing', stated Liz Bernstein, 'that
after the Khmer Rouge, one of the first things to be rebuilt by the
people were the temples and schools, village by village. It showed the
importance of the faith to them.' It also showed how many people
remembered.

After the temples came teachers and books. Here, the reopening
of the Buddhist Institute has been vital. It originally began in 1921
as the Cambodian Library. In 1930, it became the Native Institute
of Theravāda Buddhist Studies. From its birth, it encouraged
Buddhism to flourish through its specialized library, research com-
missions, a monthly publication and the reprinting of Buddhist
texts. Forced to close in 1975, it was reopened only in 1992 under
the Ministry of Religious Affairs. Situated within the premises of
Wat Unnalom in the centre of Phnom Penh, it is now working dou-
ble-time to restore what was lost. Mr Om Khem is its Director. As
in other interviews, what had been lost had to be voiced:

> During the time of the Khmer Rouge many things were destroyed,
> many books, many documents, many precious manuscripts, some
> of which were only written on palm leaves. So we can't retrieve
> them because they were never printed and, in addition, many great
> masters, great educators and great teachers were lost.

In fact, in 1979, the famous library was empty of books. The classi-
fications and catalogues had been obliterated. With the help of the
Cambodian government and foreign non-governmental organizations such as the Sotoshu Relief Committee in Japan and the
Heinrich Böll Foundation in Germany, the work of reprinting
books is again underway:

One of the most important books that we are reprinting now is the *Dhammapada*, particularly for young monks and novices. It's the first book the young monks study. We are also printing Pāli grammar books, as well as the *Vinaya*. We have reprinted over thirty titles so far for Buddhist education. Another great work, which we never dreamed we would be able to complete, we have just finished – the reprinting the *Tipiṭaka*. One thousand copies of all of the volumes of the *Tipiṭaka* were just recently reprinted. We have distributed them first to important temples throughout the country where monks are studying and then to temples where there are schools nearby.

Wat Unnalom also houses many novice monks who have come from villages throughout Cambodia. They are being trained by monks from countries such as Sri Lanka.

Books, buildings and training are essential in Cambodia if Buddhist culture is to be revitalized, but alone they are not enough. There are too many people for whom they mean nothing. As Ven. Yos Hut Khemacaro stressed, there has been internal loss as well as external, especially among the young. All the Cambodians we spoke to were aware of the culture of violence and militarism that had seeped into Cambodian consciousness, and also of the gulf which had emerged between young and old, between those who could remember life without violence and those who could not, those who had experienced the traditional centrality of the Buddhist temple and those who had not.

Some twenty kilometres outside Phnom Penh in Takhmau, deep in Cambodia's countryside, is the Vipassanā Centre for Culture and Meditation run by Mr Chheng Ponn, actor in the performing arts and an ex-Minister of Culture. In the time of Pol Pot, he had been forced to work as the driver of a bullock cart. Among trees, flowering plants and pathways stand traditional works of art evoking Cambodia's mythological and religious heritage, particularly the Angkor period of Jayavarman VII, who converted to Buddhism.[4] There is the cobra, protector of the Buddha at his enlightenment, hood raised and elaborately carved, the *garuda*, mythical bird of giant size with human characteristics, credited in Pāli literature with magical and supernatural powers, and the lion. All the carvings could grace a Buddhist temple. The peace and tranquillity is broken only by the sound of insects and birds.

The aim of the Centre is to encourage the creative springs of Cambodian culture to flow again by developing the inner spirituality

and confidence from which identity flows. Mr Chheng Ponn voiced
what he saw as the heart of it all, 'I believe that culture and
Buddhism are essential energy, a life cement in order to glue the
political parties together. I hope for the future that the *Dhamma*
will help us to develop the country.'

Courses are held at the Centre for Buddhist monks and nuns, for
teachers, university students and young people. Encouraging a culture
of non-violence is the aim. Meditation, creative arts and the teaching
of Buddhism are the means. Meditation can equip young and old to
confront themselves rather than point the finger at others, Mr Ponn
insisted. Creating new forms of theatre, he suggested, can reawaken
old springs of wisdom, re-establishing a continuity which has contemporary relevance. In 1995 at least ten Buddhist stories were per-
formed. Teachers come to gain the energy to create textbooks capable
of challenging the culture of violence. Plans are afoot to provide more
courses for educators, but young people who have known nothing
but war are especially important and Mr Chheng Ponn has two aims:
'to equip them with identity and to equip them to know and control
their mind – to raise their moral level'.

The challenge for Cambodia is one of values. What values should
govern society? Those of non-harming and respect for life or those
of division, violence and revenge? It is an urgent question. Violence
has not ended. Since the interviews were recorded, there have been
further upsurges of terror. Renee Pan works with Mr Chheng Ponn.
She is convinced that the need in Cambodia goes to the very foundation of Buddhism:

> I think that the basic teaching that Cambodia needs to know is the
> Five Precepts: not to kill, not to steal, not to lie, not to commit
> adultery and not to drink alcohol or anything that clouds your
> mind. Everywhere I go, whenever I step inside classrooms, I ask
> children whether they know the Five Precepts and which one is the
> most difficult for them. Of course, little children only have three. I
> simplify them according to their age. We must do it naturally.
> Even now, I want the Ministry of Education to have the Five
> Precepts built into the curriculum.

This does not seem an impossible hope. Mr Om Khem:

> Here in the Buddhist Institute, we believe that all of the institu-
> tions in Cambodia must work together to rebuild the country. All
> departments of government, all sections of society must depend on
> Buddhism as the foundation of our society. And Buddhism has

much to offer in the development of Cambodia in the future. So we must listen to the teachings of the Buddha and realise what we must do now, what we must do tomorrow, and what we must do later in the future in order to protect our lives, our villages and our society.

There was urgency in Mr Om Khem's words. The defeat of the Pol Pot regime and the ongoing violence has made many within the older generation in Cambodia realize that complacency about religion has no place in the modern world if the religious base of culture is to survive. The roots of religion have to be nurtured and revitalized in the very teeth of violence. Towards the end of the interview Mr Chheng Ponn expressed a grim awareness of the obstacles:

The enemy of the Buddha is ignorance. We have many temples, monks and Buddhist people. They need to be trained but we are lacking documents, schools and good teachers to teach *Dhamma*. The temple exists. What we need is knowledge. I worry so much. The war may come back. If we have a war for one year, reconstruction will take ten. The speed of destruction is faster than the speed of rebuilding. Our duty is to create an identity for our people and to create peace for each one inside – the peace which comes from the heart and mind.

CHALLENGING CULTURE

Raising a challenge to the prevailing culture within any society and revitalizing culture are firmly linked with one another. The revitalization through Buddhism to which Mr Om Khem, Mr Chheng Ponn and Renee Pan are committed is a radical challenge to the culture of violence and self-seeking gripping some parts of Cambodia. Buddhism has also helped to make both Thailand and Sri Lanka what they are. War is tearing Sri Lanka apart but Buddhism as an institution is not threatened with destruction as it was in Cambodia in the 1970s. Thailand has suffered economic recession, allegations of corruption and influxes of refugees but Buddhism remains an influential force. For some Buddhists in both these countries, the question is not so much whether Buddhism will survive but what kind of Buddhism will survive in the face of a globalized economy and growing consumerism. Will it challenge or adapt to socio-economic change? Will it become part of the consumer society or a sign of contradiction within it?

Raja Dharmapala, the Director of the Dhammavedi Institute in Sri Lanka, left the monastic *Sangha* in his twenties because he felt that Buddhists, monks and laypeople, were moving away from their roots and failing to challenge contemporary social trends. Several decades later, he cannot see much change:

> I feel that the essence of Buddhism has been distorted, even in this traditional home of Buddhism. Worth is measured in terms of wealth and power and not in terms of virtue. There is a pervasive and perverse form of consumerism, a form of hedonism, that has begun to overtake us – a love for possessions. Mansions and limousines are the defining values. Buddhism is used and manipulated by those who have wealth and power. But really, Buddhism is a doctrine to liberate the oppressed and poor.

Dr Chatsumarn Kabilsingh voiced a similar worry about Thailand:

> We have a population of sixty million. Ninety-four per cent of the people are Buddhist. But the fact that the majority of people in this country are Buddhist doesn't help us become better Buddhists. We have taken it for granted. We have become negligent of the real teaching.
>
> One side-track is that we tend to commercialize Buddhism. We observe the precepts. We go to the temple. We make a donation. But when we make a donation of, say, a hundred baht, we make a wish that we will become very rich or very successful in our business or that we will have a very big house. We make a donation of a hundred baht and ask for so many things! Expecting something in return is not the Buddhist attitude. The Buddhist attitude is to let go. If you make a donation of a hundred baht it is to help this monk or nun to do good and at the same time you are freeing yourself from clinging to money. This is the side-track in our practice – we are too concerned about merit-making. We tend to do things with the expectation of something in return and expect that something to be far larger than what we actually give. It becomes businesslike!

Dr Karunaratne in the central hills of Sri Lanka stressed misuse of sexuality rather than love of possessions:

> Now, with the new consumerism we have here, I find that the young adults forget all principles or code of ethics. There is a lot of promiscuity. A lot of them are unemployed. They take to drugs, which is common all over the world. Then, there is an uninhibited

sex life resulting in an enormous number of unwanted pregnancies. The number of illegal abortions which are done in clinics is unbelievable. There are three clinics in the vicinity of Kandy and in these three clinics, four hundred abortions are done a day. I got medical students to do a survey. It is staggering. That is not good living. Buddhism does not preach that type of thing nor does any religion. All great religions of the world must do much more. They must teach morality. It is useless for all the priests and monks to be inside their temples asking people to come. I feel that they must go out to the world. They must carry the message of good living and morality to all peoples in the world, especially in Sri Lanka. I know the same problems exist in the West but we in Sri Lanka are now progressing downwards.

Voice upon voice could be taken from the interviews with the same message: Buddhism is in danger of succumbing to the pressures of a consumerist global economy and global moral laxity. One problem mentioned by several was that the ordained *Saṅgha* in traditionally Buddhist countries had not adapted to meet new needs. Pracha Hutanawatr of Thailand:

Buddhism has great potential in this society, though as an institution it is dying. Many monks use the language of a hundred years ago and no one really understands what the monks are teaching. The younger generation is fed up with Buddhism. It is taught in school as another subject with an exam which you have to pass. It doesn't make sense for many people. I was fed up with Buddhism when I was in high school because the teaching was so boring. It devalues Buddhism.

Chapter 4 demonstrated that there are some monks who do seek to use the language of the people and to help them materially as well as spiritually. But they are in a minority, according to some of those we interviewed. So how can the challenge be mounted? Ven. Somchai Kusalacitto believes one place to start is with the training:

I try very hard to make my students understand the role of the Buddhist monk in a changing society. The monks must understand that Thai society has changed a lot. We are not an agricultural society now. We are becoming a semi-agricultural and industrialized society. Nowadays, monks cannot stay in the temple and expect everyone to come to them to listen to the teaching of the Buddha. People are in too much of a hurry. They are stuck on the roads for many hours because of the traffic jams. They are overpowered by

the westernized style of living, following the American and
Japanese way of life. They like to have money, to consume good
things. They go to department stores rather than to the temple,
they live on estates where everything is provided – swimming pool,
supermarkets, schools, hospitals – but not a temple or *Dhamma*
hall or a meditation hall for the weekends.

This means the society has changed. Forty years ago, the Thai
people were very poor. They cultivated rice and other things for their
livelihood. Even when poor, they thought of the temple. If they lived
in a hut of poor materials they would still think of the monks and
build a small hut for them also. I often emphasize that the monks
have to apply the teaching of the Buddha in a modern way. We have
to change the language and the style of teaching so that we can communicate with the people, not to sit in a very high seat or speak in a
slow, 'religious' tone with one-way communication. If we keep to the
old ways, we will not communicate with the people.

For Ven. Dr Somchai the change must also include the monks becoming more politically and socially aware so that they are able to help
people think through contemporary issues impacting on their lives.
But can Buddhism offer models to traditionally Buddhist societies so
that the race to consume and compete in an individualistic market
economy is questioned? Sulak Sivaraksa believes they can:

We must go back to the roots. The basic teaching is *dāna* [giving] –
to be generous. Buddhists must begin with this. Ultimately, we
must develop the idea of giving as more important than taking.
Consumerism wants people to take rather than to give. If we stress
giving in the modern world, we can really challenge consumerism.

But Sivaraksa was quick to add that this could not be done without
personal transformation, 'The Greens have a wonderful agenda, the
socialists also but they don't have anything to help personal transformation. This is where Buddhism can help.' A similar sentiment was
voiced by Aloysius Pieris SJ in Sri Lanka. A Christian influenced by
Marxism, who uses Buddhist insights in his meditation, he sees the
drawbacks of activism without transformation of self:

Very often we have class analysis without self analysis. We don't
introduce the idea of hidden motives, hidden agendas in our
actions. Even social work very often is an activity which we enter
into without reflection. We don't ask, 'Why am I interested in this
type of work? Am I seeking my own self-aggrandisement in this?
Are the poor just material for my self-aggrandisement?' This kind

of question constantly is necessary to find out whether our motives are pure. When you enlarge this hidden agenda to an entire movement then you find big organizations in the world which are actually entrenching people in more difficulties. I don't want to mention names. The root is wrong motivation and this is underestimated sometimes in analysis. Self-analysis has to come with class analysis.

Wongsanit Ashram embodies the ideal of *dāna* and encourages personal transformation. It does not take from nature any more than is necessary. The buildings are simple and so is the food. The members are committed to a society which does not exploit others or generate a ceaseless hunger for consumption. As the beginning of chapter 3 suggested, there can hardly be a greater contrast than between the traffic inching its way along jammed roads between high-rise buildings and construction sites in Bangkok's polluted air and the birdsong amid expanses of green at Wongsanit. Simply by existing, it offers an alternative, a sign of contradiction and it is an appealing alternative.

Wongsanit also affirms community, an ideal at the very heart of Buddhism from the beginning, as Aloysius Pieris stressed in chapter 1. He continued:

> Buddhism spread over Asia and on principle never destroyed the existing structures but absorbed them. It was the first missionary religion to give us an idea of what inculturation means. The existing community forms were absorbed into the Buddhist ethos and were influenced by the Buddhist spirit of the Five Precepts and community life. So today we can speak of the Buddhist community ethos in Asian countries. Now, this is being destroyed by technocracy, free-for-all economics and individualism. We are at the threshold of a big crisis in religion and community. This is what requires of Buddhism and other religions a greater effort to organize themselves into basic human communities to fight against this trend and recapture the concept of community.

Aloysius Pieris works closely with interfaith communities in Sri Lanka that bring together Buddhists, Hindus and Christians:

> There is a need for religion to get together, not theoretically, but in communities which are involved in fighting these waves of greedy living which are fostered as a way of life. This goes against the grain of every religion, especially Buddhism. This is not a moment to fight but to get together and really form a community force against this current. This is what some groups are trying to do in

this country. I also insist on one human achievement which is being pushed into the background in our technocracy and that is art, humanities. I am personally encouraging art, culture and music among people because that is one way in which we can bring back the greedless dimension. Aesthetics gives a sense of the transcendent.

Stressing the need for giving rather than consuming, encouraging strategies for personal transformation among social activists and forming communities as symbols of an alternative value system is one Buddhist response to the crisis of values in society. Another is to challenge from a Buddhist perspective the principles through which governance itself is carried out. Some socially engaged Buddhists believe that Buddhism can be aligned with a particular political ideology. One Thai teacher who influenced at least two of those interviewed, Pracha Hutanawatr and Ven. Santikaro, was Ven. Buddhadāsa, famous during his lifetime for his outspoken views about social issues.[5] This is how Pracha described one conversation with him:

> Ven. Buddhadāsa said to me, 'Pracha, if you want to categorize Buddhism into one of these two camps, socialism and capitalism, Buddhism cannot belong to the capitalist camp. It definitely must belong to socialism but not the Soviet model.' 'In what sense?' I asked. He said, 'In capitalism, people are motivated to work for self-interest, but Buddhism is against self. Buddhism is something which helps people get rid of the self, to make people less selfish, to develop compassion.'

Not all Buddhists would agree with Ven. Buddhadāsa, yet most Theravāda Buddhists would agree that the Buddhist texts do comment on politics. Certainly, they comment on the role of the state in providing economic justice. Chapter 4 stressed this. Mithra Wettimuny in Sri Lanka, however, went further in suggesting that built into the Pāli Buddhist texts was a blueprint for government, which stretched back to the advice given to rulers by the Buddha. Chapter 1 stressed that the Buddha was a spiritual advisor to kings and rulers. The *Mahāparinibbāna Sutta* (*Dīgha Nikāya*, ii, 72ff.), for instance, shows him suggesting political principles for the Vajjians (a republic) to follow if they were to avoid defeat at the hands of the king of Magadha. Using this and other texts, Mithra Wettimuny actually drafted a proposal for a constitution in Sri Lanka based on ten royal qualities:

The Buddha did explain how to run a country. Buddhism has a political vision based on the ten royal qualities. These are qualities embedded in the Noble Eightfold Path and they are significant for leadership, management and administration. They are: gifting; sacrifice; virtue; austerity; softness, which means to acquire a calm tranquil state of mind; uprightness, that is to safeguard the truth; non-harm or non-ill-will, which means the development of kindness; compassion, patience and forbearance; and the tenth is the avoidance of conflict. This is very important when it comes to ruling a country because conflict is the norm of the day. It is a difficult quality to develop. What it means is that you don't go into unnecessary argument and debate. You certainly discuss but you don't argue for the purpose of arguing. This also ensures the highest form of democracy. A person who practises this quality permits freedom of expression, never uses power to suppress, loves that freedom and encourages it to bring about ideas, opinions or alternative viewpoints. Of course, ultimately, a leader must make his or her decision based on what that person perceives as the truth. Unfortunately, in many governments today governments seem to sit down in order to engage in conflict. And one of the necessary qualities in order to ensure the well-being of society as laid down by the Buddha is that the rulers must gather in harmony, conduct affairs in harmony and disperse in harmony.

Just as the principle of *dāna*, generosity or giving, can challenge most traditionally Buddhist societies today, so do these ten qualities. Few countries with a democratic polity can say that its different political parties place harmony and the good of the country above gaining power. Few governments truly agree that sacrifice and austerity might be necessary and place this above vote-catching. Only if such principles are practised, Mithra Wettimuny believes, will people with integrity and wisdom enter politics. Only if such people enter politics will wholesome principles enter government.

THE CHALLENGE TO TRADITIONALLY NON-BUDDHIST SOCIETIES

EAST-WEST INTERACTION

The challenge of values such as *dāna* and the ten royal qualities is relevant not only to traditionally Buddhist countries: it is a challenge for the world. For at least a hundred years, Buddhism has been challenging countries far beyond Asia. In each non-Asian country, the story is different. For Europe, the first meaningful contact came through colonial power, and which form of Buddhism gained most exposure was dependent on which parts of the world particular countries held power over. For Britain, it was Sri Lanka and Burma, Theravāda countries; for France, it was Cambodia and Vietnam, containing both Theravāda and Mahāyāna forms. For America, there was also contact with Theravāda countries but proximity to Japan meant that Zen Buddhism became influential before it became well known in Europe.

The first Western converts to Buddhism came at the end of the nineteenth century. Some were brought to Buddhism through theosophy, spiritualism or the esoteric religious movements which flourished in the nineteenth century in reaction to the hegemony of Christianity. Others were attracted to it because of its apparent compatibility with science. The first British person to become a Buddhist monk was Gordon Douglas in 1899, in Sri Lanka. The second was Allan Bennett, in 1901. He became Ven. Ananda Metteyya and eventually led the first Buddhist mission to the West in 1908.

Much has happened since Ven. Ananda Metteyya's mission. To take Britain as an example, the Buddhist Society was the main Buddhist organization in the early decades of the twentieth century. Its principal links were with Theravāda countries and its members numbered converts, academics, theosophists and the simply curious. Now, it is one among numerous bodies. Its handbook now mentions well over three hundred. These groups cover the whole spectrum of Buddhism – Theravāda, Mahāyāna, Vajrayāna, Zen, Pure Land, groups inspired by Nichiren, and Western organisations that have carved out their own identity. Some centres specifically cater for Thai, Sri Lankan, Vietnamese, Japanese, Chinese and Cambodian groups resident in Britain, but the vast majority have grown up because of Western interest. No Asian country received Buddhism in such a variety of forms. The situation in Britain, and indeed other parts of the West, is new within the Buddhist world.

All of this has brought a new dynamic into world Buddhism. The nature of Buddhism in the West is now attracting the minds of academics and practitioners. All that can be given here are some pointers to what is drawing Westerners to Buddhism and what consequences this has both for the traditionally Buddhist East and for the West. First of all, what brings Westerners to Buddhism? Are they searching for a new set of values? Do they want to challenge society or opt out of it? Are they seeking self-fulfilment only or do they want to create a better world? Dr Helen Waterhouse has done much research on Buddhism in Britain:

The attraction of Buddhism is very diverse and that is partly because the types of Buddhism that we have in Britain are extremely diverse. This is a historically unique situation. When Buddhism has spread throughout the world, it has normally gone in one or two forms. But, in Britain, within a few decades, Buddhism arrived from all over the world, so that there are now very many different types of Buddhism which people encounter.

Some people have found Buddhism after making what they call a spiritual search. They were looking for a spiritual path which they felt they could follow. But a lot of people whom I've interviewed came across Buddhism accidentally. They perhaps saw an advertisement for a meeting and went along and enjoyed it. They might not have been very religious in their own view. They might not have been looking for a religion to follow. But they liked what they heard.

Different aspects of Buddhism appeal to different people, which is exactly what one might expect. Many people say that, when they encountered Buddhism and learnt about its doctrines, what they actually found tied in very well with what they believed anyway. So a lot of people who had been brought up in this country with the idea that one is born, lives and dies found that they actually believed, at some level of their consciousness, that we are all reincarnated. People very often say that they found that very appealing about Buddhism, while, on the other hand, there are people who find that particularly difficult and for them the appeal may have been the humanitarian aspects of Buddhism. They liked the fact that Buddhism provides a way of becoming a whole person.

This tallies quite well with the personal testimonies of those we interviewed. There was tremendous variety. First, there were a number who discovered that Buddhism was what they had been already practising in their spiritual lives:

> I don't think I ever wasn't a Buddhist. Being a Buddhist is being someone who is aware of what is happening around you and anyone who is a real Buddhist is that. I was brought up in a Christian family. And I didn't 'encounter' Buddhism. What I did do was spontaneously begin to practise meditation. Later I discovered that the form of meditation I was practising was a Buddhist form and that it had a name. What I was doing was exactly what is taught in *vipassanā* meditation but I was never taught it. This is what I mean by 'I think I was always a Buddhist.' I found out when I went to the Buddhapadipa Temple in London because I wanted to find out about Buddhist meditation, not realizing that I was

already doing it. They described a method that I recognized immediately. (Helen Jandamit)

My pilgrimage into Buddhism began in Malaysia. I was training
teachers at the university there and I spontaneously began to go
into meditation without seeking to meditate. I did not know what
it was. I was not seeking any religion. I was very happy to be an
existentialist and had rejected all religions. But the meditation
arrived. It just came and then I had to seek out what it was.
Because I was in Malaysia, it was accepted there because of the
multitude of peoples. I had a feeling that this was somehow Hindu
but the more I progressed the less sure I was. It carried on for
about two years while I was trying to find out what was happening. I then came across one of the Buddha's *suttas* and in it was the
exact wording of what I was receiving in meditation. Then, I knew
it was Buddhism. (Nyanasiri)

'Karmic synchronicity' is how Nyanasiri would now describe it. In
America, she had been busy with a family, children, a farm, editing
three magazines, being a judge for some scholarships, amateur the-
atricals, pottery, sailing. Having time in Malaysia gave her space for
something new to happen, she believes. 'But I do believe it was
kamma vipāka [the fruit of previous action]. Obviously there had
been meditation previously,' she added.

For some we interviewed, it was an experience of *dukkha* or of
deep disillusionment concerning the values they saw in society that
drew them to Buddhism:

My own suffering brought me to Buddhism and trying to overcome and work with it. I was a veteran of Vietnam and recovery
from that situation, post-traumatic stress and all that, led me to
find a solution. In Akong Rinpoché, the founder of Samye Ling, I
found a mentor, a friend and a good guide who helped me in my
spiritual path. The more I know, the more I know that I don't
know. I've been here at Samye Ling for nine years and I'm feeling
good about what I'm doing with my life. (Thom McCarthy)

I became a monk in 1985 in a new temple in one of the then northern
suburbs of Bangkok with the intention of living in a forest
monastery in the south. I came to Thailand because, after
graduating from college in the US, I didn't know what I was going
to do with my life. I was interested in being a writer but didn't
think I could make any money, so as a desperate last-minute
measure I joined the US Peace Corps – to see the world, gain

some experience, maybe find something interesting to write about. Out of choices interesting to me, I chose Thailand partly because it was a different religious context. I'd been interested in religion in college and was frustrated by the rhetoric of religious people and how little religion was lived. I was curious to see if it was any different over here.

I came to Thailand as a Christian but then I slowly came into contact with Buddhist meditation, Buddhist teachings, especially those of the monk who eventually became my teacher, Buddhadāsa Bhikkhu. But there were also other teachers such as Ajahn Chah. Meditation and some of the teachings helped me deal with some of the difficulties I was experiencing in the Peace Corps – government corruption, loneliness, having a hot Western temper in a culture where that's totally unacceptable.

I figured that after my Peace Corps time, before going back to graduate school, I would become ordained for a while, because Thailand has a tradition of temporary monkhood. So I did it as a personal retreat to develop my meditation practice and learn more about the *Dhamma* before going back. But in the trial period I started to appreciate what this way of life offered. So I stayed on and later I developed a very good relationship with my teacher, which became very important to me. So I'm still a monk. The thing which really affected me in my later Peace Corps work was the corruption. I was a school teacher but also working in the villages. I was aware of selfishness – the selfishness of government workers who took a salary and perks but did very little of service to society and also the factionalism in the villages, which got in the way of people getting together and solving their problems. I also noticed that I was selfish in pushing my ideas. It had to be my way. The selfishness I saw everywhere became a major theme for me. And I have discovered in Buddhism practical ways to cope with this. (Ven. Santikaro)

People are attracted to the Buddhism in the West because of what we call *dukkha*, unsatisfactoriness. In Western life, much emphasis is placed on the material. There's been a breakdown of values. God for a lot of people is out of the window. The new God is money. But actually money doesn't really satisfy. Either you get it and it doesn't give you satisfaction or you can't get it and you get frustrated. People come along and they are disillusioned. They feel that there is no depth of meaning to their life. They are looking for a deeper meaning that goes beyond material values and they've turned away from the Church. (Dhammacarini Sanghadevi)

Others came to Buddhism after a search for meaning and fortuitous encounter:

> Until I was eighteen I was an anarchist. I was only interested in politics and changing the world and all kinds of things like that. I was living in France. Then some friends of mine were interested in meditation and Buddhism. By accident I read a book which changed my life. In the book it said, 'Before you think of changing the world, you should change yourself.' I thought this was a good idea. So I dropped politics and got interested in meditation. This led me to Asia. I wanted to practise meditation because I thought it would transform my mind and my emotions. I ended up in Korea because of an accident over a plane ticket in Bangkok. I was going to stay there one month but I stayed ten years and became a Buddhist nun. (Martine Batchelor)

> I had been fascinated by monasticism since I was a child. I left Judaism when I was about fifteen years old. I became an agnostic at the same time as I seriously began to examine monasticism. I looked at it primarily in terms of Catholicism for a long time and was involved with some wonderful Benedictine nuns in the early 1970s. Then, as the Church shifted out of renewal into reaction, I found it harder and harder to reconcile the wonderful quality of monasticism with the demands of the Church. I came from a troubled family background and had lots of psychotherapy. I got to the point when I was becoming used to my life getting better every year. Every year, in psychotherapy I could feel strength, warmth and new depth coming into my life. When I was finished with therapy, I needed, wanted ways to continue that process. Many people I knew had shifted from the healing processes of therapy into spiritual training. So, after a few years, because of a wonderful friend of mine who had been a Zen monk under Suzuki Roshi in 1969,[7] I began to sit Zen and it was fabulous. (Beth Goldering)

Beth Goldering became a Buddhist in 1986 and was ordained as a Zen priest in 1995. She later added:

> The religious traditions in which we grew up were not addressing the realities of spiritual struggle in our lives. So we wanted to find ways of doing that. At least in Mahāyāna Buddhism, the lack of dogma – the insistence in Zen that insight is a product of experience – these were the things that made it very easy for me. I wasn't expected to believe anything. I was expected to put myself in a situation where certain things would or wouldn't happen.

Yet others were drawn intuitively by a particular teacher or image:

> Initially I came to Samye Ling three years ago to teach a Tai Chi weekend. I wasn't looking to become a Buddhist. Then I met Rinpoché. Before I left on that first weekend, I thought I must meet the person behind it all. To meet the host was simply a matter of courtesy. I didn't know who he was or anything about him. Just as well, for I had no reason to feel in awe. I booked an appointment. It was in a very little room. I realized I'd previously seen him in the garden and that we'd been eating lunch quite close to one another. He had been with his wife and family and I'd thought what a charming family they were. So, when I came into the room to meet him my opening words were, 'Oh, it's you!' And he burst out laughing and I burst out laughing and I just felt an immediate connection with him. When I got to know him a little bit better, I realized what an incredible person he was. On one hand he seems very ordinary and very practical and he doesn't blow his own trumpet. But, on the other hand, there's no mistaking his quiet power. It's a bit like the sea. When it's calm it still has the potential for power and depth. And I just felt this radiating from him. I'd never come into contact with this before, although I'd travelled pretty widely. He was the hook which brought me here. The person exemplified the message. He was the living message. (Ani Rinchen Khandro)

> My being at Samye Ling is to do with the teachers in Kathmandu when I was travelling. I'd been given a photograph of a young boy. I knew he was a Tibetan lama. I came to Samye Ling because I wanted to go to Tibet and find him. As it turned out he was the head of this particular lineage of Tibetan Buddhism, the Kagyu Lineage – His Holiness the seventeenth Karmapa. I had no idea at the time. I came to Samye Ling for four days. I was ordained and have been here for two and a half years now. I'm finally going to Tibet next month. (Ani Tsewang Chödron)

The non-dogmatic nature of Buddhism, its rationality, the possibility of a spiritual guide, the opportunity for working on oneself, changing oneself – all these appeal. The personal testimonies that emerged in the interviews were diverse but a surprising number of them speak of some kind of 'recognition' going beyond rational choice: the spontaneous arising of a certain form of meditation; an immediate bond between pupil and teacher; knowledge that 'this is right' after an accidental encounter. The nature of Western society must not be left out of the equation either. For many, the appeal of Buddhism is heightened because there is a void where religion might once have

been, and disillusionment with the search for happiness through material possessions. As Ven. Santikaro noticed on a return to America:

> The United States is a country that is hurting. I met so many people
> with money, cars and material possessions but they're tense. They
> had loads of fears and no security. They felt alienated. They're not
> connected with family. Even if they've got a good family, they have
> to work so hard to keep it together.

THE WEST THROUGH EASTERN EYES

It is interesting to look at how Eastern Buddhists see this. Sri
Lankan Buddhists often assume that what Westerners like in
Buddhism is its rationality, the fact that it does not look to a God or
a supernatural reality. Yet what Dr Asanga Tilakaratne found when
he was doing a research degree in Hawaii was different:

> In my experience I've seen several different reasons why people in
> the West like Buddhism. One very interesting thing is that we in Sri
> Lanka sometimes have the view that Westerners are rational and
> therefore that they like Buddhism because of its rational character.
> Yet I've seen the opposite. Buddhism is attracting some Westerners
> because of its rites and rituals. Tibetan Buddhism has attracted a lot
> of attention and one reason is that Tibetan Buddhism has extreme-
> ly complicated and interesting rituals. In Hawaii and on mainland
> America some Japanese sects are also very popular simply because
> they seem to provide simplistic solutions to problems, for instance,
> chanting a mantra to get whatever you want. Of course there are
> also those who are attracted to Buddhism because of its rationalis-
> tic and naturalistic nature. These are mostly people who have got
> disenchanted with monotheistic religious tradition. When they find
> that Buddhism does not accept God, does not accept creation and
> also explains things through causality – paṭiccasamuppāda – they
> are attracted. However, I would add that most of these are intellec-
> tually attracted to Buddhism. They are not necessarily opting to
> follow the teaching. They are simply attracted by its simplicity and
> modernity.
>
> Yet there is a fourth group which is highly active today and that
> is those who are practising meditation. There are so many small
> groups doing this. This is a very significant development when
> looked at from a Buddhist perspective. For that is where you can
> find people who are seriously following the Buddhist path as
> described by the Buddha, fully believing it can have consequences
> for their lives.

Dr Akong Tulku Rinpoché simply said, 'What Western people need is peace of mind. It seems to me, that is what is needed. Buddhism is perhaps the best religion to offer that.' Ven. Gnanapala in Sri Lanka gave a similar analysis:

> Westerners realize that they cannot get peace and happiness from material development itself. So they are in search of peace of mind and some sort of permanent bliss. Buddhism can bring peace of mind, the way to live a virtuous life and also a balance between materialism and spiritual growth. One-sided development can never bring peace of mind.

AUTHENTICATION AND MEMORY

Whatever the reason that new converts in a traditionally non-Buddhist country are drawn to Buddhism, the transposition of a religion into a new environment throws up issues which traditional Buddhist societies rarely have to face. For instance, there are the questions of authentication and memory. Should Western Buddhists look to the Buddhist East alone and seek to duplicate traditional Asian practices or should they aim to create something that is more in keeping with contemporary Western culture? Should there be a conscious effort to retain the 'memory' of the tradition as it stretches back into Asian history? This touches the important question of religious change and what has been termed 'inculturation'. What is certain is that when a religion moves from one culture to another it is almost impossible for it to remain static. Martine Batchelor:

> The Buddha's truth has evolved. Sometimes Buddhists assume that the Buddha said this and it has been the same ever after. But if you look, all throughout the centuries, things have moved, have changed. There is a relative context and an absolute context.

EXPERIENCING THE ROOTS

Some Western Buddhists have made Asia their home to bring greater authenticity to their practice. Nothing less than touching the roots of the tradition through immersion in Buddhist culture is enough. They feel more at home in Asia than in the West. Buddhism in the West, for some, seems inadequately grounded in tradition and cultural memory. Several such people have featured in these pages: Ven. Santikaro, Ven. Bhikkhu Bodhi, Nyanasiri, Helen Jandamit, Beth Goldering. Ingeborg and Gotz Nitsche have not been mentioned yet. Unsatisfied both with how Buddhism was prac-tised in the West and with the attitudes of German society, they

moved to Sri Lanka after full professional lives in Germany and a
particularly painful brush with the *dukkha* of existence. Gotz simply said, 'The attraction of Buddhism for Europeans is a certain idea
of freedom and peacefulness. We wanted to come closer to people
who practise this. That's why we came to Sri Lanka.' When asked
whether Sri Lanka had given what they sought, Ingeborg added:

> The first thing that really relieved me was the different approach.
> When we were in Germany we had the impression that everybody
> thought one who is meditating is mad. We didn't feel very happy
> in New Age circles because there not everything that shines is gold.
> I thought that going to Sri Lanka would be going to the roots of
> what I am seeking. I found that everybody was interested in medi-
> tation. Everybody was interested in the inner life, a meditative
> spiritual life. It is very easy to live here and do what you really
> want to do without any disturbance. Everyone helps you. That
> was my feeling in the beginning and it is still my feeling. You find
> experienced friends whom you can trust not to lead you to a point
> that is not stable. Here, we started the hard work of meditation
> and study for ourselves. We learnt Pāli for two years with
> Professor Lily de Silva. We visited the monks and nuns.

Ingeborg and Gotz's concern in Europe was the lack of Buddhist
teachers and friends of the calibre needed if both of them were to
progress along the spiritual path and not be diverted. To live in a
Buddhist context has been a tremendous source of strength to them.
With quiet humility and determination, they learn, practise and
contribute.

REMAINING IN THE WEST

Among Buddhists who stay in the West there is much diversity, both
in attitude to authority and Buddhist tradition. Broadly speaking,
three trends can be seen. First, there are those groups that attempt to
remain closely within an Asian tradition of practice, who through
their teachers and structure remain patterned on a certain country,
school or practice. Second, there are those that seek consciously to
adapt Buddhism to Western needs by distinguishing between core
beliefs and practices and what are seen to be peripheral or specific
to one particular culture. Third, there are Buddhist centres that
draw people from a variety of schools and traditions into what
might be called a Buddhist ecumenism. Within each of the three,
adaptation is necessary. It is a question of degree rather than the
presence or absence of change.

One very pertinent issue for Western Buddhism, which throws these differences in approach into relief, is the question of whether a monastic *Saṅgha* is appropriate. Helen Waterhouse:

> For some groups in the West the ordained monastic *Saṅgha* has remained extremely important. For some of the Theravāda groups, the ordained monastic *Saṅgha* is central to the kind of operation they run and they stick as rigidly as they can to the rules the Buddha laid down. But other groups don't find that to have ordained monks and sometimes nuns is particularly helpful in this culture. The Western Buddhist Order, for instance, has moved away from the traditional understanding of *Saṅgha*. Although they have a form of ordination, it does not follow the same pattern as we would see where Buddhism is practised traditionally. Some of the Tibetan groups retain the ordained *Saṅgha* but very often their monks and nuns don't take a full ordination. They take a novice ordination because, within this country, it is very difficult for people to follow all the rules that the Buddha laid down. The rules that were made were often very specific to the culture, and even to the climate in which the monks and nuns were living in Asia.

REMAINING CLOSE TO ASIA

The monasteries of The English Saṅgha Trust are one example of Buddhist communities that remain in Europe and yet are strongly attached to a particular Asian tradition, drinking deeply from its discipline and practice.[8] Few Asians in orange robes can be seen there. Most of the shaved heads are white, yet the Western monks and nuns at these centres remain closely in touch with the Thai Forest Tradition from which they grew. The rules of monastic discipline are strictly observed and a rigorous programme of meditation is followed. Adaptation, however, is present. The English Saṅgha Trust is more than a transposition of Thailand to Britain. To take a small example, verses that in Asia would be chanted in Pāli are sometimes chanted in their English translation.

Another place where Asian cultural traditions are maintained is Kagyu Samye Ling Centre, about which much has already been said. Wind chimes play in the breeze. Tibetan instruments are used in the temple and a schedule of traditional *pūjas*, acts of reverence and devotion, are held throughout each day, in the Tibetan language. Those who have become monks and nuns wear maroon robes. Some are learning the Tibetan language and even Tibetan medicine. One of the aims of Samye Ling is the preservation of Tibetan Buddhist culture, now threatened in its homeland. The Director and the Abbot

of the Centre are Tibetan and visiting Tibetan teachers such as Ringu
Tulku are frequently present.

Once again, however, the Centre is more than a transposition of
Tibet to England. Adaptation has been essential. The Westerners
who come have needs very different from those in a traditional
Tibetan society, and one of the social functions of Samye Ling is to
offer a helpline. Ani Rinchen Khandro:

> There's quite a broad spectrum of people who come here, from all
> walks of life. There are probably between 100 and 150 residents.
> Fifty of these would be ordained monks and nuns, half of them
> only ordained in the last year. Some of them might have come
> from difficult backgrounds. They might have had family problems
> or drug problems. In a way, one of the purposes of Samye Ling is
> to act as a social worker for people. I think it's very useful in help-
> ing people break bad habits or destructive patterns they might
> have built up in their lives, to dissolve these and replace them with
> a more positive way of being. That's a very practical way Samye
> Ling works in the society. As for the spiritual aspect, it is left to the
> individual. You learn as much as you want to learn. Nobody
> shoves it down your throat. If you have an inquiring mind and
> want to know more then you'll be given more. If you don't, then
> you won't.

It has already been stressed that Samye Ling allows Westerners to
become novice monks or nuns for just one year to test their commitment. Ani Tsewang Chödron:

> Samye Ling may be different from other *Dharma* centres and
> monasteries in that people can go to see Lama Yeshe, the Abbot of
> Samye Ling, and ask if they can be ordained. Usually, it's for a
> year. There's an option here of doing a trial year, which I think is
> very unusual. It has made accessible the experience of this kind of
> disciplined life to a lot of people who couldn't possible have con-
> templated taking life commitments. Having said that, I took a
> year's commitment and said quietly to myself that I would only do
> three months. I finished the year and then realized I wanted to do
> more. You have the option of another year but in my case I took
> life vows. So it's very flexible. Samye Ling is probably, in that
> sense, a good reflection of the basic thrust of Buddhism, which is
> to be realistic. So, if in dealing with Westerners the realistic thing
> to do is give them an opportunity to try out a kind of discipline
> which is quite alien to our culture, then that's what is done.

Ani Rinchen Khandro backed this up, 'Tibetan Buddhism is not an idea indigenous to our culture, so how could you possibly sign up for life to something you have no knowledge of?'

Mikmar Dorje is one person who would never have taken robes if he had had to make a long commitment. He has now been in the robes of a monk for three years but began with one. When asked what motivated him, he replied:

> Desperation, in some ways. Really not knowing what else to do. There was nowhere else to go in my life. I just felt like I'd been brought here. I had a friend who was coming up here and he was becoming a monk as well. So it just seemed like I'd been led here and that was what I was supposed to be doing. So, I spoke to the Lama and he thought it was a good idea as well. It was a good way of giving up a lot of things that weren't doing me any favours. I could see that it would have finished me off in the end if I'd carried on in the way I was going.
>
> I gave up drinking and smoking. I can't begin to explain what a difference that makes after smoking and drinking most of my life. As for other changes, there are so many. You don't really notice it happening at the time. It's completely changed my life, basically.

Dr Akong Tulku Rinpoché and Lama Yeshe are willing to give Tibetan Buddhism a face which takes Western needs into account, whilst yet making sure that the Tibetan heritage is not lost. Teachers of practices not traditionally connected with Tibetan Buddhism such as yoga and Tai Chi are allowed to lead weekends. The emphasis is on what helps, as Ani Rinchen Khandro has already stressed. Dr Akong Tulku Rinpoché has also developed a form of psychotherapy that includes writing, massage, relaxation and meditation and, through a four-year course, he trains therapists who work all over the world. Yet, all this is done without compromising religious and cultural practices the Tibetan leaders would see as central, particularly those surrounding *pūja* and meditation. They do not compromise on the robes worn or the discipline of a Buddhist way of life. They seek to keep alive Tibetan culture. Between thirty and forty students are learning Tibetan medicine at the Tara Rokpa Medical College started by Dr Akong Tulku Rinpoché. Eminent Tibetan scholars come as lecturers and all students will go to Tibet to learn about the herbs there.

Samye Ling is a dynamic centre that radiates out into society in many ways, challenging the kind of drink and drugs culture that was dragging Mikmar Dorje down, attracting a great variety of people. There is a remarkable diversity among those connected with Samye Ling, although all are united through Tibetan forms of devotion, meditation and a common teaching of the *Dharma*. Ani Tsewang Chödron provided a glimpse into this:

> I've never seen such a varied mix of people from different backgrounds and, within the same background, with completely different states of mind. There was an ordination recently and the number of different types of people was quite extraordinary. There would have been no way I would have had anything else in common with some of them if not for the fact that we're monks and nuns: someone very academically trained, somebody who had just come out of prison, someone who used to love partying – the whole young drug scene; somebody who has been a mother; somebody who's just about to retire. Almost every type of person you could think of, they're here and they live with each other in relative harmony.

Just as Wongsanit Ashram is a sign of contradiction in Thailand, so is Samye Ling. By its very success, it throws a question mark over the values that govern Western consumerist society.

ADAPTING TO THE WEST

The Friends of the Western Buddhist Order (FWBO) has already been introduced in the context of social action. It is one of the groups that has consciously attempted to make the practice of Buddhism relevant to the West through adaptation. About a year after Sangharakshita founded the FWBO in 1967, he ordained a group of men and women to begin the Order itself and since then it has grown steadily. However, from the beginning, it was very different from the monastic orders of Asia. Its members accept a rule of discipline but are not ordained in the traditional sense. Dharmacarini Sanghadevi:

> In Buddhist countries such as Thailand and Sri Lanka, when children are born into a family, they grow up as a Buddhist, thinking themselves a Buddhist. Those who become Buddhist in the West have consciously to embrace Buddhism and they can't rely on the support of the whole society for their Buddhist practice. In the Buddhist East, the monks, the full-time Buddhists, are supported by the laypeople. We haven't got that sort of context in a Western society and we don't ever expect that context. So we're looking at different models for practising Buddhism in the West, not relying on the wider society to financially support our Buddhist practice.

The model developed by the Order therefore rejects some of the signs by which Buddhism is recognizable in Asian countries. Dhammacarini Sanghadevi:

We are still developing. Twenty-seven years is not very long in the history of the development of Buddhism in a new country. The first thing is that our order is open to anyone regardless of their lifestyle. That means that a family person can make a spiritual commitment and that a single person who wishes to lead a celibate lifestyle can make a commitment. It could also be that a single person subsequent to ordination becomes involved in a family context. So we embrace what in the East would be both the lay spectrum and the monastic spectrum in one order. The important thing is to put the spiritual values embodied in the Buddha, the *Dhamma* and the *Sangha* into the centre of your life and then your lifestyle comes out of that as an expression of your commitment.

The Order therefore does not have anyone in robes supported by other Buddhists. Although there are 'friends' of the Order and Order members, the friends do not support the members financially. There are also few outward signs to mark members. Entry to the Order, however, demands training. Dhammacarini Sanghadevi:

By the time anyone enters our Order they will have been practising within our tradition for anything from three to fifteen or even twenty years. Within that, they will have done several years of meditation practice. They will have done a three-year study course which will have taken them through study texts in the different Buddhist traditions so that they get an overview of the whole Buddhist tradition as it exists already. Then, within that, they study texts that Sangharakshita has written himself. They will also have built up meaningful friendships with some people in the Order so that, when they join, they have a spiritual relationship with those other members. They feel part of a spiritual community.

As for the practice of Buddhism, the Order draws on the whole Buddhist tradition. Dhammacarini Sanghadevi:

We see Mahāyāna as an expansion and development of what already existed within the Theravāda tradition. Mahāyāna Buddhism saw itself as going further, spiritually speaking, than the Theravāda. We don't see it like that. It is more that the Mahāyāna drew out the significance of some of the original teachings which had ossified and been lost sight of at the time when Mahāyāna developed.

So, we incorporate three traditions within the Order –
Theravāda, Mahāyāna and Vajrayāna. We draw on teachings
from the Pāli Canon, Mahāyāna Sutras and Vajrayāna texts. We
teach people the mindfulness of breathing, *satipaṭṭhāna*, popular
in Theravāda Buddhism, and *mettā bhāvanā*, the meditation on
loving kindness. Those are the two meditations which everyone
learns when they come along to our movement. Our *pūja*, our
devotional practice is drawn from the Mahāyāna tradition. When
people enter the Order, they are given a further meditation practice which is taken from the Mahāyāna-cum-Vajrayāna tradition.
In the same way with the texts we study, we bring out teachings
from the different traditions.

When Dhammacarini Sanghadevi was asked whether this could not
be called searching for synthesis, she replied:

It's more that Sangharakshita has looked for the common principles
running through all the traditions and has drawn out those principles. The key principle is going for refuge. The essential act for any
Buddhist, whether they are Theravāda, Mahāyāna or Vajrayāna, is
that they go for refuge in the three jewels – the Buddha, the
Dhamma, the *Saṅgha*. So we keep emphasizing that this is what is in
common and that the different traditions can be unified through it.

We are concerned to distinguish between what are the cultural
trappings of Buddhism and what are the essential *Dhammic* principles which can be applied across cultures. On the whole, we've
been one step ahead of many other Buddhist groups in this
respect. Buddhism does express itself through cultural forms so
we have had to work on that fact. We couldn't just bring
Buddhism over and instantly overnight find a new form of expression. Some elements of the rituals we use are still embedded to
some degree in the cultural contexts that they've come from. But
we keep those elements to a minimum and, at the same time, we
encourage people to reflect on their own cultural heritage, their
own cultural roots, and, with time, to find ways of communicating the *Dhamma* through our own cultural heritage.

The Western Buddhist Order is also experimenting with new
patterns of relationship, socially and economically:

What we must work on is becoming more aware that the 'other' is
another self. We must use this to put ourselves in other people's
shoes. It comes down to very human, empathetic responses, which
can be taken to higher and higher levels. In the Order, we place a
lot of emphasis on people working together in different ways. In

Western societies there has been a breakdown of relationships. People tend to experience themselves as more and more separate. This has a positive aspect but the limitation is that people often feel isolated from other people. So we're trying to enter into deeper relationship with other people. So, in the Order, for instance, we have a lot of different forums where members of the Order come together not only to discuss their spiritual practice but also issues concerned with spreading the *Dhamma*, the work of the movement and so on. People are encouraged to engage with others in projects together, whether setting up a *Dhamma* centre to teach meditation or a team-based right-livelihood project to support themselves financially and to demonstrate to the wider world that there are other economic models of work than what is found generally. People who are single are encouraged to live together in communities where they have to share. We create situations where people are brought up against one another and sometimes it's very painful. But if you remember your own purpose you can go beyond those resistances.

The Order has one health centre and another in the process of development, a couple of arts centres, restaurants and wholefood shops as well as their teaching and meditation centres. The Order also has a large wholesale retail business in the gift trade which provides a means of financial support for many members in the movement. All initiatives are carried out with right livelihood (*sammā ājīva*) in mind.

In its exploration of forms of community that seek to break down isolation and separation between individuals, the Friends of the Western Buddhist Order is challenging British culture. In insisting that members of the Order should be financially self-sufficient, they are challenging patterns prevalent in Asia. In drawing on more than one school of Buddhism, they are claiming the right to formulate a Buddhism that is not dependent on one set of teachers or practices. It is a project that takes seriously both the need for Buddhism to adapt when it enters the West and for it to challenge certain aspects of culture. Yet, the question of 'memory' remains for the Western Buddhist Order and other Western Buddhist groups. A few Western Buddhist groups have made mistakes and some have even fallen prey to scandal. A crucial question is how far a new initiative can move away from its original religious and cultural roots and still remain within the Buddhist tradition. The Friends of the Western Buddhist Order, however, retain a tight hold over the practice of their friends and members. They are rooted in the

Buddhist textual tradition and are fully part of the Buddhist world.
It is unlikely, therefore, that their practice will diverge so much from
the Asian model that it will become unrecognizable to Asian Buddhists.

ECUMENICAL BUDDHISM

In spite of the diversity among those who come to Samye Ling, basi-
cally one Buddhist tradition is honoured: the Tibetan. Although the
Western Buddhist Order has adapted certain practices within
Buddhism to meet the new context of the West, it has a fairly strict
approach to training and practice. Sharpham College of Buddhist
Study and Contemporary Enquiry in Devon, on the other hand,
feeds on diversity. Buddhists from all traditions come and all traditions are respected. It developed out of the Sharpham North
Buddhist community, which Martine and Stephen Batchelor joined
after both had left the monastic communities they had been part of
and had become marriage partners. Martine is its Co-ordinator. She
spoke of the original vision behind the community which still continues through the College:

> Sharpham was one of those rare places in England where you didn't
> have to belong to one specific tradition. It's what we could call
> ecumenical Buddhism. We had the Buddha's teaching as the ground
> but everybody could be different. One person could be a Zen
> Buddhist. Another could be a Tibetan Buddhist or a Theravāda
> Buddhist. All of us could be together there and the thing which we
> could do together, formally, as Buddhists, was to sit in meditation,
> to share silence. For us that aspect was very important. In a tradi-
> tional Buddhist environment it is very hard to experiment and
> Stephen and I were very interested in experimenting, applying
> Buddhism to daily life.
>   Sharpham offers an opportunity. Sharpham provides a place where
> you don't have to keep to one tradition. One can explore all traditions
> and even within that you can explore the Western tradition.
>   The people who come to Sharpham will not be very orthodox
> or traditional. What will unite them will be the fact that they prac-
> tise meditation and the fact that they practise the precepts.

Academic researchers have wondered whether there is yet such a
thing as 'Western Buddhism'. Martine was quite sure that it would
be far too simplistic to speak in these terms:

> One cannot say 'Western Buddhism'. What Buddhists are interest-
> ed in in America will be quite different from what Buddhists will

be interested in in Italy or England. The connection you have is often according to your colony. In France, there are lots of Vietnamese temples. Here in Britain, there are Sri Lankan temples which you wouldn't find in France. In America, there are very few monks and nuns à la Theravāda, in other words very strict, because they are too egalitarian for a very hierarchical model unless it's a mystical model like Tibetan Buddhism. So, you can't speak of a Western Buddhism. It's too much of a generalization. It's like saying 'Eastern Buddhism'. You don't have an Eastern Buddhism. I would even say you don't have one Buddhism. You have Buddhisms. So, in each country in the East, Buddhism is slightly different and I think it could be the same in the West. Even within one country there will be tremendous variety. I don't think you will even have a British Buddhism but you will have Buddhist people and you will have Buddhist groups which will have more in common with each other than with secular society.

Sharpham aims to bring Buddhists together across traditions so that they can share, consolidate their practice and push out the boundaries in exploration. Yet, not all Buddhist groups are interested in this. Helen Waterhouse:

A lot of the Buddhist groups which practise in this country would like to be more united. Organizations have been formed so that Buddhists can get together, talk to each other, find out where there are similarities and where there are differences and discover ways around the differences. There are other groups who think this is not helpful and that, if they're to practise Buddhism, the kind of Buddhism which they practise must be pure. They insist that they must stay with the lineage which has been brought to them by their own teachers. Therefore, they don't see getting together with other Buddhists as particularly helpful to the progress that they're trying to make.

Although many Buddhists would like to see a common core of Buddhism – perhaps the Buddha's teaching of the Four Noble Truths – this is difficult for some of the other schools of Buddhism who, while not having completely moved away from the Truths, place different emphases on the Buddha's teachings. We already see this as Buddhism moved from India to Japan for instance. The emphasis in Japan is not quite the same as we might see in Theravāda countries and in Tibet. Therefore, it would be difficult to expect Buddhism as it comes into this country to necessarily look the same for the different groups and it's difficult for them to agree entirely on any kind of common core. Although they would very much like to do so, I think they will find that this is a continuing problem.

She later added:

> Lots of people would agree that there is a need for a Buddhist
> ecumenism and a lot of people would also agree that a British or,
> in broader terms, a Western Buddhism, will develop. I think from
> where we are now this is not likely to happen in the near future. If
> we look at the groups practising in this country there is a tendency
> to move away from an eclectic or ecumenical form to groups
> which have their own separate identity. I think we see this particu-
> larly among the Tibetan groups. There's been over a threefold
> increase in Tibetan groups operating in Britain in the first half of
> this decade. And many of the new groups are not really interested
> in forming a new type of Buddhism. What they're interested in is
> continuing a pure form of Buddhism which has been brought to
> them by their teacher. So, although many Buddhists would like to
> see the different Buddhist groups coming to some agreement about
> what is appropriate for Westerners to practise, there are equally
> many people who don't see this as a viable option for the future.

Yet, for Martine, 'ecumenical Buddhism' is most important:

> To me, that is the Buddhism I am interested in. Let me take my
> experience and that of my husband. I practise Korean Buddhism. He
> practises Tibetan Buddhism. He also practises Theravāda Buddhism
> and I have lots of friends who also practise Theravāda Buddhism. So
> I have seen the three practices, the three styles. And I am very
> impressed by all of them. So, although my own spiritual practice is
> Korean with a little tinge of *vipassanā* practice, at the same time I
> respect other teachers very much. Pluralism is important to me. Yet,
> at the same time there must be discrimination. There must be an
> asking, 'Is this Buddhism? Is this useful to the person or not? Is this
> making the person more wise and more compassionate?' This is the
> bottom line. I look at Buddhism in a very practical way. Ecumenical
> Buddhism is very important.

A CHALLENGE TO THE WEST

Do Buddhists in the West pose a challenge to society in the same
way that some Buddhists in Asia seek to challenge consumerism and
materialism? Centres such as Samye Ling certainly seem to mount a
challenge, so do some projects of the Friends of the Western
Buddhist Order. Yet, here again, the evidence of the interviews suggests that it is difficult to make generalizations. Certainly, Western
Buddhists are involved in charitable work. Chapter 4 illustrated this

and many of those interviewed are socially concerned and active in projects to benefit society. Beth Goldering has worked in the Middle East among Palestinians and, as this book is being written, is in Cambodia, working alongside socially engaged Buddhists and Christians there. Thom McCarthy raises money for the Holy Island Project and outreach in Moscow. Martine is active in the ecological movement. There is a Socially Engaged Buddhist Network in the West, as in Thailand and Sri Lanka. In Britain, there is also a Buddhist Prison Chaplaincy, a Buddhist Hospice Trust and a Buddhist Educational Project in Brighton. Yet, as in Asia, there are Western Buddhists who are more concerned about personal feelings of peace and well-being than with the wider society, more concerned about how Buddhism can change their own lives than about how it could change society. Martine Batchelor, however, feels that this may be simply a stage that most new Buddhists have to go through:

> Buddhism is not an intellectual enquiry. It is something which changes a person and the world. Compassion is at the root of the practice. And what is interesting is that Western people are very practical. They look at Buddhism and they start to practise Buddhism in order to help themselves. What Buddhism has is certain psychological tools for people to be more spacious in the way they relate to themselves and the way they relate to others. And, if their life is more spacious, it is easier for them to be more compassionate. Generally, that is the way it works. If you are suffering a lot, then it is very hard to go and help others. But if you feel more spacious and live a more simple and contented life, then you generally become aware of the suffering of others and ask, 'Can I do something?'

Among the Western Buddhists interviewed for the programmes, there were different viewpoints, but they were all united in believing that Buddhism was having an affect on Western society, for the better. Here, perhaps Dhammacarini Sanghadevi should have the last word:

> Buddhism can contribute meaning to the wider society, a much greater depth of meaning. Materialism is the god for many people in Westernized societies and it is not a god which really satisfies. We want to show that there is more to life than material values, that there are spiritual values, that there are higher human values and that, if you no longer believe that Christianity offers you those values, there are other options.

THE INFLUENCE OF WEST ON EAST

Another most significant question is what effect Western Buddhists
are having on the traditional Buddhist East. The world is becoming
smaller in terms of communication. No country can avoid being influenced by other countries or by global trends. Many insights came from
the interviews, both from Asian Buddhists and Westerners. From one
or two Western Buddhists came the view that Western Buddhists may
be able to call Buddhists in Asia back to their roots, a view with the
inherent assumption that Western Buddhism is somehow purer than
Buddhism in Asia. Helen Waterhouse gave an example:

> Some Western Buddhists take the view that Buddhism as practised
> in the West is a much purer form of Buddhism than the Buddhism
> which has been practised over the centuries in the East. One of the
> Tibetan groups which I've been involved in believes that the lineage
> of Buddhism which they are practising in this country is actually
> purer and therefore better, closer to original Buddhism, than the
> Buddhism which has traditionally been practised in Tibet over the
> last few centuries. It is a delight to them that some of their own
> teachers' works are being reimported into northern India where
> they think the West, and the way in which the West practises
> Buddhism, will have a rejuvenating effect on Buddhism in the East.

The Western Buddhist Order does not go as far as this, but nevertheless believes that its own practice concerning ordination could
have an empowering effect in Asia if adopted there. It sees the Asian
practice of maintaining a fully ordained, celibate *Sangha* as disem-
powering laypeople, because it has made them see themselves as
inferior, capable only of merit-making activities. It sees this as a
travesty of the original message of the Buddha, who accepted as disciples those living in the family as well as those who renounced. So
Dhammacarini Sanghadevi was able to say, 'Our own approach to
practice in the Western Buddhist Order would benefit many people
in the Buddhist East enormously.'

Some of the Westerners interviewed, however, were far more hes-
itant about whether Western Buddhists could give anything to the
East. For instance, Beth Goldering felt Buddhism was far too young
in the West to make any generalizations:

> The West cannot give very much yet to the East. We're too new at
> it. There's been horrible irresponsibility and scandal, at least in
> American Zen. I think we need generations and the development

of a much deeper strength than we have yet before we can talk about bringing things elsewhere.

She was pressed further. Did she not think that she was underestimating the revivalism that non-traditional Buddhists could bring to a tradition?

> I am not in a position to assess that. That has got to be for the country to assess. I remember in the middle of a retreat ten or eleven years ago looking at a flower and realizing that it didn't have any eyes. It had no way of knowing what colour it was. I think the world is like that. I think that what we actually bring is determined by what is there to receive not by what we think we're doing. So the fewer ideas we have about what we're doing the more we can be open to what's there and responsive to what's there. What we bring will be whatever we bring. But we're only the bearers of it. We're not what it is.

Beth touched a most important point: that it was really up to the country in question to assess what impact Western Buddhists were having on their practice. The interviews threw up some interesting views on this. A small incident related by Martine Batchelor points to one strand that emerged:

> I can remember when I was coming out of a bus one day, in Korea, as a nun, with shaved head and wearing grey clothes, a Korean woman exclaimed to me, 'If you, a Westerner, are practising Buddhism perhaps I should get interested in it too!'

Ven. Gnanapala shared a similar point from the Sri Lankan situation, 'When people here see Westerners interested in mental culture, they become more interested.' A point made by Dr Akong Tulku Rinpoché was an extension of this. He reversed the view that Westerners could only bring a corrupting materialistic influence into traditional societies. According to him, those who were themselves reacting against materialism from within the West could aid the same process in Tibet:

> Western people can help in Tibet. There's now more modern material, modern food and modern technology. When these have been introduced in Western countries they have had a positive side and a negative side. Tibetan people don't know what is the positive and what is the negative. So Westerners can help Tibetans to know what the side-effects of all this new food and new material are so that they don't have to make the same mistakes as the West. Westerners know the problems and can teach.

Ringu Tulku stressed that Westerners could give a lot of physical help in Tibet, through such things as the Rokpa Trust. He added:

> People of the East have a high esteem for the intelligence of the West. They look at the West as an ideal. Therefore, they copy almost anything that comes out of the West. Therefore, it's actually a great inspiration for the people of the East if more and more people in the West try to practise Buddhism, try to understand Buddhism and also try to teach Buddhism. It goes in a circle. I have found myself that the people in Sikkim become more interested in Buddhism because they know that the Western people are interested.

Chatsumarn Kabilsingh felt that Western Buddhists could inject a new spirit into Asian Buddhism:

> We have to learn a great deal, especially in our movement for women. Asian women tend to be subjected to traditional values. Sometimes these values are not Buddhism but we don't dare to question them. Whereas Western tradition, Western women, have a free spirit. They can ask anything. So Asian traditional Buddhists must learn this from the West – that free spirit. But the Buddha gave it to us first. He said, 'Don't believe me just because I'm your teacher. Practise first. See first whether my teaching is applicable to your life.' That spirit is in Buddhism. But people in the Buddhist tradition tend to feel they should not question the text or tradition.

What is certain is that Buddhism throughout the world is changing, and the interpenetration of East and West is part of this. Asian teachers travel West, passing on tradition but also adapting to the Western context. Western Buddhists travel to Asia and their very presence can have an influence. The result is a dynamic movement which could mount a considerable challenge to the consumerism, war and violence that threaten cultures worldwide. Yet, as in every religion, what emerges will be dependent on the commitment of practitioners. Ringu Tulku:

> It is true of all religions. The moment the followers do not practise what they teach then people lose faith. It is not because the teaching is bad but because the so-called teachers or practitioners do not practise as it is taught. The whole thing then becomes irrelevant. The only danger for Buddhism in the future is this. The teachers and practitioners, especially in the West but also in the East, must be careful that they practise what they teach.

But, he added:

> I think Buddhism can give a lot the West, actually not just to the
> West, to the whole of humanity because it teaches compassion,
> loving kindness and wisdom. Compassion and wisdom together is
> very rare and I think it is something which is very much wanting in
> the modern world. Also wanting is understanding of beings one to
> another. In Buddhism we don't have barriers of caste, colour and
> creed. Such a message is needed today. Also, Buddhism as a spiritual
> path is quite rational. It can be studied with a rational mind. It can
> be explored. Questions can be asked. It is not a system of set rules
> or beliefs but something one has to understand. It is also ecologi-
> cal. It respects the balance within nature and seeks to live in har-
> mony with nature. Again, this is a message that is very relevant at
> the moment. Then, all Buddhist ideas are based on the notion of
> tolerance. The Buddha himself taught that different people need
> different teachings. He said himself that he had taught eighty-four
> thousand different kinds of teachings.[9] That in itself eliminates
> intolerance. Taking all these things together, Buddhism is a practi-
> cal and acceptable spiritual teaching for the world.

However various the thoughts and involvements of the people we
interviewed, not one would have disagreed that Buddhism is both
an acceptable and practical spiritual teaching for the world, and one
that could benefit society tremendously if acted upon.

NOTES

1. See Kirthie Abeyesekere, *Piyadassi: the Wandering Monk, His Life and
    Times* (Colombo, Sri Lanka: Karunaratne and Sons, 1995).
2. Ibid., p.35.
3. Within Buddhist philosophy, mind is considered a sixth sense. The Pāli
    word used is *mano*, which refers to the intellectual functioning of con-
    sciousness. It is what senses rational objects and concepts. Just as the
    eye comes into contact with visual objects causing visual consciousness
    to arise, so the contact between mind (*mano*) and rational objects
    produces mental consciousness.
4. See chapter 4, note 10. Jayavarman VII is considered to be the last
    great king of Angkor. Beginning in 1181 CE, his reign lasted thirty
    years. He converted to a Mahāyāna form of Buddhism (his predeces-
    sors had been Hindu) and this religious commitment is shown in the
    temples he built at Angkor Thom.
5. Ven. Buddhadāsa was born in Thailand in 1905. He was a scholar and
    a reformist who sought to make Buddhism relevant both to modern
    philosophical and scientific thought and to social questions. He estab-

lished a centre for *vipassanā* meditation in South Thailand and wrote prolifically. The influence of his thought in Thailand and elsewhere has been considerable.

6. Ven. Ajahn Chah was a meditation master of the Thai Forest Tradition. His monastery – Wat Nong Pah Pong in Ubon Province, north-east Thailand – became an influential centre for the tradition. Many branch temples were established, including a special training monastery for Westerners, Wat Pah Nanachat. His teaching has greatly influenced a number of monasteries in the West, e.g. those of The English Sangha Trust.

7. Suzuki Roshi or Daisetz Taitaro Suzuki (1870-1966) is known for his role in making Zen Buddhism accessible to the West. He became Professor of Buddhist Philosophy at Otani University in Kyoto at the age of fifty-two after spending many years in the USA. He lectured and toured extensively in the West and wrote prolifically.

8. Monasteries (*vihāras*) associated with The English Sangha Trust can be found in Britain (four centres), Australia (two centres); Italy (one centre); Switzerland (one centre); North America (one centre); New Zealand (two centres). Wat Pah Nanachat in Thailand, the monastery set up by Ajahn Chah for Westerners, is also considered to be part of the network. *Forest Sangha Trust Newsletter* is produced from Britain: Amaravati Monastery, Great Gaddesden, Hemel Hempstead, Hertfordshire, HP1 3BZ.

9. This Mahāyāna emphasis is linked to the concept of 'skilful means', i.e. that the Buddha taught different things to different people according to their state of receptiveness in order to encourage movement away from what was unwholesome. Theravāda Buddhists use different terminology, referring to a 'gradual' path of training, i.e. the need to take learners step by step along the path rather than introducing everything at once.

APPENDIX: A BRIEF GUIDE TO THE PĀLI AND SANSKRIT BUDDHIST TEXTUAL TRADITION

THE PĀLI CANON

Traditionally, the Pāli Canon is divided into three sections and is consequently called the *Tipiṭaka*, which means 'three baskets':

1. THE SUTTA PIṬAKA

The 'basket' of *suttas* ('threads' of teaching). It contains five *Nikāyas* (bodies of texts):

1. *Dīgha Nikāya*, or the collection of long discourses.
2. *Majjhima Nikāya*, or the collection of middle-length discourses.
3. *Saṃyutta Nikāya*, shorter discourses grouped together according to subject matter.
4. *Aṅguttara Nikāya*, shorter discourses with a more scholastic approach in which subject matter is grouped according to a numerical formula.
5. *Khuddaka Nikāya*, a collection of miscellaneous books. In the Sri Lankan tradition, these number fifteen. In the Burmese, the number is higher, including some books deemed non-canonical in the Sri Lankan tradition. The following are the best known:

    Dhammapada, a collection of proverb-like verses, containing doctrinal insights;
    Udāna, verses attributed to the Buddha placed in the context of a series of narratives;
    Sutta Nipāta, considered to be an early collection of *suttas* and containing some much loved texts such as the *sutta* on loving kindness (*Mettā Sutta*);
    Theragāthā, verses of the early monks;
    Therīgāthā, verses of the early nuns;
    Jātaka, the birth stories of the Buddha, i.e. narratives of the Buddha's previous lives when he was developing the perfections.

One book accorded canonical status by the Burmese but not in Sri Lanka is the *Milindapañha* (Questions of King Milinda), a work probably compiled in the first century CE, which features a series of debates between a Buddhist monk and King Milinda (probably Menander).

2. THE VINAYA PIṬAKA

This is the 'basket' which describes the rule of discipline thought to be laid down by the Buddha for monks and nuns. It contains much narrative material. For instance, the incident which gave rise to the promulgation of each rule is described in detail.

3. THE ABHIDHAMMA PIṬAKA

This is generally conceded to be a later scholastic development, but traditionally it is considered to be the word of the Buddha and therefore became part of the Canon. It is divided into seven sections and deals predominantly with philosophical and psychological issues such as the Buddhist concept of mind.

In addition to the canonical material, a large body of commentaries on the canonical texts developed.

THE SANSKRIT CANON

No complete Sanskrit Canon now exists. Some of the texts originally written in Sanskrit are now known only in their Tibetan and Chinese translations. This means that there are two main collections of Mahāyāna literature: Tibetan and Chinese. Within these languages have been found bodies of texts similar to those of the five Nikāyas of the Pāli Sutta Piṭaka. There are, for instance, Sanskrit versions of the *Dhammapada, Theragāthā, Udāna* and *Jātaka*. In the Sanskrit tradition, there is also a Vinaya similar to the Pāli Vinaya. The Sanskrit tradition also developed literature which has no equivalent in Pāli. Among the main collections are:

1. The Perfection of Wisdom Literature, of which the oldest text is *Aṣṭasāhasrikā-prajñā-pāramitā-sūtra* (Perfection of Wisdom in 8,000 Lines), which stresses the *bodhisattva* path and the emptiness of all things. It contains the popular Diamond and Heart Sutras.
2. *Saddharmapundarīka-sūtra*, more commonly called the Lotus Sutra. It stresses the compassion of the Buddha, his use of skilful means and the *bodhisattva* path.
3. *Lalitavistara*, a poetical account of the early life of the Buddha.
4. *Avatamsaka-sūtra* (Sutra of the Garland of Buddhas), a *sūtra* which stresses the interdependence of all things. A large body of supporting literature developed around it.
5. The *Mahāvastu* (The Great Event), a work which concentrates on previous lives of the Buddha.
6. The *Buddhacarita*, a life of the Buddha by Aśvaghoṣa.

THE CONTRIBUTORS

Dr Akong Tulku Rinpoché: Director of Samye Ling Tibetan Centre, Scotland. Forced to leave Tibet in 1959 and subsequently came to Britain.

Mrs Martine Batchelor: Co-ordinator of the Sharpham College of Buddhist Study and Contemporary Inquiry in Devon. A Buddhist nun for ten years in the Korean tradition.

Ms. Liz Bernstein: Activist within the international campaign to ban landmines and co-founder of the Coalition for Peace and Reconciliation in Cambodia. Came to South-East Asia from America in 1987 to work in refugee camps on Thai border and moved from there to Phnom Penh to work closely with Ven. Mahā Ghosanandā in planning the Dhammayietras.

Ven. Bhikkhu Bodhi: President and editor of the Buddhist Publication Society, Kandy. Author of much scholarly material on Theravāda Buddhism. Left America in 1972 and gained higher ordination in Sri Lanka in 1977.

Ani Tsewang Chödron: British nun trained in the Tibetan tradition. Was resident at Samye Ling when interviewed. She is now working with local people to establish a Tibetan Buddhist Centre in Brighton whilst maintaining close links with the new Kagyu Samye Dzong Centre in London.

Lorna Devaraja: Director of the Diplomatic Training Institute, previously Professor of History at the University of Colombo.

Ven. Professor Dhammavihari: Director of the International Buddhist Research and Information Centre in Colombo, Sri Lanka. Previously Director of the Postgraduate Institute of Pāli and Buddhist Studies of the University of Kelaniya.

Mr Raja Dharmapala: Director of the Dhammavedi Institute for Communication and Development, Sri Lanka. Member of the Secretariat of the National Peace Council of Sri Lanka.

Professor Gunapala Dharmasiri: Senior academic within the Department of Philosophy, University of Peradeniya, Sri Lanka.

Mikmar Dorje: British Buddhist monk trained in the Tibetan tradition and resident at Samye Ling Tibetan Centre.

Ven. Mahā Ghosānanda: Cambodian monk born in 1929. Leader of the annual Dhammayietras and founder of the Dhammayietra Centre for Peace and Non-Violence, Wat Sam Peo Meas, Phnom Penh.

Ven. Gnanapala: Senior monk at the Vajirārāma Temple in Colombo, Sri Lanka.

Beth Goldering: American citizen ordained as a Zen priest in 1995. Meditation teacher and social activist, currently working in Cambodia in peace and reconciliation.

Professor Richard F. Gombrich: Boden Professor of Sanskrit at the University of Oxford. President of the Pāli Text Society, Oxford, UK.

Pracha Hutanawatr: A monk for eleven years in Thailand, now a layperson active within the International Network of Socially Engaged Buddhists.

Helen Jandamit: Education Editor of the *Bangkok Post Student Weekly* and teacher of meditation. Runs House of Dhamma: Buddhist Meditation and Information Centre in the northern suburbs of Bangkok.

Dr Chatsumarn Kabilsingh: Senior academic staff member of the Faculty of Liberal Arts, Thammasat University, Bangkok. Editor of *Yasodhara: Newsletter on International Buddhist Women's Activities*. An ex-president of Sakyadhītā (International Association of Buddhist Women).

Dr Nihal Karunaratne: Medical doctor in Sri Lanka committed to building ecological awareness.

Ani Rinchen Khandro: British nun trained in the Tibetan tradition. Resident at Samye Ling Tibetan Centre.

Mr Om Khem: Director of the Buddhist Institute in Phnom Penh and deputy editor of the *Kampuja Suriya Review*.

Ven. Yos Hut Khemacaro: Cambodian monk resident at Wat Lanka in Phnom Penh. Deeply involved in peace education and development work.

Ani Kunzang: British nun trained in the Tibetan tradition, resident at Samye Ling Tibetan Centre.

Ven. Dr Somchai Kusalacitto: Rector and academic member of staff at Mahachula Buddhist University, Bangkok.

Kim Leng: Activist working with the Dhammayietra Centre for Peace and Non-Violence and the Cambodian Committee for Peace and Reconciliation. One of the main organizers of the annual Dhammayietras. Educator and trainer in non-violence.

Mr Thom McCarthy: American working at Samye Ling Tibetan Centre in Scotland. Has been deeply involved in the 'Holy Island' project and establishing work in Moscow.

So Mouy: Buddhist nun since 1985. Eventually started her own nunnery. A participant in several Dhammayietras, she has also helped to form an Association of Buddhist Nuns in Cambodia.

Gotz and Ingeborg Nitzche: German citizens now resident in Sri Lanka. Lawyers by profession, they have lived and worked in Kandy since 1993.

Nyanasiri: American national resident in Sri Lanka. Worked as Secretary to Ven. Nyanaponika, an internationally recognized German monk. Now a *dasasil mātā*, living a solitary life of meditation.

Ven. Delgalle Padumasiri: Senior Sri Lankan monk who spent many years in Jaffna.

Mrs Renee Pan: President of the Cambodian Children's Education Fund. Also works closely with Mr Chheng Ponn at the Vipassanā Centre for Culture and Meditation.

Dr Aloysius Pieris SJ: Jesuit priest. Director of Tulana Research Centre, Kelaniya, Sri Lanka. Editor of *Dialogue*, the academic journal of the Ecumenical Institute for Study and Dialogue, Colombo. Has lectured on Buddhist philosophy and Asian theology in several European and American universities.

Mr Chheng Ponn: Director of the Vipassanā Centre for Culture and Meditation, near Phnom Penh, Cambodia. Ex-Minister of Culture in the Cambodian government.

Ms Niramon Prudtatorn: Journalist and freelance writer in Thailand; campaigner for women's rights; active within the International Network of Engaged Buddhists.

Ringu Tulku: Tibetan Buddhist monk, resident in Sikkim. Internationally recognized teacher of Buddhism. Makes frequent teaching visits to the West.

Mrs Monica Ruwanpathirana: Poet, development worker and researcher in Sri Lanka. Founder of PIDA, an institute for development alternatives.

Mr Godwin Samararatne: Internationally recognized teacher of meditation. Heads a lay Buddhist meditation centre at Nilambe, Sri Lanka.

Dharmacarini Sanghadevi: Senior member of the Western Buddhist Order in Britain. One of the founders of Tārāloka, a Buddhist meditation centre for women.

Ven. Santikaro: Ordained as a Buddhist monk in 1985, after serving with the Peace Corps in Thailand. Resident at Wat Suan Mok in Thailand, a temple in the Forest Tradition, influenced by the teaching and example of Ven. Buddhadāsa.

Mrs Ranjani de Silva: President of Sakyadhītā (International Association of Buddhist Women). Runs training programmes for nuns in Sri Lanka. Active in *Dhamma* education.

Sulak Sivaraksa: Prominent lay Buddhist in Thailand. One of the founders of the International Network of Engaged Buddhists. Heads Wongsanit Ashram, near Bangkok.

Geshe Lhudup Sopa: Senior Tibetan monk. Professor within the Department of South Asian Studies, University of Wisconsin.

Ven. Bhikkhu Sumedha: Swiss national and an artist, trained in Geneva and Paris. Became a Buddhist monk in 1975. Now a painter–monk–hermit living in a cave near Kandy in Sri Lanka.

Dr Asanga Tilakaratne: Senior Lecturer at the Postgraduate Institute of Pāli and Buddhist Studies, University of Kelaniya, Sri Lanka.

Dr Helen Waterhouse: Research Associate within the Study of Religions Department at Bath Spa University College, UK.

Mr Mithra Wettimuny: Chairman of a company in Sri Lanka and well-known teacher of meditation and Buddhist doctrine.

Maeji Khunying Kanitha Wichiencharoen: Advisor to the Association for the Promotion of the Status of Women, Bangkok and campaigner for the rights of women. Became a nun after a full professional life in the legal world.

Ven. Vavuniya Wimalasara: Senior Sri Lankan monk, resident at Vavuniya close to the war zone in the north of the country.

Phra Paisan Wisalo: Buddhist monk in Thailand. Active in promoting rural development and environmental awareness.

GLOSSARY

Ānāpānasati (P.), mindfulness of breathing, a form of meditation in which the breath is watched

Anatta (Skt *anātman*) no-soul, no-self, no unchanging personhood

Ani a name denoting a nun in the Tibetan tradition

Anicca (Skt *anitya*) impermanence

Apammāda (P.) earnestness, diligence, vigilance

Arahant one who has gained enlightenment through following the teaching of a Buddha (Theravāda tradition)

Aṭṭangika-magga (Skt *Aṣṭangika-mārga*) the Eightfold Path

Avalokiteśvara a *bodhisattva* in the Mahāyāna tradition, an epitome of compassion

Avijjā (Skt *avidyā*) non-knowledge or ignorance

Bhāvanā (P. and Skt) lit. to become; a word for the practice of meditation

Bhikkhu (Skt *bhikṣu*) Buddhist monk, a man who has renounced home and family

Bhikkhuṇī (Skt *bhikṣuṇī*) Buddhist nun

Bodhicitta Buddha-nature, the mind and heart of the Buddha potentially present in each human being (Mahāyāna tradition)

Bodhisatta (Skt *bodhisattva*) a being destined for buddhahood; an enlightened being who vows not to enter *nirvāṇa* until all beings have attained it (Mahāyāna tradition).

Brahmavihāras (P. and Skt) lit. dwellings of Brahma; refers to four supremely positive states: loving kindness, compassion, appreciative joy and equanimity

Citta (P. and Skt) mind and heart; rational intellectual thought and the emotions popularly connected with the heart

Dāna (P.) an act of generosity, particularly in giving to the monastic *Sangha*

Dasasil mātā lit. ten-precept mother; the name given to a contemporary nun in Sri Lanka who follows a discipline of ten rules

Deva (P. and Skt) a deity, heavenly being, a god

Dhamma (Skt *dharma*), the Truth, the way things are, the norm, the law, righteousness, what the Buddha taught; an object of mind
Dosa (Skt *dveṣa*) hatred
Dukkha (P. and Skt) unsatisfactoriness, suffering, pain

Gati (P. and Skt) the various levels or realms of existence within *saṃsāra* into which beings can be born

Jātaka (P. and Skt) lit. a birth story; stories of the previous lives of the Buddha, when he was preparing for buddhahood
Jhāna (P. and Skt) meditative absorption

Kamma (Skt *karma*) lit. action; wholesome and unwholesome volitional actions causing wholesome and unwholesome fruits which shape rebirth and human destiny
Karunā (P. and Skt) compassion
Khandha (Skt *skandha*) aggregate, the word used for the five 'groups' which make up the human person
Kilesas (Skt *kleśa*) defilements, unwholesome qualities
Koan (Zen tradition) a paradox or puzzle which cannot be solved by conventional, rational means

Lama an honorary title in Tibetan Buddhism for a person accepted as a spiritual teacher
Lobha (P. and Skt) greed

Maeji the name given to a contemporary nun in Thailand
Magga (Skt *mārga*) the path, the way
Mettā (Skt *maitri*) loving kindness, benevolence to all without discrimination
Moha (P. and Skt) delusion
Mokṣa (Skt) release, liberation
Muditā (P. and Skt) empathetic appreciation and joy at the success of others, appreciative joy

Nibbāna (Skt *nirvāṇa*) lit. extinction; the goal of Buddhist practice, the eradication or extinction of greed, hatred and delusion, deliverance from rebirth and all suffering
Nirodha (P. and Skt) cessation

Paññā (Skt *prajñā*) wisdom
Pāramitā (P. and Skt) perfection, refers to the qualities perfected by a buddha-to-be before buddhahood.

Parinibbāna (Skt *Parinirvāṇa*) full *nibbāna*, often refers to the state an enlightened being passes into at death

Paṭiccasamupāda (Skt *pratītyasamutpāda*) dependent origination, the doctrine of the conditionality of all phenomena

Pātimokkha (Skt *Prātimokṣa*) the part of the *Vinaya* which contains the rules of discipline for monks and nuns

Petas (Skt *preta*) unhappy or hungry ghosts, one of the undesirable forms of existence

Pirivena monastic school (Sri Lanka)

Pūja (P. and Skt) a devotional act of respect, reverence or worship

Rāga (P. and Skt) greed, attachment, a synonym of *lobha*

Rāja (P. and Skt) ruler, revered person, king

Rinpoché, Tibetan, lit. precious one; title of respect given to all lamas

Rūpa (P. and Skt) form, corporeality

Sākyamuni (Skt *Śākyamuni*) lit. sage of the Sakyas; a name used of Gotama Buddha

Samādhi (P. and Skt) concentration, one-pointedness of mind within the practice of meditation

Samanerī (Skt *śrāmanerikā*) novice nun

Samatha (P. and Skt) tranquillity, serenity, a synonym for *samādhi*

Samma ājīva (P. and Skt) right livelihood, avoiding work which might harm other beings

Sammā diṭṭhi (Skt *samyak-dristhi*) right view

Sammā kammanta (Skt *samyak-karmānta*) right action, in accordance with virtue

Sammā samādhi (P. and Skt) right concentration, with particular reference to the *jhānas*

Sammā sankappa (Skt *samyak-kalpa*) right thought or resolution

Sammā sati (Skt *samyak-smriti*) right mindfulness

Sammā vācā (Skt *samyak-vāchā*) right speech

Sammā vāyāma (Skt *samyak vyāyāma*) right effort, to develop wholesome states and eradicate unwholesome states

Saṃsāra (P. and Skt) lit. continuous wandering; the ceaseless process of birth, ageing, suffering, death and rebirth

Saṃyojana (P.) fetters binding beings to rebirth, ten in number in the Pāli tradition

Saṅgha (Skt *saṃgha*) lit. congregation; usually refers to the community of Buddhist monks and nuns but sometimes denotes the whole community of disciples of the Buddha

Sankhara (Skt *saṃsāra*) formation, often refers to mental formations,

the fourth *khandha*
Saññā (Skt *samjna*) perception
Saraṇa (P. and Skt) refuge, usually refers to taking refuge in the Three
 Jewels (*Buddha, Dhamma, Saṅgha*)
Sassatavāda (Skt *śāśvatavāda*) eternalism, the belief that the soul
 continues eternally
Sati (Skt *smṛti*) mindfulness, a factor of enlightenment
Satipaṭṭhāna (Skt *smṛti-upasthāna*) the foundations of mindfulness,
 traditionally a practice of meditation in which the meditator seeks
 mindfulness of four things: body, feeling, mind and mind objects
Sāvaka (Skt *śrāvaka*) lit. hearer; noble disciple of the Buddha
Sīla (Skt *śīla*) morality, virtue
Suññatā (Skt *sūnyatā*) emptiness, voidness, devoid of own-nature
Sutta (Skt *sūtra*) lit. thread; a section of teaching, discourse, sermon

Taṇhā (Skt *tṛṣṇa*) craving, the chief root of suffering
Tipiṭaka (Skt *Tripiṭaka*) the threefold collection of authoritative texts
Tiratana (Skt *triratna*) the Three Jewels (*Buddha, Dhamma, Saṅgha*)
Trikāya (Skt) the three-body doctrine within the Mahāyāna tradition
Tulku Tibetan, a reincarnate lama

Ucchedavāda (P. and Skt) annihilationism, the denial of any continuity
 or future state after death
Upāsaka (P.) layman who has taken refuge in the Three Jewels
Upāsikā (P.) laywoman who has taken refuge in the Three Jewels
Upekkhā (Skt *upekśa*) equanimity

Vedanā (P. and Skt) feelings, sensing
Vihāra (P. and Skt) lit. living-place; a monastery
Vinaya (P. and Skt) the part of the *Tipiṭaka* which deals with monastic
 discipline
Viññāna (Skt *vijñāna*) consciousness
Vipāka (P. and Skt) lit. ripen; the consequence of an action, according
 to the law of *kamma*
Vipassanā (Skt *vipaśyanā*) insight, seeing clearly into the nature of
 things
Virāga (P.) lit. without lust or greed; non-attachment, absence of greed

Wat the name given to a Buddhist temple and the living-place of monks
 in Thailand

Yama (P. and Skt) the god or lord of death

FURTHER READING

CHAPTER ONE

Carrithers, M. *The Buddha*. Oxford, Oxford University Press, 1983

Ling, T. *The Buddha: Buddhist Civilization in India and Ceylon*. Aldershot (UK), Gower, 1985 (First published Hounslow (UK), Maurice Temple Smith, 1973)

Pye, M. *The Buddha*. London, Duckworth, 1979

Saddhatissa, H. *The Life of the Buddha*. London, Unwin, 1976

Skilton, A. *A Concise History of Buddhism*. Birmingham, Windhorse Publications, 1994

Smart, N. *The World's Religions*. Cambridge, Cambridge University Press, 1989

Thapar, R. *A History of India,* Vol. 1. Harmondsworth (UK), Penguin, 1966

CHAPTER TWO

Bechert, H. and Gombrich, R. (eds) *The World of Buddhism*. London, Thames & Hudson, 1984

Bodhi, Bhikku (ed.) *The Vision of the Dhamma: Buddhist Writings of Nyanaponika Thera*. Kandy (Sri Lanka), Buddhist Publication Society, 1994

Gombrich, R. *Theravāda Buddhism: A Social History from Ancient Benares to Modern Colombo*. London, Routledge & Kegan Paul, 1988

Harvey, P. *An Introduction to Buddhism*. Cambridge, Cambridge University Press, 1980

Pieris, A. *Love Meets Wisdom: A Christian Experience of Buddhism*. New York, Orbis, 1988

Rahula, W. *What the Buddha Taught*. Oxford, Oneworld, 1997 (First published London and Bedford, Gordon Fraser, 1959)

Sangharakshita. *What is the Dharma: The Essential Teachings of the Buddha*. Birmingham, Windhorse Publications, 1998

Snelling, J. *The Buddhist Handbook*. London, Rider, 1987
    The Elements of Buddhism. Element Books, 1990
Thurman, R. A. F. *Essential Tibetan Buddhism*. New York,
    HarperCollins, 1995
Williams, P. *Mahāyāna Buddhism: The Doctrinal Foundations*.
    London and New York, Routledge, 1989

CHAPTER THREE

Carrithers, M. *The Forest Monks of Sri Lanka: An Anthropological
    and Historical Study*. Delhi, Oxford University Press, 1983
Chah, Ajahn, *A Taste of Freedom*. Thailand, Wat Pah Nanachat,
    Ampher Warin, Ubon Rajathani, 1980
Goldstein, J. *The Experience of Insight: A Natural Unfolding*. Santa
    Cruz, Unity Press, 1976 (and Kandy [Sri Lanka], Buddhist
    Publication Society, 1980)
Jandamit, H. *The Path to Peace Within: A Guide to Insight Meditation*.
    Bath (UK), Gateway Books, 1997
Khema, Ayya. *Who Is My Self: A Guide to Buddhist Meditation*.
    Somerville (Mass.), Wisdom Publications, 1997
Nhat Hanh, Thich. *Living Buddha, Living Christ*. London, Rider, 1995.
    The Miracle of Mindfulness. London, Random House, 1991
Nyanaponika, Thera. *The Heart of Buddhist Meditation: A Handbook
    of Mental Training based on the Buddha's Way of Mindfulness*.
    London, Rider, 1962 (and Kandy [Sri Lanka], Buddhist Publication
    Society, 1992)
U. Pandita, Sayadaw. *In This Very Life: The Liberation Teachings of
    the Buddha*. Boston, Mass., Wisdom Publications, 1992
Suzuki, D. T. *An Introduction to Zen Buddhism*. London, Random
    House, 1991
Trungpa, Chogyam. *The Heart of the Buddha*. Boston, Mass.,
    Shambhala, 1991
    Meditation in Action. Boston, Mass., Shambhala, 1969
Wilson, B. and Dobbelaere, K. *A Time to Chant: The Soka Gakkai
    Buddhists in Britain*. Oxford, Clarendon Press, 1994

CHAPTER FOUR

Batchelor, M. and Brown, K. (eds) *Buddhism and Ecology*. London,
    Cassells, 1992
Chandler, D. *The Tragedy of Cambodian History*. New Haven and
    London, Yale University Press, 1991

Eppsteiner, F. (ed.) *The Path of Compassion: Writings on Socially Engaged Buddhism*. Berkeley, Parallax, 1988

Ghosānanda, Mahā. *Step by Step*. Berkeley, Parallax, 1992

Jones, K. *Beyond Optimism: A Buddhist Political Ecology*, Oxford, John Carpenter, 1993
The Social Face of Buddhism. Boston, Wisdom Publications, 1989

Macey, J. *Dharma and Development: Religion as Resource in the Sarvodaya Self-Help Movement*. West Hartford, Conn., Kumarian Press, 1983

Matthews, B. 'Buddhist Activism in Sri Lanka' in *Questioning the Secular State: The Worldwide Resurgence of Religion and Politics*, ed. D. Westerlund. London, Hurst, 1996, pp. 284–96

Nhat Hanh, Thich. *Being Peace*. Berkeley, Parallax, 1987
For a Future to be Possible: Commentaries on the Five Wonderful Precepts. Berkeley, Parallax, 1993

Queen, C. S. and King, S. B. (eds) *Engaged Buddhism and Buddhism Liberation Movements in Asia*. New York, State University of New York Press, 1996

Sivaraksa, S. *A Buddhist Vision for Renewing Society*. Bangkok, Thai Inter-Religious Commission for Development, 1994
'Liberation from a Buddhist Perspective' in *World Religions and Human Liberation*, ed. D. Cohn-Sherbok. New York, Orbis, 1992
Seeds of Peace: A Buddhist Vision for Renewing Society. Berkeley, Parallax, 1992

Sivaraksa, S. (ed.) *The Quest for Just Society: The Legacy and Challenge of Buddhadasa Bhikkhu*. Bangkok, Thai Inter-Religious Commission for Development, 1995

Tambiah, S. J. *Buddhism Betrayed? Religion, Politics and Violence in Sri Lanka*. Chicago and London, University of Chicago Press, 1992

Tucker, M. E. and Williams, D. R. (eds) *Buddhism and Ecology: The Interconnection of Dharma and Deeds*. Cambridge (Mass.), Harvard University Centre for the Study of World Religions, 1997

Wickremaratne, A. *Buddhism and Ethnicity in Sri Lanka*, Kandy (Sri Lanka), International Centre for Ethnic Studies, 1995

CHAPTER FIVE

Bartholomeusz, T. *Women under the Bo Tree: Buddhist Nuns in Sri Lanka*. Cambridge, Cambridge University Press, 1994

Dresser, M. *Buddhist Women on the Edge: Contemporary Perspectives from the Western Frontier*. Berkeley, North Atlantic Books, 1996

Gross, R. *Buddhism after Patriarchy: A Feminist History, Analysis and Reconstruction of Buddhism.* Albany, State University of New York Press, 1993

Horner, I. B. *Women under Primitive Buddhism*, 2nd edition. Delhi, Motilal Barnasidass, 1975

Kabilsingh, C. *A Comparative Study of the Bhikkhuṇī Pātimokkha.* Varanasi, Chaukhamba Orientalia, 1984
  Thai Women in Buddhism. Berkeley, Parallax, 1991

Murcott, S. *The First Buddhist Women.* Berkeley, Parallax, 1991

Paul, D. *Women in Buddhism: Images of the Feminine in the Mahāyāna Tradition.* Berkeley, University of California Press, 1985

Tsomo, Karma Lekshe. *Sisters in Solitude: Two Traditions of Buddhist Monastic Ethics for Women.* Albany, State University of New York Press, 1996

Tsomo, Karma Lekshe (ed.) *The Feminisation of Buddhism.* New York, Snow Lion, forthcoming
  Sakyadhita: Daughters of the Buddha. New York, Snow Lion, 1988

CHAPTER SIX

Books by Sulak Sivaraksa listed in the section for chapter 4 should be referred to.

Almond, P. C. *The British Discovery of Buddhism.* Cambridge, Cambridge University Press, 1988

Batchelor, S. *The Awakening of the West: The Encounter of Buddhism and Western Culture.* London, HarperCollins, 1995

Fields, R. *How the Swans Came to the Lake: A Narrative History of Buddhism in America.* Boulder, Colo., Shambhala, 1981

Humphreys, C. *Sixty Years of Buddhism in Britain (1907–1967): A History and Survey.* London, The Buddhist Society, 1968

Oliver, I. *Buddhism in Britain.* London, Rider, 1979

Subhuti. *Bringing Buddhism to the West: A Life of Sangharakshita.* Birmingham, Windhorse Publications, 1995

Waterhouse, H. *Buddhism in Bath.* Leeds, Community Religions Project, Department of Theology and Religious Studies, University of Leeds, 1997

INDEX